Reason and Sexuality in Western Thought

Reason and Sexuality in Western Thought

David West

polity

First published in 2005 by Polity Press

Polity Press
65 Bridge Street
Cambridge CB2 1UR, UK.

Polity Press
350 Main Street
Malden, MA 02148, USA

ISBN: 0-7456-2421-9
ISBN: 0-7456-2422-7 (pb)

A catalogue record for this book is available from the British Library.

Typeset in 10.5 on 12 pt Sabon
by SNP Best-set Typesetter Ltd, Hong Kong
Printed and bound in Great Britain by TJ International Ltd, Padstow, Cornwall

For further information on Polity, visit our website: www.polity.co.uk

For Paul

Contents

Acknowledgements

This project was initially provoked by Robert Aldrich, who asked me to write a series of short articles on philosophers for the two volumes of *Who's Who in Gay and Lesbian History* (edited with Garry Wotherspoon, Routledge, London and New York, 2001). He should not, of course, be blamed for the result. I am grateful for conversations at an early stage with Richard E. Flathman, who alerted me to the importance of Montaigne whilst reassuring me that the topic was worthwhile. Over a number of years, Barry Hindess has always responded helpfully and insightfully to my not always clear ruminations. Moira Gatens has helped me to a more adequate understanding of Simone de Beauvoir, Spinoza and Mozart. The Australian Research Council awarded me a Small Research Grant towards the completion of an extensive bibliography on 'Reason and Sexuality in Western Thought', which provided the basis of my research for this book, as well as for research on the Bentham manuscripts at University College, London.[1] I am grateful to the Bentham Project for allowing me (and my optician for enabling me) to examine these manuscripts. I would like to thank Robert Aldrich, Peter McCarthy and Kevin White for their detailed comments and helpful suggestions about a complete draft of this book, and my editors at Polity Press, Andrea Drugan, Justin Dyer and John Thompson. I am also grateful for the constructive suggestions and helpful criticisms of an anonymous reviewer, without whom my argument would be even more incomplete. I owe a particular debt to Glenn Worthington, who not only compiled much of the online bibliography for *Reason and Sexuality in Western Thought* and read and commented on the entire manuscript, but who also contributed during many conversations a wealth of suggestions, ideas and encouragement.

Introduction

> There is *only* a perspective seeing, *only* a perspective 'knowing'; and the *more* affects we allow to speak about one thing, the *more* eyes, different eyes, we can use to observe one thing, the more complete will our 'concept' of this thing, our 'objectivity', be.
>
> Friedrich Nietzsche[1]

The aim of this book is to explore the relationship of reason and sexuality within the western tradition of philosophy. It explores some of the manifold interactions and relations, some of the major 'constellations' of reason, sexuality and the self. The discussion is developed both historically and thematically, focusing on a number of decisive approaches and turning-points. Three major constellations are explored. Chapter 1 considers the transcendent 'reason' and 'ascetic idealism' of Plato, Aristotle, Augustine, Aquinas and Kant. The contrasting 'hedonist realism' and conceptions of instrumental 'rationality' in the thought of ancient Epicureanism and the philosophies of Hobbes, Hume, Bentham, La Mettrie and Sade are examined in chapter 2. Chapter 3 looks at a number of Romantic and post-Romantic approaches which, in different ways, subordinate reason or rationality to some manifestation of passionate love or sexual desire, most notably the Christian mysticism of St Teresa of Ávila and the thought of Rousseau, Friedrich von Schlegel, Schopenhauer and Freud. The final part of *Reason and Sexuality in Western Thought* addresses a series of alternative philosophical perspectives, which go beyond the clearly defined but one-sided constellations previously considered. These perspectives contribute to a more holistic and multidimensional understanding – and perhaps a *more* complete concept and objectivity – of reason and sexuality, situating them in the context of society, history, the subject and power.

This four-fold organization is intended primarily as a convenient way to identify a series of philosophical 'ideal types' of reason and sexuality. It is, of course, just as important to notice the tensions and inconsistencies *within* each constellation. The representative thinkers considered in each chapter are chosen in order to explore these variations on the common theme. It turns out that opposing constellations sometimes share common assumptions as well. So, for example, both ascetic idealists and hedonists tend to agree in according sexuality a fairly lowly status as the expression of an animal instinct, but evaluate it as either dangerously corrupting or harmlessly pleasurable. By contrast, some Romantics regard sexual passion as the key to a meaningful life. Although a chronological order is followed within (but not between) the main chapters, this does not imply any straightforward historical development or evolution of ideas. Any attempt to provide a continuous and reasonably inclusive history of this topic would clearly be beyond the scope of this project. The aim is rather to identify some of the most significant approaches and some of the more striking and interesting relations and contrasts between them.

It may be helpful, by way of introduction, to provide some preliminary explanation of what is meant by 'reason' and 'sexuality'. The reference to either 'reason' or 'rationality' signals the main emphasis here on philosophical approaches to sex and sexuality, although in some instances literary and theological variations are considered as well. The broadness of these terms reflects the fact that our concern is as much with alternative forms of reason as with the understanding of sex and sexuality. No single, well-defined conception of reason is presupposed, as the aim is precisely to consider the characteristics and implications of alternative conceptions. Since a philosophical understanding of any subject is presumably closely related to a rational or reasoned understanding of it, this project also involves an inescapable circularity. A philosophical understanding of the relations of reason and sexuality to the self will inevitably reflect the particular conception of reason implicit in the chosen philosophical approach. Reason is thus both an object of the inquiry and, at the same time, one of its essential conditions or presuppositions.

From this point of view, the topic of sexuality provides a helpfully concrete context and testing-ground for different conceptions of philosophy and reason. For one thing, sex is an area of human experience that delivers notably sharp and insistent intuitions – sometimes uncomfortably so – against which the abstractions of philosophy can more readily be understood and assessed. More pointedly, it turns out that the western philosophical tradition has to a considerable degree *defined* reason in opposition to sensual, sexual impulses and behaviour. In the dominant tradition of ascetic idealism, sexuality is devalued at the same time as rationality is purified and idealized. The outcome is not only a deep gravitational pull towards asceticism but also a skewed conception of reason. As Robin May Schott puts it, 'the interpretation of emotion, desire, and sexuality as polluting has in fact been central to the construction of rationality on the basis of purity'.[2] So reason and sexuality cannot be regarded as completely independent terms. Any conception of sexuality says as much about reason or rationality, intellect or mind as it does about the body and sex.

The range of approaches to reason within the western philosophical tradition also brings a variety of different and less abstractly philosophical issues into play. In its most modest, most 'realistic' manifestation, what I shall refer to as mere, or instrumental, '*rationality*' is defined simply in terms of certain human capacities of analysis, reasoning and calculation, memory and foresight. In this version, rationality itself is morally neutral, serving only as an instrument for the maximization of individual or collective pleasures. More ambitiously, an idealist conception of what I shall call '*reason*' refers not just to certain reasoning abilities associated with human intelligence, but also to something less tangible, something higher. Reason is identified as what is most valuably human about human beings, what is most genuine or true about the self. Far more than a mere instrument in the service of animal inclinations, reason is something that raises human beings above their merely animal natures. The 'life of reason' is then regarded as the proper object of human aspirations. More than a simple faculty or set of capacities that we happen to have at our disposal, reason is something to which we must *aspire*.[3]

Reason in the latter, idealist sense is clearly more metaphysically contentious than the calculating faculty of instrumental rationality. Not surprisingly, associated philosophical approaches strain the boundaries of philosophy in its contemporary sense as a clearly demarcated and, above all, secular intellectual discipline. Philosophies of idealist reason invoke ideas of a 'real' or 'essential' and morally valuable self, and, as such, are not easily separated from religious forms of thought. Philosophers like Plato and Kant seem to be motivated by religious or, at any rate, extra-philosophical metaphysical and moral considerations which, for a different philosophical tradition, are clearly *beyond* reason. The relationship between religion and philosophy is further complicated by the fact that Christianity, as the dominant religion of the western tradition, has evolved through frequent interaction and mutual inspiration with philosophy. This relationship is apparent both in the deep influence of Platonic and Aristotelian ideas on Christian theology and in the importance of theology itself within the Christian religion. Accordingly, religious and theological conceptions of self and sin will be considered alongside philosophical conceptions of reason, morality and pleasure.

The case of Romanticism further stretches the sense in which this book is concerned with different conceptions of reason. Romantic currents of thought both react against and are inspired by the traditions of philosophical and religious idealism. But in the process, they develop accounts of love, passion, sex and sexuality that are significantly independent of, and sometimes even explicitly opposed to, reason. They are concerned with reason primarily in the mode of criticism, opposition or denial. Some strands of Romanticism identify the essential self, or what we truly are, with our loving, passionate or sexual selves rather than with reason or even what is compatible with rationality. They do so despite centuries of ascetic condemnation and hedonist cynicism about our erotic nature. Romantic commitments may require us to endure unhappiness or even to die for their sake. Marriage, family and social order are potentially sacrificed for the sake of the individual's amatory or erotic attachments. Significantly, these Romantic motifs are expressed not only through the medium of art and literature but also within the seemingly less congenial confines of philosophy. In the latter case, reason not only is present as an object of criticism but also paradoxically provides the medium for its own correction.

Nor can a philosophical discussion of reason exclude consideration of *political* issues of order and power. Philosophical constellations of reason and sexuality can as little be separated from politics and society as they can be abstracted from religion. In the intellectual tradition of the West, the requirements of reason are closely connected with notions of order, whether within the individual or society. For Plato, both forms of order are related, since the proper order of the individual's inner life, which requires the supremacy of reason over will and appetite, is directly analogous to the proper organization of a well-ordered society. The notion of social order is important in a different way for the realist tradition of instrumental rationality, whose radically hedonist implications are, with Hobbes and Hume, almost immediately cancelled for the sake of family stability, inheritance and the King's peace. Conversely, Bentham's consistently radical hedonism leads him to an alternative conception of social order. Romantic views are politically more ambivalent, sometimes challenging the restrictions of the bourgeois family and merely conventional marriage, sometimes approving both as the apotheoses of eternal love.

If various notions of reason are in these ways hostages to a variety of long-standing philosophical, religious and political disputes, *sexuality* has in recent decades become a no less complex and contested term. It is now difficult to talk about sexuality other than in the wake of Foucault's and Foucauldian discussions of recent decades. Foucault attempts to show how a specifically modern construction of 'sexuality' has come into being as the privileged expression of the 'subjected subjectivity' of the modern individual. Certainly, sexuality in this special sense represents an important configuration of reason and sexuality in the West.[4] In the present context, the widespread influence of the Foucauldian argument calls for the immediate proviso that the term 'sexuality' will be used, at least initially, in the more straightforward sense as whatever pertains to sex, the sexes and things sexual. Understood in this theoretically innocent (or naïve) way, it is then considered as the variable and evolving partner of reason and the self. Thus conceived, sexuality has a past as well as a genealogy.

Further terminological cautions follow from the same basic point. If sexuality has a distinctive genealogy and assumes a distinctive form in the modern West, then so do its variants and sub-categories. David Halperin has argued, for example, that there have only been (now somewhat more than) one hundred years of homosexuality.[5] But for the sake of an uncluttered discussion, 'homosexuality', 'heterosexuality' and their cognates and cousins are used here to refer simply to sexual behaviour involving partners of the same or opposite sex, respectively. There is no assumption that the partners in such transactions identify as, or even are aware of, being homosexual or heterosexual. In these theoretically innocent terms, homosexuality has existed for considerably more than one hundred years. But neither is this usage intended to rule out arguments for the social construction of sexuality. It does not imply, for example, that it has always been possible to be gay or lesbian, categories that will be reserved for self-identifying or, at least, self-conscious homosexuals. The intention is only to avoid an endless and potentially confusing proliferation of sexual categories and terms at the outset. These loose and approximate definitions of the concepts of reason and sexuality will, it is hoped, provide some idea of the field within which the following discussion will take place.

However, for a topic of such breadth and historical range, it is surely also prudent to indicate some significant omissions and exclusions. Certainly, the areas omitted or treated only cursorily here are the subject of a wealth of analysis, commentary and argument elsewhere. Any serious encounter with the wide-ranging theories of gender, sex, desire and the body produced by recent and contemporary feminist theorists is beyond the scope and, indeed, outside of the central focus of the present work. These feminist theories evidently deserve separate and direct treatment in their own right.[6] This work is intended to *complement* rather than to encompass or engage directly with feminist discussions of patriarchy and gender. Although sexuality is clearly at issue in both areas, it will be considered here mainly in the sense that cuts across divisions of gender between the male and female 'sex'. Even the legacy of gay and lesbian liberation and the ever-expanding fields of gay and lesbian studies and queer theory, which are more directly relevant, will not be directly addressed. They also deserve separate treatment. This book is therefore best considered as a preparation or propaedeutic for a more adequate study of contemporary theories of sexuality.[7]

The place of reason and sexuality in the western tradition of philosophy is such a large topic that it is also inevitable that even directly relevant thinkers and theories have to be treated selectively or not at all. The psychoanalysis of Sigmund Freud, his followers and successors has obviously exerted a major influence, albeit sometimes by way of reaction or outright opposition, on the contemporary understanding and even practice of sexuality. This legacy will be considered only in two respects: first, in so far as Freudian concepts can be understood as an indirect expression or outcome of Romanticism and post-Romanticism; secondly, as applied, developed and criticized by philosophers like Sartre, Beauvoir, Marcuse and Foucault.[8] Nor will there be any detailed examination in what follows of the historical and conceptual intricacies of sexology and other biological and medical studies of the phenomena of sex. Instead, their philosophical and moral implications, whether legitimate or specious, will be briefly considered.[9]

A more surprising omission, perhaps, is the thought of Friedrich Nietzsche, who is the first philosopher (to my knowledge) who commonly refers to 'ascetic idealism' as a prominent and highly problematic feature of the western cultural and intellectual tradition. Nietzsche has, I now believe, exerted a considerable subterranean influence on the perspective that emerges from the present study.[10] But his thought is so complex and many-faceted that it would inevitably be distorted by being forced into the clear confines of an 'ideal type' or constellation of reason and sexuality. Nietzsche's complex relationship to asceticism deserves, once again, independent discussion. This omission is, perhaps, somewhat mitigated by the fact that Nietzsche has had a profound effect on the thought of Foucault, who *is* discussed in this volume.[11] Foucault's history of sexuality might even be described as Nietzsche by other means.

One final question needs to be addressed at this stage. Why, it might be asked, should we look back at all to earlier philosophical conceptions of reason and sexuality, if not to provide a systematic and chronological history of this topic? One overriding and critical aim is to avoid some of the distorted understandings of sexuality and the self which have been perpetrated by western philosophical and theological traditions to profound and largely detrimental effect. These distorted understandings reflect a recurring and pernicious tendency within western thought to elevate and absolutize some particular, limited dimension of human experience at the expense of its overall richness and coherence. The specific critical intention of the present argument is, in these terms, to disable rationalizing, theologizing but also biologizing, individualizing, naturalizing and similarly reductive treatments of sensual and sexual experience. Within idealist philosophy, sexual desire is subordinated to the requirements of transcendent reason. Within Christian theology, sexual pleasure is sacrificed for the sake of a rationalized conception of divinely ordained nature and the narrow goal of procreation. To very different effect, naturalism and hedonism tend to rely on an unhelpfully one-dimensional and detached standard of satisfaction. Some Romantics have even been prepared to abandon life itself for the sake of passionate love rendered absolute.

The more positive and ambitious goal that ultimately inspires the ensuing historical and philosophical exploration is to point towards alternative and richer conceptions of reason and sexuality. Central to the approach advocated here is a holistic conception of reason. Reason is understood not as a separate faculty – whether of idealist inspiration or mere rational calculation – but as a capacity or set of capacities that only exists in the articulation and complexity of human experience as a whole. The rational articulation of experience is, further, something that is ultimately inseparable from the social situation and historical unfolding of intellectual and cultural life. It is, in that sense, not just conceptions of reason but reason itself that has a history and a past. To that extent, the approach adopted here evidently has some affinities with Hegelian philosophy.[12] But Hegel's social and historical perspective must also be supplemented and, in part, corrected by the insights of existentialism and phenomenology. From the existentialism of Kierkegaard and Sartre to the sexual politics of Beauvoir, Marcuse and Foucault, the sexual subject is situated within the matrix of history, society and power.

A further important implication of a holistic approach to reason, philosophy and the self is that sexuality is not only limited or contained, but also potentially *enriched* by demands and interests stemming from complementary spheres of human experience. Rather than being forced to sacrifice sex for the sake of reason or reason for the sake of passion, these and other areas of our experience are mutually illuminating and enriching. We approach something like an 'objective' knowledge or 'concept' (in Nietzsche's sense) of reason and sexuality not by isolating them from this wider experiential context, but by remaining open to the manifold perspectives, the sometimes indefinable 'affects' of these different orders of meaning. In other words, the interpretation of sexual experience is one part of a broader and ultimately infinite task of understanding or interpretation.

At this stage, the most telling feature of this 'hermeneutic' task is the familiar problem of circularity – a feature of any systematic attempt to understand a meaningful text or human artefact. A certain circularity is unavoidable in any process of interpretation, where the understanding of some *part* of the work – for example, a sentence in a work of literature – depends on understanding the *whole*, but where understanding of the whole itself depends on a prior understanding of its component parts, and so on.[13] Put more positively, interpretation advances in an 'upward' spiral of understanding which, at best, is always improving but, in the meantime, is never perfect or complete. As Hegel famously said, 'The owl of Minerva spreads its wings only with the falling of the dusk'.[14] It would be more accurate, if less inspiring, to say merely that a *more* adequate knowledge and a *more* complete concept can be expected at the conclusion. After all, the conclusion is not the end, just another beginning.

1

The Ascetic Idealism of Reason

> . . . if a man has seriously devoted himself to the love of learning and to true wisdom, if he has exercised these aspects of himself above all, then there is absolutely no way that his thoughts can fail to be immortal and divine, should truth come within his grasp. And to the extent that human nature can partake of immortality, he can in no way fail to achieve this: constantly caring for his divine part as he does, keeping well-ordered the guiding spirit that lives within him, he must indeed be supremely happy.
>
> Plato[1]

1 Eros and the Idealism of Platonic Reason

Contemporary western thought still bears the clear marks of a distinctive conception of reason and philosophy that received its first and most systematic expression in the philosophical schools of ancient Greece. The rationalist, idealist and at least tendentially ascetic treatment of sexuality in the thought of Plato and Aristotle represents a decisive formative moment in the genealogy of a constellation of reason, sexuality and the self that is then consolidated, if not petrified, and propagated by Christianity in the West. Western attitudes to sex and sexuality have been profoundly and, let us be clear, detrimentally affected as a result. At the same time, a longstanding relationship within western culture and thought associates the classical world and, in particular, ancient Greece with dissidence against the western sexual syndrome. For those frustrated by the unnecessarily repressive morality of the western tradition or, at least, for those whose social, academic or artistic status gave them access to unexpurgated classical texts and sexually explicit artefacts, ancient Greece has long represented an inspiring beacon of sexual freedom.

In fact, the classical associations of sexual dissidence are virtually as old as the restricted sexual morality it has reacted against. This should not be surprising. Ancient Greek art and literature portray a variety of sexual acts and reflect a 'polymorphous perversity' of sexual inclination that was shocking to conventional western sensibilities for some two thousand years. Homosexual relations are particularly prevalent. Even more disturbing to some, Greek culture is replete with images, stories, poetry and even learned discourse and serious moral reflection concerning 'pederasty' or men's love of young men. Even when homosexuality is mocked in the plays of Aristophanes or ostensibly condemned in Plato's *Laws*, the inevitability of such a common human foible is rarely questioned. What is more, the classical associations of unorthodox sexuality persist to this day. Terms such as 'Greek' and 'Socratic' love, 'Ganymede', 'Sapphic', 'tribad', 'lesbian' and 'pederast' are just a few of the many classically inspired euphemisms for male and female homosexuality. These terms were kept alive through centuries of indirect reference and allusion, whether learnedly obscure or snidely condemnatory, to 'illicit' sexual activity. As a result, the traces of ancient Greek sexual mores and peccadilloes persist into the present time, despite the Christian West's long and violent campaign to extirpate all traces of sexual deviation.

But the relatively unconstrained sexual mores of ancient Greek society, portrayed in its art and literature and celebrated in the subsequent tradition of sexual dissidence, contrast with the rationalism and ascetic idealism that also found expression in the thought of Greek philosophers and, most definitively and influentially, with Plato. Over the course of his life, Plato (*c*.427–*c*.348 BC) fashioned a remarkable series of philosophical works that have influenced the western intellectual tradition so profoundly that A. N. Whitehead described subsequent western philosophy as 'footnotes to Plato'. In fact, Plato himself was almost certainly homosexual, and although he gradually changed his views on a wide range of subjects, including sexuality, many of his writings reflect the homophile sexual mores of Athens. He wrote an epigram imbued with recollections of passionate feeling for his friend Dion who, as a twenty-year-old youth 'made my heart mad with love'.[2] Plato had hoped to collaborate with Dion on his plans for political and social renewal. His early dialogue *Lysis* is notable for its portrayal of the male lovers Lysis and Hippothales, who are depicted in conversation with Socrates. The dialogue itself consists of a series of inconclusive reflections on the nature of love and friendship between a male 'lover' (*erastes*) and his similarly male 'beloved' (*eromenos*). Some of the perennial problems of pederastic relationships are explored, from the importance of a close relationship between friendship and virtue to the more pragmatic concern not to flatter or spoil one's beloved.[3] But homosexual friendship is not presented as being in any way dubious and there is no suggestion that physical relations should be avoided.

For the classical tradition of sexual dissidence, however, it is Plato's *Symposium* that has exerted a particular fascination, inspiring generations of thinkers and poets. This text was recognized not only as one of the greatest works of ancient philosophy but also as a treatise about love which offered a refreshing alternative to the drier concerns of much academic philosophy, a philosophical style more attuned to the interests of artists, poets and the general reader. The *Symposium*'s open discussion of homosexual love inspired those of homophile inclination as much as it troubled those committed to conventional sexual morality. In this work from Plato's middle period, homosexual friendship is still taken to be the most obvious example of the power of Eros, the Greek god of love. But although prized for its homosexual ambience by a long line of sexual dissidents, the *Symposium*'s canonical expression of the Platonic 'doctrine of eros' also turns out to be one of the main sources of the tradition of ascetic idealism in the West. Although the drive and energy, the sometimes awe-inspiring power of eros is still valued as the force driving human aspiration to higher things, the foundations of a less positive attitude to erotic desire are also laid.

The *Symposium* is most often remembered for Aristophanes' beguiling, mythical explanation of love as 'our pursuit of wholeness . . . our desire to be complete'. Aristophanes relates that originally there were three sexes of 'doubled' human beings, each with two sets of limbs, heads, genitals, and so on.[4] One sex was male, one female and one 'man–woman'. But as a punishment for conspiring against the gods, these doubles were eventually split into their parts, resembling the sexed human beings we know today. Ever since, each part has longed to be reunited with its 'other half', a longing that we know as love. A further implication of the myth is to explain the origin of heterosexual and homosexual desire. Only individuals derived from the 'mixed' male–female doubles desire someone of the opposite sex. The parts of the male–male and female–female doubles pursue homosexual reunions. If anything, Aristophanes' myth seems to imply that homosexual relationships between men are the best. Young men interested in other men are described as 'the best of boys and lads, because they are the most manly in their nature' and as 'the only kind of boys who grow up to be real men in politics'.[5] The story is even radical in the context of ancient Greek pederasty, since it implies that love between men of the *same* age – lovers are 'people who finish out their lives together' – may be as natural as the conventionally approved relationship between an older 'lover' and younger 'beloved'.[6]

This homophile reading is, however, undermined by Plato's further discussion of eros, which reflects broader moral and metaphysical intentions. Although the *Symposium* includes a wide range of serious and humorous opinions on love, it is Socrates, the last major contributor to the discussion, who is the most likely mouthpiece for Plato's own doctrine of eros. Through his recounting of the sayings of the priestess Diotima, Socrates presents a quite different view of eros as an almost mystical force. For the Greeks, eros or desire found its natural object in all beautiful things. But according to Diotima, eros finds its proper purpose only when it ascends from *particular* beautiful things, such as young men, to more *abstract* and *universal* ideals of beauty and goodness:

> This is what it is to go aright, or be led by another, into the mystery of Love: one goes always upwards for the sake of this Beauty, starting out from beautiful things and using them like rising stairs: from one body to two and from two to all beautiful bodies, then from beautiful bodies to beautiful customs, and from customs to learning beautiful things, and from these lessons he arrives in the end at this lesson, which is learning of this very Beauty, so that in the end he comes to know just what it is to be beautiful.[7]

The ideal manifestation of love, therefore, is a spiritual communion between souls who are attentive to Truth and Goodness in their abstract and universal form. The bodily, sexual expression of love is not completely abolished but must be restrained for the sake of the higher ideals of the philosophic soul.[8] Significantly, although there is no conclusive evidence that the historical Socrates always treated sexual activity as a distraction from higher pursuits, the dialogue concludes with a long encomium by Alcibiades on Socrates' impressive mastery of his carnal desires.[9] Platonic love points beyond the significance of inter-personal love affairs to the love of an abstract, universal ideal.[10]

A similar doctrine is developed in *Phaedrus*, where Plato's ideas about love emerge from a more mundane and characteristically Greek discussion of some of the problems of pederastic relationships. Lovers can be irrational and even mad, they boast in public, they are possessive and jealous.[11] The lover, in other words, will not necessarily benefit his beloved as the latter might expect: 'Consider this, fair youth, and know that in the friendship of the lover there is no real kindness; he has an appetite and wants to feed upon you. As wolves love lambs so lovers love their loves.'[12] Eros is a powerful and potentially dangerous force whose excesses must be kept in check by 'temperance'.[13] It is also a deeply *ambivalent* force. Love is madness, but madness is divine and has kinship to prophecy, ritual and poetry. The 'divine' and the 'evil and foul' manifestations of eros are represented by two horses who either lift the 'winged chariot' of the soul higher towards the divine or drag it down to the realm of earthly lust and ambition. It is reason as the charioteer of the soul who must tame the unruly horse of lust and harness the horse of spiritual love.[14] Only then will the divine madness of eros transport us beyond 'the beauty of the earth' to 'the true beauty' of the divine. The souls who are able to go beyond the enjoyment of mere earthly beauty will be inspired to recollect the beauty of the divine world whence they came before being 'imprisoned in the body, as in an oyster-shell'.[15] The philosopher, whom the 'vulgar deem mad', is really someone who ascends towards divinity and eternity in this way.[16]

Plato's views on love and desire are reinforced by other metaphysical doctrines. In the same middle period as the *Symposium*, he developed his famous 'theory of Forms', notably in the *Republic*.[17] Sometimes called a theory of 'universals', the theory of Forms is an attempt to explain our ability to judge particular things or properties to be of the same general or 'universal' kind as philosophers or chairs, green or tasty. It is intended above all to explain our ability to make aesthetic and moral judgements about goodness, justice and beauty. Plato's solution is to explain these abilities as the result of our intellectual access to a transcendent and eternal, non-material world of Ideas or Forms (*eidos*). In thought we apprehend the eternal and essential attributes or Forms of particular kinds of things and qualities, Forms that we can then apply in our judgements about the world.

But for Plato, the theory of Forms is also a metaphysical explanation of reality. Particular beautiful things 'participate' in the Form of Beauty, particular good things participate in the Form of Goodness. By implication, the ordinary reality of the material world is an illusory, inferior reality. According to Plato's famous analogy of the cave, we encounter in our ordinary experience of a changing and imperfect material world no more than the projected shadows of perfect and unchanging Forms. Only the philosopher is equipped to undertake the arduous ascent to the higher Reality and Truth beyond the cave.[18] Because the theory of Forms posits the real existence of universals, medieval scholastics described Plato's doctrine as 'realism'. This term is misleading, however, since the implication of his theory is that ordinary reality is *not* real, so it is closer to *idealism* in the contemporary sense. The medieval term for the opposing doctrine was 'nominalism', which deemed universals to be no more than the names we employ to talk about particular collections of real things (a doctrine closer to the contemporary meaning of 'realism').

The theory of Forms confirms the hierarchical relationship between reason and the passions, between the intellectual or spiritual and the merely physical life of the individual. In the *Republic*, Plato goes on to describe the proper organization of the individual soul as an analogy for the proper ordering, or 'justice', of the state.[19] According to Plato's account, the soul comprises three parts: the rational, thinking element of reason; the 'spirited' part that incorporates emotion; and the 'appetitive' principle of desire. The proper organization of both the soul and the state requires the subordination of 'appetite' and 'spirit' to reason:

> Therefore, isn't it appropriate for the rational part to rule, since it is really wise and exercises foresight on behalf of the whole soul, and for the spirited part to obey it and be its ally?
>
> . . . And these two . . . will govern the appetitive part, which is the largest part in each person's soul and is by nature most insatiable for money. They'll watch over it to see that it isn't filled with the so-called pleasures of the body and that it doesn't become so big and strong that it no longer does its own work but attempts to enslave and rule over the classes it isn't fitted to rule, thereby overturning everyone's whole life.[20]

The bodily pleasures, which figure so largely in the appetitive element, must be kept sternly in check. But it is equally important to notice that the bodily pleasures are still tolerated in their proper place of subordination to reason. It is only when appetite threatens to 'usurp a dominion to which it has no right' that the proper ordering of the soul is endangered. In the *Gorgias*, Socrates similarly maintains that the disciplined individual is not a slave to his passions, which must be subjected to the requirements of virtue. But the disciplined man does not shun pleasure altogether either. Rather, he must choose appropriately.[21] Plato's aim is not to expunge passion and desire entirely, but to control and exploit them through the force of the 'spirited element' of the soul.[22] The rationalist idealism of *Symposium* and *Republic* is thus not yet a thoroughly *ascetic* idealism.

However, the body and sensual pleasures are further devalued by Plato's later metaphysical doctrines, which may have been influenced by the teachings of so-called 'Orphic' and 'Pythagorean' cults. Orphism emphasized the importance of religious rituals and asceticism as means to obtain the favour of the gods in the after-life. Important in this regard was the Pythagorean belief in metempsychosis or the migration of souls. Orphism contributed the further ideas that it is only as a result of sin that the soul is condemned to an earthly existence in the prison of the body, and that it is only through punishment in the underworld and the cycle of incarnation and reincarnation that the soul is able to return to the divine realm. The other-worldly outlook of Pythagoreanism devalued worldly life and goods at the same time as it evinced faith in the effectiveness and inescapability of divine justice and firm belief in the divine nature and origin of the soul.[23] There is certainly some evidence to suggest the possible influence of Orphism and Pythagoreanism on Plato. In contrast to his early concern to distinguish between religion and philosophy in *Euthyphro*, in dialogues of Plato's middle period the relation of knowledge and wisdom to the immortality of the soul is discussed in terms compatible with Pythagorean doctrine. In *Meno*, Plato explains the possibility of our *a priori* knowledge of mathematical truth as recollection of knowledge acquired by the soul before its incarnation. The *Phaedo* teaches that the philosophical pursuit of wisdom can lead to immortality.[24]

The ascetic implications of this world-view are developed in the cosmology of Plato's *Timaeus*. According to this late dialogue, the process of Creation has housed the immortal soul in a perishable, earthly body. The hierarchical relation between body and soul is reflected in a corresponding hierarchy ordering the different parts of both. The only immortal and genuinely rational part of the soul is located in the head, whereas its two lesser, mortal parts, the seats of emotion and appetite, are lodged in the heart and belly, respectively.[25] Once again, the proper relation between these parts requires the supremacy of the rational part of the soul and the subordination of the emotional and appetitive parts. Virtue still requires the control of soul over body and reason over desire for the sake of Truth and Goodness. But now the necessary 'food' of the rational part of the soul is provided by religious contemplation of the harmonies of the divine universe. And the proper ordering of the soul is held to be the secret of immortality:

> . . . if a man has seriously devoted himself to the love of learning and to true wisdom, if he has exercised these aspects of himself above all,

> then there is absolutely no way that his thoughts can fail to be immortal and divine, should truth come within his grasp. And to the extent that human nature can partake of immortality, he can in no way fail to achieve this: constantly caring for his divine part as he does, keeping well-ordered the guiding spirit that lives within him, he must indeed be supremely happy.[26]

The view of sexuality briefly adumbrated in the concluding paragraphs of *Timaeus* follows from the hierarchical subordination of body to rational soul with the aid of a further misogynist premise. The origins of women and sex are unflatteringly derived from Plato's specific doctrine of reincarnation: 'According to our likely account, all male-born humans who lived lives of cowardice or injustice were reborn in the second generation as women. And this explains why at that time the gods fashioned the desire for sexual union, by constructing one ensouled living thing in us as well as another one in women.'[27] Sexual reproduction is incorporated into the physical organization of male and female bodies as an independent 'living creature'. But the sexual instinct is significantly located beyond the sphere of rational control. Indeed, the urge to reproduce is so powerful as to be almost uncontrollable: 'This is why, of course, the male genitals are unruly and self-willed, like an animal that will not be subject to reason and, driven crazy by its desires, seeks to overpower everything else.'[28] A man's sexual urges are so powerful that his 'sexual incontinence' – his lack of control over his sexual appetites – should be judged leniently as a 'disease of the soul' induced by some 'corrupt condition of his body' or 'an uneducated upbringing'.[29]

In Plato's last dialogue *The Laws*, the prizing of virtue as manly self-control in the face of disruptive bodily passions comes even closer to the later Christian doctrine that sex is only acceptable as a means of procreation. To support his preferred law of sexual conduct, Plato refers to 'nature's rule' and the evidence of animals, where 'the males do not have sexual relations with each other, because such a thing is unnatural'. This law would prohibit the sowing of 'illegitimate and bastard seed in courtesans, or sterile seed in males in defiance of nature'. Even his alternative proposal, which more pragmatically insists only that privacy be maintained in matters adulterous and perverse, still casually proposes 'suppressing sodomy entirely'.[30] No doubt, as John Boswell suggests, Plato's hostility to sexual relations *beyond* nature (*para physis*) must be understood in the context of his conviction that human beings are superior to animals and, in that sense, unavoidably beyond nature. Plato does not describe such sexual relations as *against* nature, the term that would be used to condemn a wide range of non-reproductive sexual activity during the long hegemony of Christian asceticism. When he admits that his argument may not be well received in Crete and Sparta, where pederasty is particularly in vogue, Plato seems to acknowledge that sexual relations between men are so common and irrepressible as to be beyond any hope of legal control.[31] Still, his condemnation of homosexuality remains difficult to deny and, in any case, is eminently consistent with the metaphysical dualism and religious idealism of his later writings. Perhaps Plato found it easier as an old man to condemn affairs of the kind he had enjoyed as a youth.[32]

The connection between Platonic idealism and Christian asceticism becomes even clearer with Pierre Hadot's wide-ranging account of the moral and spiritual, 'life-philosophical' intentions of classical Greek and Hellenistic philosophy. Despite the impression caused by our reliance on a few surviving texts, ancient philosophical discourse was primarily oral and 'persuasive' rather than scientific or theoretical. It was designed to 'form rather than to inform'.[33] Epistemological and metaphysical doctrines are intended to transform our way of being through an overall conception of the cosmos. Plato's Socratic dialogues can be seen as records of a spiritual practice that 'turns the soul away from the sensible world, and allows it to convert itself towards the Good'. They are intended to contribute to 'the spirit's itinerary towards the divine'.[34] In these terms, the topic of eros has particular heuristic (or maieutic) value, because it offers a spiritual path that leads from the interlocutors' human (perhaps all-too-human) desires to a higher spiritual goal. Asceticism is not an extraneous intrusion – whether deriving from idiosyncratic personal inclination or independent religious conviction – into Plato's otherwise objective and soberly theoretical metaphysical and epistemological doctrines. Rather, it corresponds to the deeper ethical and spiritual import of the epistemological and metaphysical doctrines themselves.

Plato's idealization of reason lays clear foundations for the asceticism which, through subsequent philosophy and Christian theology, came to dominate the sexual morality of the West. There is some irony here, since *askesis* originally referred to the physical training of the gymnasium, literally the place for exercising naked and a favourite site of homosexual encounters. It was Christianity that turned ascetic self-discipline so decidedly *against* the body. The metaphysical foundations for Christianity's suspicion of the body and sexuality are supplied by Plato's determined elevation of soul, reason and 'Platonic' love above body, desire and lust. What is more, Platonism created an intellectual force-field that has influenced even western philosophies that are otherwise of a very different complexion, and even when they are concerned with issues other than sex. The West's dominant conception of reason was, in other words, fashioned under the influence of certain quite distinctive attitudes to the body and sexuality, desire, pleasure and the soul. Platonism is the decisive matrix for much of subsequent western philosophy. From this perspective, the decisive question becomes not simply whether Plato and subsequent philosophers wielding the Platonic conception of reason themselves approved or disapproved of particular sexual acts. It is rather how a certain sexual stance has informed and perhaps deformed the dominant conception of reason in the western intellectual tradition.[35]

2 Aristotelian Virtue, Love and the Ends of Nature

Aristotle (384–322 BC) was Plato's most famous student and successor. But he diverges from Platonic doctrine in a number of important ways, particularly in his view of the nature of human knowledge and his ultimate vision of the ends of human life. Aristotle has been regarded as the advocate of a more balanced and worldly view of morality as well as the pioneer of a scientific approach to the study of nature and even sex. At the same time, he retains important features of Platonism. Most influentially, he fashions the idealism of Platonic reason into a powerful idea of the good life and a persuasive ideal of love or friendship (*philia*).[36] It is important to note, however, that what follows is a discussion as much of Aristotelianism as of Aristotle. The latter's intellectual legacy is complicated by the considerable scholarly difficulties of distinguishing his original words from the later omissions, interpretations and elaborations that resulted from a long history of early neglect, the loss of many important texts and the translation of his works from Greek into Latin, Hebrew, Arabic and sometimes between these languages. As a result, there is considerable uncertainty about Aristotle's ultimate position. It is unclear, for example, whether his apparent departures from Platonic doctrine should be seen as a clear break or merely a matter of emphasis. There is even debate about the direction of Aristotle's development – whether through the course of his life he moved further away from, or returned towards, Platonism.[37] In what follows, a number of salient differences between Plato and Aristotle are alleged in the full knowledge that they are by no means immune to scholarly correction.

At its most fundamental, the divergence between Plato and Aristotle concerns Plato's epistemological and metaphysical theory of Forms. The mature Aristotle rejects this centrepiece of Platonic doctrine.[38] For his more worldly, empirical temperament, there is nothing to be gained by positing an eternal realm of ideal Forms beyond the reach of ordinary observation and experience. Plato's solution to the problem of universals just pushes the epistemological problem one step further away. If the theory of Forms is supposed to explain our general knowledge of things and qualities in the world, it surely leaves us with the more difficult problem of explaining how we can have knowledge of a transcendent realm of abstract Forms.[39] In broad terms, Aristotle seeks instead to account for knowledge and judgement by bringing together 'form' and 'substance' in the world of ordinary reality. Forms represent the generic features or 'essence' of particular things, allowing us both to classify them and to explain their behaviour and interactions with other things. Particular things combine some form or essence with 'substance', Aristotle's term for the unformed matter common to every thing. Forms correspond to universals or concepts and are the object of our general knowledge of the world as an orderly cosmos.[40]

Fortunately, the metaphysical intricacies of Aristotle's theories of form and substance need not detain us here. The important point is that his rejection of Plato's theory of transcendent Forms ultimately translated into a more worldly, less ascetic view of human life and its flourishing. The moral conditions for a fully realized human life are investigated in one of Aristotle's greatest and most influential works, the *Nicomachean Ethics*. Aristotle retains some features of Plato's conception of reason, but at the heart of his distinctive approach to ethics is a refusal to regard reason as a universal faculty that can be applied to all objects, questions and areas of investigation. Aristotle emphasizes the different methods appropriate to different areas of inquiry and, in the process, effectively founds the disciplines of logic, metaphysics, physics and biological science. Such 'theoretical' inquiries are in turn distinguished from moral and aesthetic questions involving 'practical judgement' or *phronesis*.[41]

Practical judgement involves applying universal moral rules to particular instances and so can never hope to deliver the exact and certain answers delivered by theoretical sciences, which work in the opposite direction.[42] Such judgement also differs from theoretical judgement in its greater dependence on practical experience. We cannot make moral judgements or identify the ultimate end of human life without being practically engaged ourselves in both life and the society of the *polis* (the ancient Greek city-state). Practical judgement is unlike theoretical knowledge in its intimate relationship with the common opinions of our fellow citizens, which provide its ultimate standard. The task of the philosopher is not to identify a completely autonomous moral standard on the basis of reason alone but, more modestly, to resolve the difficulties and inconsistencies in these common judgements.[43] It is this conception of practical judgement that plays an important role in, as Gadamer puts it, 'circumscribing the intellectualism of Socrates and Plato'.[44]

Aristotle's more worldly, less extremely rationalist approach to human life is expressed in three principal topics of the *Nicomachean Ethics* concerning pleasure, friendship and happiness or the fulfilled life. Aristotle's view of pleasure returns to the more moderate opinions of Plato's earlier works as against the strongly other-worldly and ascetic tendencies of the later ones. Pleasures are not always impediments to higher things.[45] The philosopher should surely be the first to recognize the pleasures of 'theoretical wisdom', the pleasures of thinking and intellectual contemplation. Pleasure is not intrinsically opposed and does not always have to be sacrificed to the life of reason and virtue. Rather, the virtuous individual is someone who feels pleasure and pain *appropriately*, finding pleasure in virtuous actions and pain in vicious ones. The appropriate relationship to pleasure also involves balance and moderation or 'temperance' (*sophrosune*), which is 'a mean with regard to pleasures'.[46] But such virtuous dispositions do not occur naturally. They must be inculcated to become habit: 'Hence we ought to have been brought up in a particular way from our very youth, as Plato says, so as both to delight in and to be pained by the things that we ought; for this is the right education.'[47]

At the same time, some pleasures must be recognized as frequent sources of error: 'In most things the error seems to be due to pleasure; for it appears a good when it is not.'[48] Aristotle follows the overwhelming tendency of classical philosophy not only in regarding physical pleasures as the most dangerous but also in singling out certain physical pleasures for special caution. Of the pleasures of the senses, the pleasures associated with sight are less threatening. We must especially beware of *tactile* pleasures concerned with taste and touch, for example 'in the case of food and in that of drink and in that of sexual intercourse'.[49] These pleasures not only tend intrinsically to insatiability and excess, they are also pleasures shared with our inferior fellow creatures and children: '. . . self-indulgence would seem to be justly a matter of reproach, because it attaches to us not as men but as animals. To delight in such things, then, and to love them above all others, is brutish.'[50] The appetite for such sensual pleasures should be 'chastened' or, like children and animals, kept on a short leash. An appetite that is indulged is boundless and insatiable unless it is subjected to the 'ruling principle' of reason.[51]

The vice of self-indulgence, which is the opposite of temperate self-control, is particularly blameworthy, because it results from a deliberate and self-conscious decision and so is unlikely to be cured.[52] But most instances of excess are the result of weakness of will or what Aristotle calls 'incontinence' (*akrasia*). Much bad behaviour is the result of 'morbid states', 'disease' or bad habits and so is effectively beyond the control of an individual's will. Aristotle refers predictably to 'the habit of plucking out the hair or gnawing the nails, or even coals or earth, and in addition to these paederasty'. These states 'arise in some by nature and in others, as in those who have been the victims of lust from childhood, from habit'. In either case, they are 'beyond the limits of vice' because beyond the control of will.[53] Excess is less common with 'natural appetites' for food and drink than it is in the case of 'pleasures peculiar to individuals', which include the pleasures of the flesh.[54] Even so, Aristotle accepts that sexual pleasure is intrinsically good and does not value sex solely for the sake of procreation. He recommends moderation rather than sexual abstinence.[55]

A second major dimension of Aristotle's moral philosophy, which had enormous influence on the subsequent history of sexuality and what have been called homosocial relationships, is his account of love or friendship (*philia*).[56] Aristotle famously distinguishes between three kinds of love or friendship. *Philia* can be understood as a relationship of mutual goodwill with someone who is regarded as either 'good, pleasant or useful'. But goodwill based on usefulness or pleasure is fundamentally self-interested and does not amount to true love. Goodwill of these kinds ceases as soon as one's friend ceases to be useful or enjoyable. It is 'incidental' and 'easily dissolved'.[57] Friends who are pleasant or useful are valued for the sake of a quality they possess rather than for their own sake. We might just as easily value the same quality in another person. And if our friend ceases to possess that quality, he will presumably cease to be our friend as well. Both kinds of friendship fail to meet the highest ideal of genuine friendship, which involves valuing our friend for his own sake.

According to Aristotle, perfect friendship of the latter kind can only be based on virtue. One loves the other person for the sake of his goodness. Only then can we truly say that we love him for himself: 'Perfect friendship is the friendship of men who are good, and alike in excellence; for these wish well alike to each other *qua* good, and they are good in themselves.'[58] Such friendship is certainly rare, but once found it is likely to be long-lasting, since it does not depend on transient qualities of beauty or expediency. True friendship cannot exist apart from a common aspiration towards the good. For friends 'the most desirable thing is living together'.[59] Friendship is a relationship between good individuals who are dedicated to a life of virtue and are drawn to that quality in their friend. So friendship in virtue also includes all the advantages of the other two kinds. The virtuous friend is useful and pleasant for someone who is himself virtuous in Aristotle's sense, that is, someone who finds pleasure in virtue. But if the true friend is useful in that sense, still dependence on one's friend is something to be avoided. Friendship in adversity may be commonly regarded as useful, but the friendship in prosperity of self-sufficient and independent individuals is more noble.[60]

The tension between Platonic and non-Platonic elements in Aristotle's thought evidently pervades his ideal of friendship as well. The Platonic, idealizing element in Aristotle's notion of friendship is his emphasis on the common devotion to goodness as an essential condition of true friendship. As with Plato, love remains inseparable from the pursuit of virtue.[61] But in contrast to Plato's view of the goal of eros as a transcendent absolute that is beyond mere humanity or contingent existence, Aristotle's ideal remains within the domain of this-worldly human activities and relationships. Personal friendship is not important merely as a step on the upward path towards absolute and eternal Goodness. It is an essential condition of a happy and fulfilled human life: 'For without friends no one would choose to live, though he had all other goods.'[62]

Both aspects of Aristotle's ideal of friendship are nevertheless in tension. His account sets out to combine a commitment to universal goodness and virtue with the personal nature of human relationships. According to Jaeger, Aristotle 'retains the kernel of Plato's notion – the basing of friendship on the ethical principle of the Good – but he makes the Good a concrete moral value developing within the character of the man himself.'[63] But if one loves another primarily for his virtue, in what sense does one love another truly for himself? There seems to be no secure place here for the uniqueness of the friend as a particular individual. What happens to love, if one's friend ceases to be virtuous? Even if virtue might be regarded as a necessary condition of a genuine friendship, it is not obvious that it is sufficient. Ironically, though, the ambivalence of Aristotle's conception of friendship only seems to have reinforced its influence. On the one hand, this conception has persisted throughout the western tradition as a powerful expression of idealism in human relationships. At the same time and for that very reason, the same conception has acted as a helpful alibi for less spiritual, even distinctly sensual, homosocial or even homosexual relationships.[64]

There is further ambivalence in the third and most comprehensive topic of the *Nicomachean Ethics*, its ultimate conception of happiness or the good life for human beings. For Aristotle, both pleasure and virtue depend on activity, and the particular happiness of any creature depends on its fulfilling the activities distinctive to its kind. What is most distinctive of human beings is their capacity to reason. It is the 'rational principle' that represents one's most essential self and should be the object of self-love.[65] It appears to follow that, as Plato himself maintained, the highest activity for human beings is the contemplative activity of theoretical wisdom. At its best, this activity is pure, does not depend on other people, is loved for its own sake, is leisurely and, unlike the courageous actions of the warrior or statesman, is not wearisome.[66] Even the practical life of moral virtue seems to represent a level of human existence below the philosophical life of pure contemplation.

But Aristotle also lends support to a more qualified conclusion. Humanity is superior to other animals, which cannot contemplate or reason at all. But by the same token, humanity is inferior to God, for whom contemplation is the *only* essential activity. This suggests that human beings should *aspire* to a life of contemplation without ever being able to achieve it entirely: 'Therefore the activity of God, which surpasses all others in blessedness, must be contemplative; and of human activities, therefore, that which is most akin to this must be most of the nature of happiness.'[67] It would seem to follow that human beings live in the highest, most divine way possible when they live the life of contemplation to the greatest extent possible for such an imperfect creature: 'Happiness extends, then, just so far as contemplation does, and those to whom contemplation more fully belongs are more truly happy, not accidentally, but in virtue of the contemplation; for this is in itself precious. Happiness, therefore, must be some form of contemplation.'[68] But equally, Aristotle makes clear that the life of rational contemplation presents an unattainable ideal for the majority of human beings.

It is here that Aristotle's conception of practical judgement or *phronesis* plays an important role. Unlike 'wisdom' (*sophia*) for Plato, the conclusions of practical judgement cannot be detached from the ordinary concerns and common judgements of people. Practical wisdom offers guidance to human conduct that is substantially independent of any 'higher insights' that might be delivered by pure philosophy. As Jaeger says of *phronesis*: 'The philosophical knowledge of God is no longer its essential condition. That knowledge is a source of higher insight revealed to a few mortals, but this does not mean that practical wisdom is confined to the narrow circle of philosophers.'[69] It is never enough simply to set out a rational ideal of life. Practical judgement always depends on the feasibility of this ideal, how closely it conforms with the 'facts of life':

> ... the truth in practical matters is discerned from the facts of life; for these are the decisive factors. We must therefore survey what we have already said, bringing it to the text of the facts of life, and if it harmonizes with the facts we must accept it, but if it clashes with them we must suppose it to be mere theory.[70]

The contemplative theoretical life of the philosopher may be a particularly or even supremely valuable form of life. But this does not mean that it is the proper aim for every human being.

Nor does Aristotle share Plato's belief in the moral effectiveness of philosophical arguments for ordinary human beings: '... with regard to excellence, then, it is not enough to know, but we must try to have and use it, or try any other way there may be of becoming good.'[71] The virtuous life depends on character and habit or disposition. The source of moral behaviour is not the Platonic contemplation of Forms but good habits: 'we become just by doing just acts', and virtuous dispositions or 'states arise out of like activities'.[72] To that end, what is most important is private moral education within the family household and rule of law in the *polis*.[73] As a 'social animal' (*zoon politikon*), a human being has social and material needs and can thrive only in a well-ordered community. It is therefore no coincidence that the argument of the *Nicomachean Ethics*, which ends with the words 'Let us make a beginning of our discussion', runs seamlessly into the social and political issues of Aristotle's *Politics*.[74]

At the same time, Aristotle's description of 'man' as a social *animal* also recognizes the biological basis of his behaviour. Aristotle's more worldly philosophy is reflected in his systematic, scientific interest in the natural world, with a substantial proportion (about a quarter) of the surviving Aristotelian corpus consisting of studies of animate and inanimate nature. His biological studies of plants and animals made an enduring contribution to botany and zoology. He bequeathed to European and to Middle Eastern, Arabic traditions a systematic division and hierarchy of distinct 'inquiries' (later 'sciences') as well as detailed accounts of logical and scientific method. He was an assiduous gatherer of observations and anecdotes, even conducting dissections of animals. It is perhaps not surprising, then, that Aristotle's empirical temperament was also expressed in a number of interesting, if now seemingly quaint, attempts to explain homosexual behaviour as the result of organic malformations or incomplete or degenerate reproductive functions.[75]

Aristotle's 'scientific' account does not, however, substantially affect the moral position developed in the *Nicomachean Ethics*, where pederasty is mentioned as an example of a morbid or pathological condition. The general implication of Aristotle's explanation of homosexuality is to exculpate what he evidently regards as at best a morally risky form of relationship. To the extent that lovers err morally, they do so from weakness of will, which may be corrigible, rather than from deliberate, wilful and presumably incorrigible self-indulgence. At the same time, Aristotle does not rule out the possibility of genuine friendship between 'lover' (*erastes*) and 'beloved' (*eromenos*), the usual Greek terms for the older, active and younger, passive partners in an approved pederastic relationship.[76] He tends to associate pederastic relationships with relationships of pleasure and utility rather than the more perfect friendship based on virtue and the love of goodness.[77] But perfect love may still be possible, as long as the lovers are not led astray by the passionate feelings generated by their abnormal physiology. Such a relationship would certainly be preferable to the more common kind of pederastic relationship, in which the lover seeks only pleasure, and the beloved hopes for gifts and other advantages.[78] *Philia* is a more permanent 'moral state' and so more valuable than passionate love, which is a merely transient 'feeling'.[79]

Overall, Aristotle's substantial qualification of Plato's idealist and ascetic conception of reason leads to greater acceptance of pleasures, including sexual ones, and even a degree of tolerance of non-normative expressions of sexuality. His inspiring (if not unproblematic) transmutation of Platonic idealism into the realm of personal friendship would provide a degree of moral shelter for subsequent homosocial and even homosexual relationships. It can be argued that Aristotelian principles are at least compatible with a relaxed view of sexuality.[80] But ironically, a significant aspect of Aristotle's proto-scientific approach to the study of nature was to have a less happy influence. For Aristotle, the nature of each thing, its particular 'essence', is understood as a potentiality that implies a process of development towards a particular goal or end (*telos*). As he remarks in the *Politics*, 'the nature of a thing is its end. For what each thing is when fully developed, we call its nature.'[81] In these terms, a fully formed plant or animal is the goal or *telos* of the seed or embryo that will develop into it. Aristotle's work on the 'Parts of Animals' similarly treats bodily organs as differentiated by their function or purpose within the greater whole of the organism.[82] Harmless when applied to plants and animals, Aristotle's teleological conception of nature would supply the rationale for Christianity's unsparing condemnation of homosexuality as a sin 'against nature'.

3 God, Will and Unruly Sex

It is not uncommon to regard religion in general and the Christian religion in particular as primary sources of an unnecessarily repressive sexual morality in the West. Although there is undoubtedly some truth in this belief, it is important to remember that the belief in supernatural forces and agencies, spirits and gods has just as often been associated with an enthusiastic celebration of sexuality. Fertility rites, the worship of genitalia in the form of symbolic representations of the phallus and vagina, and orgiastic rituals culminating in a sexual ecstasy venerated as a supernatural escape from the individual self and prosaic reality have all been regarded as privileged expressions of religious belief.[83]

So perhaps it is only Christianity and related monotheistic religions such as Judaism and Islam that are the sources of sexual asceticism? But Christianity has itself, during more than two millennia, accommodated a wide variety of attitudes to sexuality. The Judaic Old Testament condemns onanism and homosexuality in the terms of ritual purity and pollution as 'abominations': 'If a man also lie with mankind, as he lieth with a woman, both of them have committed an abomination: they shall surely be put to death; their blood *shall be* upon them.'[84] But as John Boswell has pointed out, similar ritual offences were shaving and the eating of shellfish, which contemporary Christians no longer tend to regard as problematic. The dreadful vice responsible for the destruction of the 'cities of the plain', Sodom and Gomorrah – another potent source of Christian homophobia – was arguably inhospitality to strangers rather than sodomy.[85]

The New Testament is not single-mindedly hostile to sex either. Jesus did not preach asceticism and, far from being a woman-hater – a common feature of Christian asceticism – he treated women with a considerable degree of equality and respect. In the Gospel of St Mark, love between men and women is understood as a redemptive union of two souls in 'one flesh' rather than as something justified only by its contribution to reproduction.[86] Jesus' close friendships with some of his disciples have even given rise to the suggestion that he was homosexual. As Bentham, who himself raised this possibility, cautiously argued some two centuries ago, it is St Paul rather than

Jesus who introduced asceticism and misogyny into Christianity.[87] Even despite this problematic influence, some early Christian sects exhibited a wide range of attitudes to sexuality, from the orgiastic rituals of some Gnostics to self-castration.[88] According to Boswell, even the established Church did not enforce strict standards of sexual behaviour until the thirteenth century.[89]

Christian theology is relevant in the present context, because its sexual asceticism is significantly marked by its incorporation of a Platonist conception of reason. Platonism is introduced to Christianity through the teachings of St Paul as well as through the ongoing influence of the Neoplatonism of the first three centuries of the Christian era. Platonist influence is particularly apparent in the thought of St Augustine of Hippo (AD 354–430). But Augustine himself reads Plato largely through the lens of Plotinus (AD 204–70), who emphasized the closeness of Plato to the monotheistic principles of the Judeo-Christian tradition. Plotinus develops Plato's idealist theory of Forms into a complex hierarchy of gradations of Being extending from the eternal and ideal to the merely material. At the pinnacle of this hierarchy, above the realm of Platonic Forms, he posits the existence of a supreme being or 'One', which Augustine readily identifies with the unique and personal God of Judaism and Christianity.[90]

Viewed through the lens of Plotinus, it is not surprising that Plato seemed so much closer to Christianity than did other ancients. In *City of God* Augustine remarks that no other philosophers 'come nearer to us than the Platonists'.[91] Augustine heartily approves what he understands to be the Platonists' acknowledgement of a supreme God.[92] Some evidence for this view can certainly be found in Plato's dialogue *Timaeus*. In contrast to traditional Greek cosmology, which posited an original matter existing in chaos before the arrival of the gods, Plato claims there that the world was created by an intelligent being. Plato's Creator, being limited by his material and acting within a pre-existing space and time, is not the omnipotent Creator of the Judeo-Christian tradition. Augustine also rejects Plato's pantheist belief that the Creator was aided by the minor divinities of ancient Greek religion.[93] Still, Augustine discerns significant parallels with the Creator-God of Genesis. He also approves of Plato's view of the created world as something good: 'Plato indeed is bold enough to go further, and to say that God was actually delighted when the whole scheme of things [Creation] was finished, and rejoiced in the created world.'[94]

It was Plotinus' elaboration of Platonism, rather than Plato's own writings, which gave Augustine the essential weapon in his early struggle with Manicheanism. Manicheanism was an offshoot of

Christianity founded by the prophet Mani (AD 216–76), from Ctesiphon on the Tigris. Influenced by Zoroastrianism, Manicheanism preached a radical theological and metaphysical dualism of 'Light' and 'Darkness', Good and Evil. It abandoned any attempt to reconcile the manifest evils and calamities of existence with the absolute goodness and omnipotence of God. Instead, the Manicheans attributed the evils of humanity and the world to the workings of Satan or the Devil, an independently powerful though ultimately inferior cosmic force of Evil and Darkness. So great was their contempt for ordinary reality that they regarded the incarnation of Christ as only apparent. The world was simply too inferior a setting for the Son of God (a view associated with the later heresy of Docetism).

The Manichean cosmology corresponded to an extremely negative view of the human body and sexuality. Like many Christians, the Manicheans advocated sexual abstinence. The devotees or the 'Elect' should remain completely chaste. If a man married, he should avoid sexual relations with his wife. But in contrast to later Christian orthodoxy, the Manicheans' objection to sexual intercourse was precisely its tendency to lead to reproduction and so perpetuate the fallen, earthly existence of humanity: 'Sexuality was a principle of mindless proliferation.'[95] Manicheans even imagined an originally hermaphroditic state of innocent asexuality.[96] As a result, Manicheans and later Manichean heretics such as the twelfth-century Cathars were often suspected of the non-reproductive sexual sin of sodomy.[97]

Augustine's theology substitutes Plotinus' gradations of Being for the cosmological dualism of Manicheanism. Rather than being the result of a cosmic struggle between Good and Evil, the world and humanity manifest different degrees of goodness. Referring to his earlier Manichean tendencies, Augustine admits that he did not then 'know that evil has no existence except as a privation of good, down to that level which is altogether without being'.[98] This implied a very different view of the world. Although nature is the scene of human imperfection and wickedness, it is also the divinely ordained site of human redemption. Not everything that happens in the natural world is morally acceptable. But it is nonetheless the product of a beneficent and omnipotent Creator and so intrinsically susceptible to the moralizing force of the Church as God's representative on earth. So although there is a gulf between the corrupted realm of natural happenings and the absolute perfection of God, the two realms are nevertheless inextricably linked and interrelated. Augustine's identification with an alternative and superior reality or world thus leads not to the outright rejection of this world, and with it human sexuality, but rather to their moralization. Nature is conceived as a hierarchically structured moral order, witness not only to the pervasive corruption and wickedness of humanity, but also to anticipatory signs of divine goodness. The Creation can remind us of a loving God at the same time as we are constantly in danger of being distracted into loving nature for its own sake.[99]

But if Augustine can be understood as a kind of Neoplatonist, it is equally important to recognize his rejection of Platonism's key assumption that philosophical reason is by itself an effective moralizing force. Philosophy on its own no longer provides the sufficient basis for the 'spiritual exercises' of the soul. The human will can make its way back to the City of God only with the help of God and the Church. It is God's grace and religious faith, rather than reason, that play the decisive role in the individual's salvation. Augustine's 'religious turn' poses the intractable theological problem recognized by St Paul, namely how to reconcile human freedom and moral responsibility with the essential agency of divine grace.[100] The sinful will is somehow responsible for its choice between good and evil, even though it can only choose by the effective grace of God. Even more problematically, the individual soul's eventual choice between eternal salvation and perdition must be known in advance by an all-knowing and eternal God.

For present purposes, however, the important point is that Augustine's theology displaces moral questions from the domain of reason and knowledge to that of will and grace. This displacement has momentous consequences for the understanding of human sexuality. For Augustine, our fallen sexuality is a pre-eminent instance of the potential pathologies of our will – as well as being the vice to which he was probably most susceptible himself. Sex differs from other occasions of sin in its peculiar demonstration of the vulnerability of the human will.[101] Plato and other ancients had recognized that the intensity of sexual pleasure, like the passions, tended to cause an 'extinction of mental alertness'.[102] But for Augustine, there is no longer any possibility of harnessing eros for the ascent to eternal truth. Sex only distracts us from God. The main problem with sexual urges is that, because they escape the control of the human will, they cause human beings to fall short of that freedom of will intended for us by God. Fallen sexuality is thus a most appropriate punishment for the wilful disobedience of the Fall. Erection, orgasm, impotence and frigidity are important not as bodily events but as so many symptoms of an underlying pathology of will.

Augustine considers the lamentable disobedience of flesh exclusively in terms of the sexual situation of the male.[103] Recalling Plato's remark in the *Timaeus* that 'the male genitals are unruly and self-willed, like an animal that will not be subject to reason and, driven crazy by its desires, seeks to overpower everything else', Augustine finds the source of shame in a 'genital organ' that refuses to bend (or unbend) to the direct control of the will: '. . . the genital organs have become as it were the private property of lust.'[104] The potent male's experience of uncontrollable arousal is as relevant here as the contrary problem of impotence: 'Sometimes the impulse is an unwanted intruder, sometimes it abandons the eager lover, and desire cools off in the body while it is at boiling heat in the mind.'[105] The case of 'nocturnal emissions' provides further corroboration: 'From the wide gulf between these occurrences and our will, we discover that we did not actively do what, to our regret, has somehow been done in us.'[106]

Sexuality is particularly shameful, because it involves the will's loss of control not just over its emotions but over the even lowlier body and the lowliest parts of the body at that. The insubordination of the body subverts the proper dominion of mind or soul, which is fundamental to Platonist and Christian assumptions alike.[107] How else to explain the seemingly universal feelings of shame associated with male and female 'pudenda' (literally 'shameful things') and the activities in which they are employed? How else to explain the apparently universal insistence on privacy for sex, including 'lawful and respectable' conjugal intercourse as well as the 'legalized depravity' of fornication?[108] The brazenness of the cynic Diogenes, who reputedly sought to establish the mere conventionality of social manners by masturbating in public, was an exception imitated by few and, for Augustine, scarcely credible: 'I doubt whether the pleasure of that act could have been successfully achieved with spectators crowding round.'[109]

When judged by the religious standards of his time, however, Augustine is not absolutely opposed to sex. Against the Manicheans, he insists that marriage, procreation and so inevitably sex were divinely ordained even before the Fall. Even fallen human sexuality is part of God's plan for the world, which anticipated sin but still envisioned sex as the means 'whereby he might complete the fixed number of citizens predestined in his wisdom, even out of the condemned human race'.[110] But the shamefulness of fallen sexuality is contrasted with the innocent, indeed to contemporary tastes somewhat clinical, sex originally intended by God for Adam and Eve in the Garden of Eden. Reproduction in paradise is not yet associated with any 'morbid lust', so man's sexual organ remains entirely subject to his will.[111] The prospect of 'propagation as a deliberate act undisturbed by passion' is something the wise man must surely prefer:

> Now surely any friend of wisdom and holy joys who lives a married life but knows, in the words of the Apostle's warning, 'how to possess his bodily instrument in holiness and honour, not in the sickness of desire, like the Gentiles who have no knowledge of God' – surely such a man would prefer, if possible, to beget children without lust of this kind. For then the parts created for this task would be the servants of the mind, even in their function of procreation, just as the other members are its servants in the various tasks to which they are assigned. They would begin their activity at the bidding of the will, instead of being stirred up by the ferment of lust.[112]

A hard price to pay, it might be thought, for a more obedient penis. But such bliss is, in any case, no longer possible except in the after-life.

The close relationship between lustful sexuality and the confused state of the fallen human will takes narrative form in Augustine's early work of personal and spiritual *Confessions*. There he relates his not inconsiderable sexual lapses as a youth who famously prayed: 'Grant me chastity and continence, but not yet.'[113] Although his sexual adventures all apparently involved women, Augustine admits to a very close male friendship. Some of the most moving passages of the *Confessions* concern the death of this young man, whose companionship 'had been sweet to me beyond all the sweetnesses of life that I had experienced'.[114] When this friend dies, Augustine is utterly distraught:

> 'Grief darkened my heart' (Lam. 5:17). Everything on which I set my gaze was death . . .
>
> I had felt that my soul and his soul were 'one soul in two bodies'. So my life was to me a horror. I did not wish to live with only half of myself, and perhaps the reason why I so feared death was that then the whole of my much loved friend would have died.[115]

Augustine even compares himself unfavourably with the bravery of two legendary friends and, perhaps, lovers of antiquity, Orestes and Pylades, who 'were willing to die for each other together, because it was worse than death to them not to be living together'.[116] There is little justification for suspecting a sexual dimension to this relationship, even though earlier he confesses to polluting 'the spring water of friendship with the filth of concupiscence'.[117] But it is perhaps ironic that Augustine continues and even intensifies the Aristotelian tradition of friendship in this way.

In his later Christian teachings, Augustine reproduces Judaic and Pauline hostility to homosexuality despite being an early critic of a facile universalism. He criticizes the Manichean tendency of assessing 'the customs of the entire race by the criterion of their own moral code', affirming instead the 'true inward justice' of God, which is deeper and more enduring than the passing customs of human societies.[118] The eternal truths of God's laws may have different implications in different times and conditions. Unfortunately, Augustine makes an exception for certain allegedly universal rules of sexual morality. In a less than obvious application of the injunction to love God and our neighbour as ourselves, he castigates the sin of sodomy:

> Can it be wrong at any time or place to love God with all your heart and with all your soul and with all your mind and to love your neighbour as yourself (Matt. 22: 37, 39)? Therefore shameful acts which are contrary to nature, such as the acts of the Sodomites (Gen. 19: 5ff.), are everywhere and always to be detested and punished. Even if all peoples should do them, they would be liable to the same condemnation by divine law; for it has not made men to use one another in this way. Indeed the social bond which should exist between God and us is violated when the nature of which he is the author is polluted by a perversion of sexual desire.[119]

More than a shameful expression of lust, homosexuality is a flagrant violation of God's law.

In *City of God*, hostility to homosexuality is strongly associated with Augustine's condemnation of paganism. His long and involved vituperation against pagan rituals is peppered with expressions of outrage at the 'immodest' and 'shameless' activities demanded by pagan gods. An example he finds particularly disgusting is the fertility rite associated with Liber, the Roman god of 'liquid seeds', which involved the prominent display and worship of effigies of the 'male organ'.[120] He evinces equal venom at the 'obscene rights of the Great Mother', whose acolytes were the 'effeminates' of Carthage:

> The same applies to the effeminates consecrated to the Great Mother, who violate every canon of decency in men and women. They were to be seen until just the other day in the streets and squares of Carthage with their pomaded hair and powdered faces, gliding along with womanish languor, and demanding from the shopkeepers the means of their depraved existence.

These effeminates are self-mutilated eunuchs, 'a degradation which outdid all the carnal excesses of Jupiter himself', who 'only once disgraced heaven with a Ganymede'.[121] But again, it is worth noting that this is an indirect attack on the extreme asceticism of some Christians, who were also known to practise self-castration. In effect, Augustine appeals to the conservative social and sexual morality of his Roman readership in order to discredit both pagans and certain rival Christian sects.

Augustine's overall attitude to sexuality corresponds to his qualified view of the goodness of God's creation. The world threatens to inflict 'worldly stains' on the soul striving after light and purity, but nature remains the indispensable scene for the aspiring life of the Christian. The ideal of goodness enshrined in the person of the one God does not serve to devalue nature as such, but rather to establish a moral vector, clear lines of ascent and descent for nature's human inhabitants:

> As for us, what we are looking for is a soul which puts its trust in true religion and does not worship the world as good, but praises the world as the work of God and for the sake of God. Such a soul, when purified from worldly stains, may come in purity to the God who created the world.[122]

For Augustine the soul is not simply the prisoner of a body tainted by sex. He retains an essential, if strictly confined, place for sexuality in human life. Although he is highly suspicious of our 'morbid' and 'sinful' lusts, his suspicions are nevertheless moderate in comparison to the radical asceticism of some early Christian sects. But the body and its lusts are still the greatest threat to the ideal espoused by Augustine. In Peter Brown's words,

> Quite as much as the little group of monks and continent clergymen gathered around him in the bishop's palace, the dignified concord of married couples, from whom the mists of sexual desire would soon blow away, summed up for Augustine the great hope that had begun to fill his mind – the ideal of the total transparency of all human will within the City of God.[123]

4 Divine Order of Nature

Augustine's theology of God, will, nature and human sexuality was developed but not fundamentally revised by later Catholic tradition. The most important contributor to that later tradition was the theologian and philosopher St Thomas Aquinas (*c.*1225–74), the founder of Thomism. Although he aroused controversy in his day,

Aquinas was able to forge an impressive synthesis of Christian and Aristotelian ideas, above all in his *Summa Theologiae* (1266–73), which came to form the bedrock of Catholic theological orthodoxy.[124] One of his main legacies was to entrench within that orthodoxy a highly systematic, coherent and above all durable sexual morality.

Whereas Platonist and Neoplatonist doctrines figure largely in the thought of Augustine, Aquinas was more directly influenced by Aristotle. He benefited from the rediscovery from mainly Arab sources of a number of Aristotle's works previously unknown in the West. These works became available in the middle of the twelfth century, complementing the mostly logical works extant since the early Middle Ages. The discovery of Aristotle's extensive and systematic treatments of natural philosophy, metaphysics, ethics and politics represented an important new opportunity and challenge for Christian thought. With access both to Aristotle's more descriptive or 'scientific' works of natural philosophy and the expanded intellectual world made possible by the rise of the universities during the thirteenth century, Aquinas set out to produce a detailed synthesis of the philosophical and 'scientific' findings of 'reason' with the religious truths supplied by revelation and faith.[125]

With his strong Aristotelian heritage, Aquinas is often contrasted with the Platonist Augustine. Augustine is one of the founders of 'fideism', the theological belief that faith is an essential condition of salvation which depends on God's beneficent grace. Salvation cannot be achieved by relying on the unaided cognitive powers or reason of human beings. Aquinas, on the other hand, is regarded as a protagonist of a Christian *rationalism*, because his theology is founded on the complementarity of faith and reason. In fact, the two theologians have much in common.[126] As a Neoplatonist, Augustine recognized the philosophical and even moral achievements of the ancient world, even though he insisted that the heritage of pagan philosophy must be corrected by divine revelation and supplemented by grace. Roman virtue and Greek philosophy were only pointers to Christian truths that surpassed them.

In fact, Aquinas preserves the essentials of Augustine's religious rather than philosophical vision of humanity's moral condition and fate. Aquinas not only recognizes the importance of grace and will, but his view of free will is deeply and explicitly indebted to Augustine.[127] Like him, Aquinas is eager to distinguish Christian moral and religious doctrine from Platonic moral cognitivism. Where Platonism regards virtue as the inevitable consequence of moral knowledge and, as a result, sees weakness of will as equivalent to ignorance, Aquinas draws on Augustine in order to explain the independent possibility of weakness of will.[128] In religious matters, or those matters concerning 'things that are above us', we must acknowledge the greater importance of will as opposed to knowledge and reason.[129] Aquinas' debt to the earlier theologian is also apparent in his metaphysical account of evil as the absence of goodness rather than as an independent force opposed to God and goodness.[130] Aquinas is able to rebut the dualistic metaphysics and hostility to reproductive sexuality of Albigensian and Cathar heretics of the thirteenth century with the same Plotinian metaphysics that Augustine deployed against the Manicheans in the fifth.[131]

Although Aquinas adopts an essentially similar attitude to Augustine on the relationship between philosophy and religion, reason and faith, his more detailed encounter with Aristotelian natural philosophy influences his distinctive contribution to Christian theology. Impressed by Aristotle's achievements, Aquinas could be more confident that the particular sciences of nature would provide reliable knowledge of the material world. Although such knowledge is derived independently of faith and revelation, it should complement rather than contradict the knowledge we obtain directly through revelation from God.[132] Faith and reason will ultimately give the same result, though most people may have no practical alternative but to accept truths on faith. For Aquinas, therefore, the project of theology is able to expand to take in the entire range of human knowledge.

The greater interest taken by theology in science would have contradictory effects. Although Aquinas is keen to reconcile the revealed truths of religion with humanly derived truths about nature, his conception of nature is deeply imbued with Aristotle's teleological and implicitly normative conception,[133] and is still a long way from the thoroughly secularized world-view of modern philosophy and natural science, which regards the physical world as a complex of morally indifferent causal relations. That world-view gained authority only gradually after the Renaissance.[134] Whereas modern science perceives nature as an elaborate mechanism which, at most, might be attributed to an inventive, but remote and abstract, deity, nature remains for Aquinas an essentially meaningful and purposive order. Nature still represents an obvious manifestation and proof of the existence of a beneficent and all-powerful God. The world is not merely a product, but the meaningful expression of its Creator.[135]

For Aquinas, therefore, the organization of the natural world is a moral fact. This conviction is reflected in his conception of 'natural law'.[136] Aquinas believes that through a careful consideration of the order of the natural world, human reason can discern universal values and moral principles. The order of the world manifests a 'law of nature' or 'natural law' that supports and complements the moral teachings of the Church, which are otherwise based on the authority of biblical revelation, commentary and interpretation. Human moral judgements are pale reflections of the 'divine light' of God's eternal law. The divine law manifests itself throughout Creation in the form of laws of nature, which govern the behaviour of animate and inanimate entities. For human beings, God's law takes the further form of natural law. Natural law is distinguished by the fact that it is accessible only to rational creatures with free will. They can make a choice whether or not to obey the divine law, whereas non-rational creatures can offer only unthinking obedience:

> All things subject to divine providence are ruled and measured by the eternal law, and consequently it is clear that somehow they share in the eternal law, for under its influence they have their propensities to their appropriate activities and ends. Among all the rest, rational creatures most superbly come under divine providence, by adopting the plan and providing for themselves and for others. Thus they share in the eternal reason and responsibly pursue their proper affairs and purposes. This communication of the eternal law to rational creatures is called the natural law. The natural light of reason, by which we discern what is right and wrong, is naught else but the impression on us of divine light.[137]

The determination of natural law thus performs an analogous role in the area of morality as the identification of causal laws of nature does in the area of natural science or 'theoretical reason': 'The precepts of the natural law are to the practical reason what the first principles of science are to the theoretical reason.'[138]

The moral reasonings determining the natural law are thus the distinctly human extension of the divinely ordered regulation of the natural world. But since human beings are still animals, albeit *rational* animals, divine law operates within them in a dual way: both through deliberate human reasoning and unthinkingly in the form of instinctual animal behaviour. An example of the former is the institution of private property, which follows from the reasoned judgement that it is an essential condition for the flourishing of human societies. Aquinas' example of natural law operating 'without deliberate adjustment' in all animals, both rational and non-rational, concerns the 'generative complementarity of the sexes' and the rearing of children, or, in other words, sexual relations within the family: '. . . as male is adapted to female for generation and parent to child for comfort in the very nature of things'.[139]

Aquinas goes on to apply the apparatus of natural law to human sexual behaviour in considerable detail and to powerful effect. Like Augustine, he defends the place of sexuality within human life against the extreme asceticism of Albigensian and Cathar heresies, which had gained considerable popularity. Cathars, like the Manicheans attacked by Augustine, were hostile to reproductive sexuality as a result of its role in perpetuating the enslavement of human souls in a corrupt material world. In fact, Aquinas' emphasis on the divinely ordained order of nature leads, if anything, to a more positive attitude to procreative sexuality than Augustine's. As Aristotle taught, pleasure is natural and often a symptom of natural flourishing: '. . . pleasure arises from being established in a condition that is in harmony with one's nature.'[140] Sexual pleasure belongs not to the rational part of us that is unique to human beings but to the animal part that we share with other animals: 'In that sense, we call things "naturally" pleasurable which are especially bound up with physical preservation, either of the individual – e.g. food, drink, sleep, and the like – or of the species – e.g. sex.'[141] The pleasures of sex, like those of eating and drinking, are essential to that part of our nature 'which men have in common with other creatures'.[142]

Abandoning Augustine's deep theological suspicion of the very mechanism of sexual desire and arousal, Aquinas is able to discuss love and sex in a surprisingly relaxed manner. He is happy to reproduce the Aristotelian account of friendship and even the language of 'lover' and 'beloved', which, for the Greeks, had more than grammatically homosexual implications. He closely follows Aristotle in preferring the idealized friendship of virtue over friendships based on pleasure and desire: 'Friendship is love simply speaking; desire is love in a qualified sense.' Indeed, for Aquinas the only truly appropriate object of love is God. And it is presumably in this way that we should understand his description of the lover's striving for 'intimate discovery', which recalls mystical accounts of union with God as Beloved: 'The lover is not content with superficial knowledge of the beloved, but strives for intimate discovery and entrance.'[143] But at the same time, Aquinas has no difficulty discussing ordinary sexual relations. He is able to refer, for example, to that 'imperfect reciprocity' that occurs when, 'as sometimes in erotic love, a couple are not enjoying the same thing'.[144]

Less happily but consequentially, Aquinas' defence of reproductive sexuality as an expression of natural law is complemented by stern condemnation of any *non-reproductive* sex. Only monogamous heterosexual activity answers to our moral duty to produce and rear children. Consistent with Aquinas' general approach, his moral position is grounded in both natural law and the perspective of faith. He is able to refer to the usual biblical passages, which enjoin us to 'Be fruitful, and multiply', condemn Onan's masturbatory wasting of his seed, and so on.[145] But the dual structure of Aquinas' understanding of natural law – corresponding to the duality of our animal and rational natures – delivers a much more elaborate and graduated catalogue of sexual sins. Sexual sins like adultery and even incest are to be condemned, because they violate the laws of human reason. They defile the institutions of marriage and exogamy, which represent the rationally justifiable, distinctively human way of organizing the bearing and rearing of children. But adultery and incest still conform to our animal nature, because they are consistent with the reproductive goal of natural sexuality.

Far more horrifying are the so-called sins 'against nature', which not only contravene the rational principles constitutive of human families but also wilfully ignore the reproductive goal habitually recognized even by animals:

> . . . where there is an especial ugliness making sex-activity indecent there you assign a determinate species of lechery. This may crop up in two ways. The first is common to all sins of lechery, namely that they are in conflict with right reason. The second, which comes on top of this, is that they are in conflict with the natural pattern of sexuality for the benefit of the species: it is from this point of view that we talk about unnatural vice.[146]

Aquinas is appalled by these sins 'against nature', even though he is clear-sighted enough to acknowledge that, unlike rape and adultery, they may not harm anyone else and so may *seem* to be lesser sins: 'The more sin is against charity the worse it is. Now adultery and seduction and rape harm our neighbour, whereas unnatural sin injures nobody else, accordingly it is not the worst form of lust.'[147] We should not, however, be confused by Aquinas' scholastic dialectic, which advances a particular proposition only to refute it. Despite its apparent harmlessness, unnatural vice is in fact truly the worst, because it is an affront not merely to human institutions but also to God's law:

> Since, then, unnatural vice flouts nature by transgressing its basic principles of sexuality, it is in this matter the gravest of sins. . . .
>
> The developed plan of living according to reason comes from man; the plan of nature comes from God, and therefore a violation of this plan, as by unnatural sins, is an affront to God, the ordainer of nature.[148]

Never squeamish in such matters, Aquinas goes so far as to rank all the various sins of unnatural lechery according to their degree of deviation from the natural aim and object of sexual activity:

> And so, to compare unnatural sins of lechery, the lowest rank is held by solitary sin, where the intercourse of one with another is omitted. The greatest is that of bestiality, which does not observe the due species. . . . Afterwards comes sodomy, which does not observe the due sex. After this the lechery which does not observe the due mode of intercourse, and this is worse if effected not in the right vessel than if the inordinateness concerns other modes of intimacy.[149]

According to this reasoning, only bestiality turns out to be more horrifying than homosexuality, which is no longer equated with the solitary sin of Onan.

Aquinas' cool and explicit reasoning would have dire consequences for the sexual heretics of Christendom. According to Boswell, Aquinas' view of homosexuality is best understood as a rationalization of an intense wave of prejudice against 'sodomites', Muslims and Jews, lepers and heretics that swept across Europe in the late thirteenth century: 'Between 1250 and 1300, homosexual activity passed from being completely legal in most of Europe to incurring the death penalty in all but a few contemporary legal compilations.'[150] The baneful legacy of Aquinas' sexual moralizing was certainly made worse by the simultaneous rise of the Catholic Inquisition, with its increasingly systematic, cruel and profitable imposition of religious orthodoxy. Aquinas' theological account of sexuality has also proved remarkably resilient. His principles have been reproduced with relatively little emendation through generations of Catholic doctrine on contraception, abortion, masturbation, homosexuality and adultery. Even attempts to challenge Thomist sexual morality are still couched in very similar terms. There have, for example, been casuistic attempts to justify a not unusual form of sexual activity, where intercourse occurs 'in the manner normally associated with procreation' but without the real possibility of procreation.[151] But Aquinas' legacy more widely was to systematize and solidify a morally charged conception of nature rigorous enough to condemn much that happens naturally. Still loyal to Aristotle, Aquinas is able to admit that 'unnatural' acts may be natural for a particular man, if 'in him nature is ailing'. But nature as a quasi-judicial order must prevail. Accordingly, homosexuality is condemned with cannibalism and bestiality as the worst of all possible sins.[152]

5 Intolerance of Universal Reason

The Aristotelian and Thomist conception of nature as a meaningful teleological order, which directly implied the strict system of sexual morality so clearly formulated by Aquinas, was gradually undermined by the scientific world-view of modern philosophy. That world-view is associated with philosophical nominalism, an 'empiricist' emphasis on experience as the essential source of our knowledge of the external world, materialism and sometimes atheism. It is also associated with hedonism and a more permissive approach to sexual morality.[153] The explicitly *religious* foundations of the dominant sexual morality of the West were also increasingly eroded by these intellectual developments, which reached their clearest expression in the European Enlightenment of the eighteenth century. But the association between idealist reason and sexual asceticism is preserved, in purified and even more virulent form, in the philosophy of Immanuel Kant (1724–1804), undoubtedly one of the most penetrating intellects of the eighteenth century.

Kant sets out to secure a place for religion and morality in the face of a scientific world-view that regards human beings simply as physical entities in a world governed by deterministic causal laws. How can such a world-view account for our moral and religious experience? Scientific determinism undermines our conception of ourselves as free and potentially responsible moral agents. The dominant currents of Enlightenment philosophy seem to lead either to an atheist and potentially amoral materialism or to an abstract and morally indifferent deism. At the same time, Kant recognizes the impressive achievements of the natural sciences within their proper domain and is committed to a rigorously rational solution to the modern moral predicament. Kant's 'critical philosophy' is designed to define the proper limits of scientific inquiry, metaphysical speculation and religious experience in order to establish their validity within their proper domain and, at the same time, to prevent the improper incursion of these modes of thinking into areas that they are ill equipped to address. The essential structure and limits of human knowledge and experience are established in three major works. The *Critique of Pure Reason* (1781/1787) considers the 'pure' employment of reason in the study of the natural phenomena of the external world or, in other words, natural sciences. The *Critique of Practical Reason* (1788) examines the moral or 'practical' employment of reason in moral judgement. The third and more elusive *Critique of Judgement* (1790) looks at our capacity to identify ultimate purposes in nature and make aesthetic judgements of the beautiful in both art and the natural world.

The details of Kant's philosophy, which is both original and difficult, are beyond the scope of the present discussion. Of particular interest here are the ways in which Kant perpetuates and even intensifies the ascetic and sexually repressive tendencies of western thought. Each of the different dimensions of human experience is subordinated to a conception of reason purified of 'sensory' contamination. Kant's account of theoretical knowledge demonstrates a systematic suspicion of human emotion and mere 'feeling'. In his *Critique of Pure Reason*, as Robin May Schott has pointed out, Kant excludes certain sensations from the domain of genuine experience, even though they are surely an important part of the 'empirical receptivity' that is essential to genuine knowledge of the world. For Kant, genuine knowledge depends on *Anschauung* ('intuition') rather than 'feeling' (*Gefühl*), which involves pleasure or pain, or merely subjective 'sensation' (*Empfindung*): '. . . the sensations of colours, sounds, and heat . . . since they are mere sensations and not intuitions, do not of themselves yield knowledge of any object, least of all any *a priori* knowledge.'[154] In other words, the objectivity of theoretical knowledge depends on detached 'perceptions' or 'observations' of reality, which must remain undisturbed by merely 'subjective' feelings and emotions.

Kant's suspicion of feeling is reinforced by his epistemological preference (shared with much of the western philosophical tradition) for some senses rather than others. The sensory experience most appropriate to knowledge derives from sight rather than touch, let alone smell and taste, which are merely 'subjective senses' that provide no valid empirical content for theoretical knowledge. Not unrelatedly, pleasure is dismissed as a mere distraction without cognitive content. The pleasures of touch and taste are, as Aristotle had noted, those most liable to encourage vicious excess.[155] In Schott's words, 'the cognitive portion of sensibility, to which Kant ascribes the immediate apprehension of an object, excludes the feeling of pleasure as a subjective interference with external sensation.' Experiences of pleasure and pain are regarded as purely internal, self-related affairs without generalizable cognitive import: 'Since pleasure is cut off from the perception of an external object, it becomes a completely self-related experience.'[156] The world of objective sensory knowledge is, it seems, devoid of sensuality. In the *Critique of Judgement*, Kant similarly, if even less plausibly, excludes sensual gratification from the domain of *aesthetic* experience and judgement as well. Aesthetic pleasure is not seen as a direct corollary of the sensory content of a beautiful work of art or aspect of nature. Rather, aesthetic experience is essentially intellectual. Aesthetic judgement is merely 'occasioned' by sensation of the beautiful object: '. . . the senses do not themselves provide gratification but merely serve as the occasion for the mind to reflect on the form of purposiveness in the representation of the object. It is the free play of the cognitive faculties that produces the feeling of pleasure in the harmony of the faculties.'[157]

The ascetic implications of Kant's conception of reason flow most directly from his moral philosophy. His attempt to account for human freedom and moral responsibility in the face of scientific determinism relies on a dualistic metaphysics. Reality comprises both the 'phenomenal' world of 'appearance' and a rational or 'noumenal' world of 'things-in-themselves'. The phenomenal world of appearances corresponds to the material world of ordinary sensory experience and scientific knowledge. But according to Kant's 'transcendental idealism', we can have no immediate sensory experience or knowledge of things as they are in themselves or what he also terms 'noumena'. The problem of human freedom and morality is resolved in these terms. Freedom is understood as an attribute of the noumenal or 'intelligible' self rather than the causally determined phenomenal self of ordinary reality. The noumenal self is somehow connected to the causally determined phenomenal self of the 'world of appearances' whilst at the same time remaining sufficiently independent of that world to be understood as a free and responsible agent.

Kant's dualist metaphysics readily translates into his conviction that we act freely and morally only when our actions are based purely on reason, only when they are entirely independent of any merely 'empirical' motivation. A moral action must be motivated by reason alone, that is, by the moral intention to do what is right, not by the desires, impulses or inclinations of our phenomenal self. This does not, as some critics have suggested, mean that a morally justified action must necessarily be *incompatible* with one's particular inclinations or desires.[158] Rather, Kant believes that the principles of morality and hence the maxims of our actions must be able to be derived from the abstract notion of a rational self or will, a will devoid of distinguishing individual features such as personal desires or inclinations. The individual acts freely and morally, then, only when he acts purely in obedience to a universal moral law that is the product of reason alone. Kant calls this universal moral law the 'categorical imperative', which requires that 'I ought never to act except in such a way that I could also will that my maxim should become a universal law.'[159]

The formal and abstract nature of Kant's moral philosophy raises a number of difficulties. Hegel was one of the first to criticize Kant's moral philosophy as devoid of any substantive moral implications and content.[160] The principle of universalization does not by itself rule out any particular action. It is not obvious why we cannot 'universalize the maxim' of an *immoral* action, provided that we are willing to accept that other agents are entitled to act according to the same maxim. This is, in effect, the stance assumed by the Marquis de Sade.[161] Hegel even suggests that the very abstraction of Kantian morality could have dangerous consequences. A purportedly abstract and universal morality ignores all the subtleties of inherited social practices, which Hegel terms 'ethical life' (*Sittlichkeit*). But what is worse, the attempt to follow the dictates of abstract morality in isolation ends in destruction The abstract universality of absolute freedom is, for Hegel, the ultimate source of the French Revolutionary Terror: 'Universal freedom, therefore, can produce neither a positive work nor a deed; there is left for it only *negative* action; it is merely the *fury* of destruction.' [162]

Less dramatically, Kant's assertion of the priority of reason over inclination can reasonably be interpreted as reviving a long tradition of ascetic idealism. Like Plato, Kant equates morality with rigorous self-mastery, with the absolute dominion of autonomous reason over unruly, merely animal inclinations. This dominion is, at the same time, understood as preserving one's true or essential self: 'The principle of self-mastery is universal respect for one's own person in relation to the essential ends of humanity or human nature. . . . This discipline is the executive authority of the prescription of reason over the acts whose origin is in sensibility.'[163] Kant also echoes Plato's political analogy between the proper political order of the state and the moral order of the individual. Inclination or 'sensibility' is a kind of 'rabble' that must be vigilantly kept in check by the rational will: 'Our sensibility is a kind of rabble without law or rule; it requires guidance even if it is not rebellious.' Indeed, the rule of reason should permit no democratic deviation from the 'autocracy' of free will.[164] The emotions and passions are ever-present and disruptive threats to the calm sovereignty of reason: 'Emotion produces a momentary loss of freedom and self-control. Passion surrenders both, and finds pleasure and satisfaction in a servile disposition.'[165] Cold rationality is a necessary condition for the independence of the free citizen.

For Kant's discussion of friendship, love and sexuality, an alternative version of his categorical imperative is most helpful. According to this version, 'So act that you use humanity, whether in your own person or in the person of any other, always at the same time as an end, never merely as a means.'[166] Respect for oneself as a 'rational person' implies universal respect for all rational persons. This version of the categorical imperative finds direct application in Kant's account of friendship. Friendship is that state 'in which self-love is superseded by a generous reciprocity of love': 'The maximum reciprocity of love is friendship, and friendship is an Idea because it is the measure by which we can determine reciprocal love.'[167] The ideal of perfect friendship contrasts with the ulterior motivations of 'real empirical friendships'.[168] Like Aristotle, Kant recognizes that ordinary human relationships are often determined or, at least, influenced by motivations other than friendship or love for its own sake. Actual friendships are based on uniformity of interest or need, on common tastes and enjoyments, on the useful complementarity of capacities, and so on. In the context of eighteenth-century political economy, it is not surprising that Kant places particular emphasis on the countervailing power of self-interest. In a phrase that anticipates Marx's description of the family, he describes friendship as 'man's refuge in this world from his distrust of his fellows, in which he can reveal his disposition to another and enter into communion with him'.[169]

If Kant elevates love and friendship to the status of an ideal, it is, however, only on condition that any sexual or erotic taint is thoroughly expunged. Unmarried and childless himself, Kant does not hesitate to deploy his universal rational principles in support of Christian sexual morality. He reproduces the traditional Christian sexual prohibitions in words that often recall Aquinas' canonical version. In fact, Kant goes further than Augustine and Aquinas in his hostility to sex, regarding even procreative sex as intrinsically degrading. In the absence of extraneous moral justification, sex is a 'principle of the degradation of human nature'.[170] The sexual impulse is condemned, because it necessarily involves treating another person as a mere object rather than as a rational end. To treat another as end necessarily involves treating that person as a rational rather than merely corporeal self. As an activity directed to the body rather than the rational self, sexual activity reduces the other person to the status of a mere means to selfish gratification. As Kant acidly remarks, 'Sexual love makes of the loved person an Object of appetite; as soon as that appetite has been stilled, the person is cast aside as one casts away a lemon which has been sucked dry.'[171]

Sexual love can only be redeemed when it occurs within the context of marriage. But Kant does not rely here on the traditional Christian view of marriage as the only proper context for the bearing and rearing of children, let alone on the Lutheran understanding of marriage as a guarantee of loving mutuality. Rather it is the marriage *contract* that makes the sexual act compatible with a proper moral relationship between rational selves. Only the marriage contract preserves our freedom in the midst of sexual commerce. As Kant lucidly (if not very enticingly) states:

> The sole condition on which we are free to make use of our sexual desire depends upon the right to dispose over the person as a whole – over the welfare and happiness and generally over all the circumstances of that person. If I have the right over the whole person, I have also the right over the part and so I have the right to use that person's *organa sexualia* for the satisfaction of sexual desire. But how am I to obtain these rights over the whole person? Only by giving that person the same rights over the whole of myself. This happens only in marriage. Matrimony is an agreement between two persons by which they grant each other equal reciprocal rights, each of them undertaking to surrender the whole of their person to the other with a complete right of disposal over it.[172]

This view of marriage does not, of course, place it in any essential relationship with love or friendship.

It is a relatively straightforward matter for Kant to derive from the categorical imperative understood as a principle of universalization the further principle that only procreative sex can be redeemed in this way. A non-procreative sexual act must be wrong, because it is contrary to 'the end of humanity in respect of sexuality', which 'is to preserve the species without debasing the person'.[173] Were everyone to act on the principle derived from universalizing the maxim of a non-procreative act, then the human species would inevitably fail to be reproduced. Of course, Kant does not consider here the possible universalization of an alternative maxim to act according to one's sexual inclinations, whether these are homosexual or heterosexual. It is only on the presumably false premise that everyone's sexual inclinations are really homosexual that the universalization of *this* maxim would have deleterious consequences – assuming that the disappearance of the human race is something to be avoided. It nevertheless follows for Kant, as it did for Aquinas, not only that any sexual activity outside the sanitizing bonds of matrimony is *ipso facto* a 'misuse of sexuality', but that any *non-procreative* sexual activity is to be doubly condemned.

Kant further classifies and castigates a variety of *crimina carnis* or 'crimes of the flesh' in terms that closely resemble those employed by Aquinas. Like Aquinas, Kant distinguishes between sexual acts that are simply 'against reason' and those that are also crimes 'against nature' (*crimina carnis contra naturam*). Sexual crimes such as concubinage and adultery violate the requirement of marriage but are otherwise 'according to nature' and so only 'contrary to sound reason'. Crimes 'against nature', however, must also be deemed 'contrary to our animal nature'.[174] Kant differs from Aquinas only in regarding such violations of our animal nature as affronts to humanity rather than God. But Kant's typically Enlightenment commitment to 'humanity' inspires a hostility to non-procreative sex that would have impressed any medieval theologian. Such acts include masturbation and what Kant discreetly terms intercourse between *sexus homogenii* ('people of the same sex'). Wrongly assuming, like Aquinas, that other animals are quite innocent of such acts, Kant repeats the old accusation that these forms of sexuality degrade human beings even below the level of animals.

The intensity of Kant's homophobia is most blatant in his unfavourable comparison of homosexual acts to what he describes as the 'most dreadful' crime of suicide. Suicide clearly violates the rational end of humanity, which must include a duty to oneself and one's life. But sexual crimes against nature are far worse:

> All *crimina carnis contra naturam* degrade human nature to a level below that of animal nature and make man unworthy of his humanity. He no longer deserves to be a person. From the point of view of duties towards himself such conduct is the most disgraceful and the most degrading of which man is capable. Suicide is the most dreadful, but it is not as dishonourable and base as the *crimina carnis contra naturam*. It is the most abominable conduct of which man can be guilty. So abominable are these *crimina carnis contra naturam* that they are unmentionable, for the very mention of them is nauseating, as is not the case with suicide.[175]

It is only, Kant assures us, because such sexual crimes are of surprisingly 'frequent occurrence' that the philosopher must reluctantly mention them, albeit behind the protective veil of Latin terminology and only in order to condemn them. It is difficult to avoid the conclusion that Kant was, in effect, recommending suicide to those young men attending these lectures on ethics who might otherwise be tempted to indulge in that even more 'dreadful', 'dishonourable' and unmentionable crime.

Against the moral scepticism unleashed by Enlightenment materialism and hedonism, Kant's philosophy as a whole is designed to preserve the rational core of the tradition of ascetic idealism. His elevation of the autonomous will above the body's irrational and subversive inclinations allows him to reconstruct Christian sexual morality on seemingly more rational foundations. Sensuality is a prime obstacle to the intellectual and moral clarity that we might otherwise attain. Sexual impulses and activities enslave the will in the mire of natural necessity. But this rehabilitation of idealist reason also institutes a significant innovation. Though religious himself, Kant demonstrates that an idealist and ascetic constellation of reason and sexuality is capable of surviving independently of religious premises. In the process, the ascetic demands of reason are internalized. No longer the external impositions of a harsh and perhaps vengeful deity, sexual proscriptions are understood henceforth as products of the *self*-legislation of a rational self.[176] Sexual asceticism is, as a result, even more difficult to overcome. The self is no longer entitled to maintain any kind of separation or distance from injunctions that are now revealed to be its own.

2

Rationality in the Service of Desire

> *Love* of persons for pleasing the sense only, *natural lust*. *Love* of the same, acquired from rumination, that is, imagination of pleasure past, *luxury*. *Love* of one singularly, with desire to be singularly loved, *the passion of love*. The same, with fear that the love is not mutual, *jealousy*.
>
> Thomas Hobbes[1]

1 Epicureanism and Sexual Realism

A second major constellation of reason and sexuality retains a significant role for a diminished faculty of what will here be called *rationality*. In contrast to the ambitious claims of idealist reason, which is regarded as the source of transcendent values for an idealized self, rationality is more sceptically and modestly conceived as an intellectual instrument of organization and calculation in the service of a natural, bodily self. The tradition of *realist* rationalism associated with this conception of rationality is typically also linked to some form of materialism and empiricism. Empiricists regard sensory experience rather than innate reason or divine revelation as the ultimate source of human knowledge. Materialists regard the ordinary material world as the only significant reality, rejecting idealist claims that we should orient our lives to some higher or 'ultimate' reality or truth. Realist rationalism has also tended to encourage a more accepting attitude to the body and sexual pleasure in some version of hedonism. Realist rationalism comes most clearly into focus after the Renaissance with the rise of modern science, scientific rationalism and Enlightenment, but this occurs only as the culmination of a long and difficult genealogy. Like the ascetic idealism of reason, realist rationalism has ancient origins.

The classical sources of realist and scientific rationalism can be found in the early literature of sexual realism. Sexual realism can be understood as an expression at the level of culture and everyday morality of those more relaxed pagan attitudes to sexuality that were gradually overwhelmed by the ascetic idealism of Platonism and Christianity. On a variety of grounds, sexual realists are inclined to accept the facts of sexuality without seeking to impose more demanding moral standards or ideals. In the literary works of sexual realism, the highlights and vicissitudes of sexual activity are described and explored rather than evaluated, let alone condemned. Sexual realism assumes a sceptical or cynical rather than idealizing attitude to love. Far from understanding love as a 'higher' and worthier substitute for sex, love is regarded as a pathological manifestation of excessive desire.[2] A further common element of classical sexual realism is humour. In a connection that has a long history in western culture, humour signals and even effects greater tolerance in sexual matters. Humour indicates acceptance of the realities of human weakness and folly. The comparison with the moral strenuousness and limited tolerance of sexual idealism could not be more striking.

The Roman poet Publius Ovidius Naso (43 BC–AD 17/18), better known as Ovid, wrote a number of poetic works on love and sex, notably the *Amores* and *Cures for Love*. Indeed, in sexual-realist spirit he makes little attempt to distinguish between the two. From the outset, the sexual desires and erotic infatuations of his nominally male readers are regarded as natural and inevitable. In a manner helpful and humorous in equal part, Ovid describes the various strategems of sexual conquest and the complementary 'remedies of love'. The latter are required to cure the enamoured individual of the unfortunate side-effects of what always threatens to become an obsession or even madness. The guiding intention is at all times the purely pragmatic one of securing the greatest amount of pleasure and the least frustration for his readers. From this perspective, restrictive sexual prohibitions and even sexual possessiveness are just self-defeating. The imposition of chastity is a spur to desire – one 'shouldn't encourage vice by veto':

> We're all rebels against restriction – in love with the illicit –
> sick men craving the fluid they're forbidden.[3]

The sexually active are willing devotees of Eros, who do not deserve the harsh and unjust punishment meted out to them in the form of obsessive love:

> No terms could be strong enough, Cupid, to express my resentment
> At the treacherous way you've settled yourself in my heart.
> What's your grudge against me? Have I ever once deserted
> Your standards? Then why should I
> Be the one who gets shot from behind? How come your torch and arrows
> Are turned against friends?[4]

Ovid's realism is simply descriptive without any pretension to penetrate to any underlying reality or truth about sex or love. He is satisfied with the superficial 'phenomena' of sex, uncritically reproducing the cultural assumptions of men of his time. Eternal truths about unrequited love jostle with joking references to hairy armpits and legs.[5] Ovid mocks the idealizing pretensions of his time, but he never seriously sets out to immunize his audience against the inevitable symptoms of the folly of love.

Many features of sexual realism in literary form are theoretically elaborated in the philosophy of Epicureanism. This current of thought is named after the Greek philosopher Epicurus (341–270 BC), though few of his own writings survive. Epicurean principles were given elegant and more systematic expression some two centuries later by the Roman poet Lucretius (Titus Lucretius Carus, *c.*95–*c.*55 BC) in his philosophical poem *On the Nature of Things* (*De rerum natura*). In contrast to Platonist idealism, the Epicureans based their ethics on empiricist epistemology and materialist metaphysics. Sensation is regarded as the basis of our knowledge of an external world that is understood in strictly secular terms, as an arrangement of material particles and forces. The pagan gods of ancient Greek and Roman religion may still be deemed to exist, but they are not taken as seriously. The pagan gods exhibit most human vices, so they are hardly suitable candidates for moralizing uplift. In any case, Epicureanism's materialist metaphysics implies that the world and human life can be understood without reference either to such divinities or to the eternal realm of ideas posited by Platonic idealism.

Epicureanism resembles Platonism, however, in the way it links epistemology and metaphysics with ethics and an overall philosophy of life. The Epicurean picture of the world, and humanity's place in it, is designed not simply to represent philosophical truth but, above all, to enable its followers to live a good and happy life. As Epicurus remarks in his letter to Pythocles: 'First of all then we must not suppose that any other object is to be gained from the knowledge of the phenomena of the sky, whether they are dealt with in connexion with other doctrines or independently, than peace of mind and a sure confidence, just as in all other branches of study.'[6] Philosophical understanding provides the means to overcome the fears and pitfalls of life. The metaphysical contemplation of nature is an effective means to this end. True piety is not found in ritual observances or sacrifice but rather, as Lucretius puts it, in the ability 'to survey all things with tranquil mind'.[7] Knowledge of the 'aspect and law of nature' dispels fear.[8]

The most straightforward application of materialist principles serves to dispel superstitious anxieties aroused by religious belief. Epicurus claims that the true philosophy can deliver us from the belief that the heavenly bodies are gods and related fears of death and punishment in the after-life.[9] Death cannot be something evil, because it is really nothing at all: 'For all good and evil consists in sensation, but death is deprivation of sensation. . . . So death, the most terrifying of ills, is nothing to us, since so long as we exist, death is not with us; but when death comes, then we do not exist.'[10] It is important to overcome the fear of death above all, because this fear is not only the source of much human suffering in its own right, it is also the cause of many other ills and wrong-doings, countless futile efforts and false beliefs.[11] Like Epicurus, Lucretius believes that materialism removes any legitimate ground for fearing the 'nothingness' of death. Even the prospect of reincarnation would give us no legitimate reason for either hope or fear. We exist only as a 'compacted' whole of 'spirit' and 'body', so we can have no possible reason for concern about any future or past incarnations. Without memory or consciousness (*repetentia*) – 'when the recollection of ourselves has once been broken asunder' – we lose any reason to identify with 'our' reincarnation.[12]

Liberation from the prospect of eternal damnation also removes one of the main motivations for conventionally pious behaviour and opens the way for a morality centred instead on the individual's happiness and 'peace of mind'. It is important, however, to avoid the common misunderstanding – fostered mainly by their enemies – that Epicureans advocated unfettered indulgence in sensual pleasure. That position is more correctly associated with the cynic Diogenes, who, as we noted in the previous chapter, is reputed to have masturbated in public in order to demonstrate his relaxed attitude to natural human pleasure.[13] Like Plato and Aristotle, Epicurus and Lucretius are critical of over-indulgence and share similar fears about the insatiability and corruptibility of sensual desires. Lucretius expresses the more sober Epicurean aim of enjoying a simple life through avoidance of unnecessary pain and suffering, which is caused not only by fear of death but also by selfish and destructive passions for wealth, power or fame.[14] Happiness is secured by avoiding unnecessary desires and the frustrations they inevitably bring, not by the active pursuit of pleasure. Only the simplest and most natural pleasures should be indulged. As Epicurus puts it, 'The happy and blessed state belongs not to abundance of riches or dignity of position or any office or power, but to freedom from pain and moderation in feelings and an attitude of mind which imposes the limits ordained by nature.'[15]

Epicureanism's balanced attitude to pleasures in general is applied to the topic of *sexual* pleasure. Pleasure remains as essential to the Epicurean conception of a good and happy life as it is for Aristotle. And this applies, according to Epicurus, even to physical pleasures: 'I know not how I can conceive the good, if I withdraw the pleasures of taste, and withdraw the pleasures of love, and withdraw the pleasures of hearing, and withdraw the pleasurable emotions caused to sight by beautiful form.'[16] Nor are sexual pleasures intrinsically bad either, though there are potential dangers and pitfalls that should not be overlooked:

> You tell me that the stimulus of the flesh makes you too prone to the pleasures of love. Provided that you do not break the laws or good customs and do not distress any of your neighbours or do harm to your body or squander your pittance, you may indulge your inclination as you please. Yet it is impossible not to come up against one or other of these barriers. . . .
>
> Sexual intercourse has never done a man good, and he is lucky if it has not harmed him.[17]

Epicurus apparently assumes that if we obey nature, we will not be in danger of violating 'laws' and 'good customs'. But as sexual realists always emphasize, love is a risky business that can cause conflict, dissension and disappointment. These dangers can be mitigated if the incitements to excessive desire associated with love are avoided and only 'natural desires' pursued: 'We must not violate nature, but obey her; and we shall obey her if we fulfil the necessary desires and also the physical, if they bring no harm to us, but sternly reject the harmful.'[18]

Lucretius, closer in this respect to Ovid than Epicurus, provides more practical advice on dealing with potentially risky sexual and amatory involvements. He understands sex as a fairly straightforward product of human physiology. Sexual attraction in men results from the sight of a human form, which provokes an accumulation of seed near the generative organs, leading to the 'desire to emit it towards that whither the dire craving tends'.[19] This urge is associated with a particular person as a result of beautiful images emanating from the object of love, which arouse lust. The gender of sexual partners is not treated as an issue of any importance. Lucretius acknowledges matter-of-factly that the beloved may be either male or female.[20]

Of greater concern is the risk of erotic obsession and consequent dependence on the object of one's affections. Although sexual attraction can lead to painful dependence on another person, the passion of love is altogether more dangerous. In the spirit of sexual realism, Lucretius recommends 'frequent sexual intercourse' and 'promiscuous attachments' as the most effective cure for obsessions of either kind.[21] He admits, though, that this remedy is not guaranteed to work. Love, in particular, is a delusional state that often persists after the otherwise therapeutic release of accumulated male seed. Love induces cravings for fulfilments that prove illusory: '. . . so in love Venus mocks lovers with images, nor can bodies even in real presence satisfy lovers with looking . . . but all is vanity, for they can rub nothing off, nor can they penetrate and be absorbed body in body; for this they seem sometimes to wish and to strive for.'[22] More psychological remedies may also be called for. One should do the opposite of most people 'bewitched by Venus' and try to dwell on 'all faults of mind and body in her whom you prefer and desire', recognizing the girl who is 'dirty and rank', 'stringy and wooden' or a 'squat little dwarf' for what she is.[23]

The often misogynist sexual realism and Epicureanism of the ancient world were relentlessly suppressed at the hands of Christian ascetics and idealists. During the Middle Ages, sexual realism was also challenged by rival chivalric traditions, which put forward demanding and sometimes chaste ideals of courtly love.[24] But sexual realism nevertheless persists throughout the medieval period. A fascinating text in this regard is the thirteenth-century *Romance of the Rose* (*Roman de la rose*), a long and involved allegory of love that is further complicated by its dual authorship – the first 4,028 verses of the poem (around a fifth of the final version) were written by Guillaume de Lorris between 1225 and 1230, the rest by Jean de Meun (*c.*1269–78). The earlier part appears to celebrate the ideals of courtly love in such a way that C. S. Lewis could detect the 'peculiar charm of medieval love poetry – that boy-like blending . . . of innocence and sensuousness which could make us believe for a moment that paradise had never been lost'.[25] But the contribution of Meun strikes quite a different, decidedly realist and even cynical note.

Lorris explores some of the difficulties and untoward circumstances on the path to true love through a series of allegorical encounters between the Lover and a number of other characters, including Fair Welcome, Rebuff, Jealousy, Hope and Despair. Meun is more direct though by no means concise. After a long disquisition by Reason, two further allegorical figures appear in the second portion of the *Romance*: Nature and Genius. At considerable length and with only lightly disguised vulgarity, they argue for the natural, reproductive necessity of sex and the consequent innocence – or at least veniality – of fornication: 'Lift the stilts of your ploughs with your two bare hands, support them firmly on your arms and make an effort to thrust the ploughshare straight along the right path, the better to penetrate the furrow.'[26] Sex is a natural and productive pleasure that should be encouraged. Condemnation is reserved for 'those who are so blinded by their sin and misled by pride that they despise the furrow of the fair and fertile field; those wretches who go tilling the desert ground where their seed is wasted'. The punishment for these rebels against nature is severe. They should be excommunicated and 'lose the purse and testicles that are the sign of their manhood'.[27]

A century later, the licentiousness and apparent misogyny of Meun provoked a reaction from a woman who has been described as the first feminist, Christine de Pizan (1365–*c*.1430). As a woman writing openly at this time in defence of women, she was certainly remarkable. She is most famous for her involvement in the so-called 'debate of the Rose', which arose from a letter she wrote criticizing Meun's *Romance*.[28] She is particularly critical of his apparently insulting view of women, expressed (though indirectly) through the character of the Friend, who relates the speeches of Nature and Genius. As well as advocating promiscuity, the Friend is seemingly indifferent to the value of marriage and expresses a very low opinion of women. Pizan's defence of women is developed in many of her subsequent works.[29] But what the debate of the Rose also confirms is the extraordinary resilience of sexual realism in the western tradition.[30]

2 Renaissance and the Humanization of Eros

The Renaissance is often associated with the flourishing of Italian culture and intellectual life in the *Quattrocento* or fifteenth century. It is more accurately seen as the culmination of a series of developments gathering pace in the later stages of the medieval period from around AD 1200, which eventually brought about a decisive shift in the social, cultural and intellectual life of Europe.[31] The term 'Renaissance' refers to the apparent 'rebirth' of classical learning and the renewed influence of pagan culture. Certainly there was during this period a renewed interest in classical philosophy, partly inspired by the rediscovery from the twelfth century of some significant

Aristotelian and Platonic texts, mainly from Arab sources. But the Renaissance should not be understood as an abrupt turn from Christianity to paganism. Sexual realism and other aspects of classical culture had, as we have seen, survived throughout the medieval period. But they were always subordinated to the priorities and prohibitions of religion. Augustine and Aquinas were inspired by Plato and Aristotle, but they adapted classical philosophy to the theological demands of the Church. By the same token, important figures of the high Renaissance such as Petrarch, Erasmus, Valla and Ficino remained firmly Christian.

Characteristic of the Renaissance is rather the gradual emergence of a very different intellectual approach. For R. G. Collingwood, this transformation involves, above all, the greater independence from religion of the different elements of intellectual and cultural life, including art, history, philosophy and science. Medieval Christendom was characterized by a 'unity of the mind' whereby '[n]o mental activity . . . existed in its own right and for itself. Art was always working hand in hand with religion, religion hand in hand with philosophy.'[32] The Renaissance is the period when the 'voices' of art, science, philosophy and, to a lesser extent, history begin to be liberated from their subservience to religion. This development is the basis of our 'modern' (and now taken-for-granted) experience of science, art, philosophy and history as independent modes of experience and knowledge associated with potentially conflicting standards of value.[33] This independence represents the essential meaning and achievement of modern intellectual freedom: 'Freedom, the watchword of the Renaissance, meant freedom for all the different activities of the mind from interference by each other.'[34]

Perhaps the most well-known manifestation of the process described by Collingwood is the liberation of art and aesthetics from their subservience to religion. From the Renaissance, art is increasingly free to explore non-religious and even pagan themes, albeit subject to moralistic interventions like that of Girolamo Savonarola (1452–98) in late fifteenth-century Florence. Freed from the obligations of religious worship and piety, art unashamedly celebrates the vigour and beauty of the human form, sometimes in strikingly erotic terms. Artistic beauty comes once again to be associated less with religious worship than, as for the ancient Greeks, with desire. Art resumes its long and complex relationship with sexual experience. Exploits of unconventional sexuality certainly figured prominently in the lives of a number of Renaissance artists. Magnified through the homoerotic sensibilities of later historians and art critics such as J. J. Winckelmann in the eighteenth century, and Walter Pater and J. A.

Symonds in the nineteenth century, art entered its long career in the West as a respectable cover and voice for sexuality in both conventional and unconventional modes.[35]

The shift from an hegemonically religious culture and consciousness and the liberation of art are part of the more general flourishing of *humanism*. Humanism is closely related to revived interest in classical thought and culture and, in a practical sense, has been defined as 'a liberal education centred on authoritative texts in Greek and Latin that taught grammar, rhetoric, poetry, history, and moral philosophy'.[36] But humanism was far more than a curriculum. The gradual emancipation of classical studies from the control of religion allowed the emergence or re-emergence of a distinctively *human* perspective on the world. A significant element of this was greater confidence and even pride in humanity's unaided cognitive powers. But humanists still followed Aristotle and religious orthodoxy in distinguishing between technical or scientific knowledge and moral or practical wisdom. Technical knowledge was the domain of the emerging natural sciences of astronomy and mechanics, which came into increasing conflict with the cosmological doctrines of the Church.

But *moral* judgement was not yet seen to be amenable to the analytical, calculating methods of science. Where they did not still defer to Church teaching, humanists relied for their knowledge of 'man' on the corpus of classical literature and learning supplemented by anecdotes from history, folk wisdom and travellers' tales of 'savages' and the 'new world'. Humanism did not, at first, directly impinge on western sexual morality, which remained within the sphere of religious authority.[37] At the same time, the 'new science' did begin to lay the foundations of a less moralistic account of *nature*, which had obvious implications for the understanding of sexuality. Although the Renaissance did not have an immediate effect on social mores, let alone repressive sexual norms, it did contribute to an increasingly 'scientific', secular and morally neutral conception of nature. The removal of the earth from its privileged position at the centre of a divinely ordered cosmos would eventually set morality loose as well, as suggested by the Catholic Church's harsh treatment of cosmological heretics like Galileo and Giordano Bruno.

Gradually, sexual-realist themes from classical antiquity were able to resurface along with greater acceptance of the realities of human sinfulness and imperfection. The liberation of culture from religious strictures encouraged non-religious subjects and even the portrayal of classical episodes of dubious respectability. The idea that literature might portray reality rather than having to serve some higher religious or moral purpose made it less problematic to mention 'immoral' sexual behaviour, as long as suitably moralistic commentaries were inserted as well. In Chaucer's *Canterbury Tales*, Rabelais's *Gargantua and Pantagruel* and Boccaccio's *Decameron*, the earthy realities of human sexuality are portrayed for all their humorous and sensationalist worth, albeit with occasional lip-service to traditional Christian pieties. In the process, the classical tradition of sexual dissidence was also kept alive. But Epicurean materialism, empiricism and moral hedonism gained ground only slowly. Even a nominally Epicurean work such as Lorenzo Valla's *On Pleasure* identifies the ultimate pleasure for human beings as divine love (*caritas*).[38]

In fact, it was Neoplatonism rather than Epicurean nominalism that was still the dominant party in Renaissance thought and the main influence on the nascent scientific revolution. It was not until sixteenth- and seventeenth-century thinkers such as Francis Bacon and Pierre Gassendi that nominalism, materialism and empiricism came to the fore and, even then, still with persistent theological concerns.[39] Certainly, unlike their medieval forebears, Neoplatonist humanists proudly celebrate human cognitive capacities. But this occurs within the context of metaphysical and cosmological views that are still decidedly Christian. Accordingly, humanity is celebrated not as an already perfect creature but as a being capable of aspiring to the higher moral demands of religion. Beauty and heroism are similarly seen to reflect humanity's connection with higher things. At the same time, Neoplatonism had the effect of reviving discussion of classical figures and texts with sometimes heterodox sexual associations. This encouraged a subtle softening and humanizing of the otherwise harshly ascetic sexual morality of Christianity. Plato was perceived not just through the lens of a Christian theology partly inspired by Platonism but also through the eyes of the more permissive pagan culture that Platonism helped to displace.

The Christian Neoplatonism of Marsilio Ficino (1433–99) intriguingly combines idealism, humanism and allusions to pagan sexuality in a way characteristic of the Renaissance. Ficino is a major figure in the revival of Neoplatonism that was spurred by the rediscovery of major Platonic texts. He produced the first complete translation of the works of Plato into Latin as well as translations of other Platonist texts. Ficino's interpretations of Plato reconcile the high contemplative ideals of Platonism with the worldly lives of his contemporaries in Florence. The philosophical transcendence of lower levels of human existence remains the ultimate goal, but worldly concerns are still valued in their place. At the same time, Platonist ideas are reconciled with Christian doctrine, reuniting the wisdom of philosophy with religion – the *pia philosophia* (pious philosophy) and *docta religio* (learned faith).[40] In his interpretation of Plato's works, Ficino seeks a deeper poetic and allegorical significance that turns out to be religious. For Ficino, as for Augustine, the obscure wisdom underlying the sometimes morally unsettling discourse of Plato and other ancient philosophers is essentially Christian.

Ficino's allegorical hermeneutics is much in evidence in his *Commentary on Plato's Symposium on Love*. Here Ficino recounts Aristophanes' famous story of the origins of both heterosexual and homosexual love.[41] Despite the intense homophobia of Christian teaching at the time, Ficino does not deny the possibility of homosexual love:

> Hence certainly a reciprocal love is innate in men, the conciliator of their original nature, striving to make one out of two and to heal the nature of men. For each of us is half of a man. . . . But each human half seeks its own half. And so whenever his own half meets someone, of whichever sex he may be desirous, he is most violently aroused, clings to it with burning love, and does not even for a moment permit being separated from it. And so the desire and longing for the whole to be restored received the name of love.[42]

But Ficino quickly substitutes a more spiritual interpretation that is far less shocking to Christian sensibilities. Like Plato, he regards human love as the confused stirring of a deeper need to be reunited with divine truth, but Ficino's God is firmly identified with the God of Christianity:

> When souls, already divided and immersed in bodies, first have come to the years of adolescence, they are aroused by the natural and innate light which they retained (as if by a certain half of themselves) to recover, through the study of truth, that infused and divine light, once half of themselves, which they lost in falling. This once recovered, they will be whole, and blessed with a vision of God.[43]

According to Ficino's re-reading, male and female in Aristophanes' story are intended to represent not the erotic relations of ordinary human beings but rather the relationship between different kinds of *virtue*. The male represents courage, the female temperance and the union of both is justice.

Ficino interprets in similarly allegorical terms Plato's contrast between two kinds of love, one desiring progeny of the soul and the other progeny of the body. He agrees that the vulgarly reproductive kind is inferior to the spiritually productive variety that Plato associates with relationships between men.[44] But the *Symposium*'s apparent approval of homosexual relationships is really just an allegorical way of advocating the life of reason and a higher form of love. Any other interpretation is ruled out for Ficino by the simple fact that Socrates was never charged with 'immoral loves': 'Now do you think that if he had polluted himself with a stain so filthy, or rather, if he had not been completely above suspicion of this charge, he would have escaped the venomous tongues of such detractors?'[45] To the contrary, Socrates exerted a benign influence on young men, attracting them towards philosophy and away from those 'wicked men' who are flatterers, away from 'lascivious men' interested only in physical copulation.[46] It seems all the more ironic, then, that Socrates' pre-Christian and non-ascetic contemporaries took a different view and, perhaps puzzled by his sexual restraint, condemned him to death for 'corrupting the youth of Athens' with abstract philosophy.

At the same time, Ficino's commentary finds room for a 'scientific' explanation of homosexuality in astrological terms. The reproductive drives are, it turns out, particularly vulnerable to mistakes of the kind familiar from ancient Greece:

> But since the reproductive drive of the soul, being without cognition, makes no distinction between the sexes, nevertheless, it is naturally aroused for copulation whenever we judge any body to be beautiful; and it often happens that those who associate with males, in order to satisfy the demands of the genital part, copulate with them. Especially those at whose birth Venus was in a masculine sign and either in conjunction with Saturn, or in the house of Saturn, or in opposition to Saturn. But it should have been noticed that the purpose of erections of the genital part is not the useless act of ejaculation, but the function of fertilizing and procreating; the part should have been redirected from males to females. . . . We think that it was by some error of this kind that that wicked crime arose which Plato in his Laws roundly curses as a form of murder.[47]

A further medical explanation for the attraction between men is also adduced. The effect of 'spirit' and 'blood' passing through the eyes to the heart is not to be resisted: witness the example of Phaedrus and Lysias. The sexual attraction between men may even be stronger than that aroused in men by women, who are themselves particularly attractive when they resemble boys: 'Women, of course, catch men easily, and even more easily women who display a certain masculine character. Men catch men still more easily, since they are more like men than women are, and they have blood and spirit which is clearer, warmer, and thinner, which is the basis of erotic entrapment.'[48] Some of Ficino's remedies for excessive physical attachments of this kind also bespeak a surprisingly Epicurean tolerance for this 'filthy' vice. As he helpfully reminds us, 'Lucretius also prescribes frequent coitus.'[49]

Both idealist and realist tendencies of the Renaissance come together, if somewhat uneasily, in its strong cultural and intellectual emphasis on friendship. Renaissance ideas of friendship were influenced directly by classical ideals and especially Aristotle's idealization of friendship as a communion of virtue. This ideal had never been repudiated by the Church but rather, as with Platonic idealism more generally, was reinterpreted in religious terms as the communion of God's Church or even as communion between man and God. Under the sway of Renaissance humanism, ideals of love and friendship are reconciled with the possibility of a *human* object, albeit one that is still required to stand in for higher things. As Irving Singer puts it, 'things and persons in the world are to be loved only for the sake of a spiritual beauty that transcends them, and yet the beautiful cannot be appreciated unless we love its manifestations in matter.'[50] As with the ancients, Renaissance humanists tended to believe that the higher spiritual ideals of friendship could only be attained between men or sometimes in any same-sex relationships *ipso facto* presumed asexual.[51] At the same time, under the countervailing sway of Renaissance sexual realism, the possibly physical and sexual dimension of these friendships is close at hand. Ficino's Platonic defence of spiritual love between scholars devoted to truth was highly suspect to his cynical or, perhaps, observant contemporaries. What Ficino defended as a chaste Socratic love (*amor socraticus*) had become a synonym for sodomy within fifty years of his death.[52]

The Renaissance's 'homosocial' ideal of friendship is represented in similarly ambiguous terms in the life and writings of Francis Bacon (1561–1626). Himself reputedly homosexual, Bacon combines praise of the Renaissance ideal of perfect friendship in the Aristotelian tradition with what is presumably merely conventional condemnation of unnatural and 'unlawful' sexual desires.[53] His essay 'Of Friendship' catalogues its many benefits, including the opportunity to express otherwise pent-up emotions and the sharing of grief. Not unusually for the humanist and classical traditions, his essay on 'Beauty' concerns itself with exclusively male examples. The essay on 'Marriage and Single Life' finds no necessity and some disadvantages in marriage. At the same time, Bacon elsewhere warns of the dangers of natural bodily inclinations. Nature is viewed as something to be controlled and repressed. The value of spiritual friendship in the Aristotelian sense is contrasted with reprehensible 'masculine loves'. The idealized inhabitants of his mythical New Atlantis value marriage as, among other things, 'a remedy for unlawful concupiscence'.[54] They approve of true friendship but know nothing of sexual relations between men: 'As for masculine love, they have no touch of it; and yet there are not so faithful and inviolate friendships in the world again as are there. . . .'[55]

The uncertain distinction between friendship and sexual love can be explored further in relation to Desiderius Erasmus (1466–1536), who was one of the most influential figures of the Renaissance. A humanist cleric and scholar born in Rotterdam, Erasmus is now most famous for his satirical work of Christian humanism, *In Praise of Folly* (1509). He was a prolific writer in a wide range of genres as well as translator of the Greek New Testament. Although he pioneered a more humanist attitude to faith, he remained a faithful Catholic throughout his life, successfully side-stepping the Church's controversy with Luther and Protestantism. The letters of Erasmus provide a striking example of a passionate discourse of friendship between men. After entering a monastery in 1487, he wrote a series of 'love' letters to a young man called Servatius Rogerus. The sexual inference that a contemporary reader would be likely to draw is, however, uncertain. According to prevailing conventions of letter-writing catalogued in Erasmus's own work *On the Writing of Letters*, these letters could be interpreted either as passionate avowals of homoerotic love or merely as formal exercises in a popular Renaissance genre of friendship letters. Certainly, Erasmus's use of the female gender to refer to his (male) 'tigress' and nonchalant citing of famous homosexual lovers of antiquity do not betray awareness of any rigid ban on love or courtship between men. Perhaps, as Alan Bray suggests in his work on Renaissance homosexuality, the prevailing culture consigned 'sodomy' to a region of infernal wickedness and depravity hard to connect with those things that 'one does with one's friend'.[56]

3 Hedonism within the Bounds of Rational Order

Although the Renaissance was still predominantly Platonist and Christian, the greater recognition of human cognitive powers that came with humanism ultimately encouraged the rise of a more robustly secular and scientific rationalism. In the process, the ascetic rationalism of Platonism and Christian theology was gradually challenged. The new rationalism was based on Epicurean, materialist and nominalist philosophical principles and was inspired by the impressive successes of Copernican astronomy, Newtonian mechanics and mathematics. The world that comes into view with the sciences and philosophy of the modern period is, to use the term made famous by Max Weber, thoroughly 'disenchanted' (*entzaubert*). The world of nature is no longer understood as a meaningful whole with moral and religious significance for humanity. Rather, as Charles Taylor puts it, the world familiar from modern philosophy and science is 'a world of ultimately contingent correlations to be patiently mapped by empirical observation'.[57]

The shift from a religious to a scientific world-view is associated with a strongly contested but ultimately decisive transition from the metaphysical ambitions and moral demands of 'reason' to the instrumental benefits proffered by calculating 'rationality'.[58] For the most durable currents of modern philosophy, there is no longer any convincing role for a quasi-divine faculty of reason. Rather, the calculating intelligence of a more modestly conceived human rationality is valued in instrumental terms as the means to greater control over the material world. Francis Bacon expresses, in explicitly patriarchal terms and still within the context of religious belief, his hope 'that knowledge may not be, as a curtesan, for pleasure and vanity only, or as a bondwoman, to acquire and gain to her master's use; but as a spouse, for generation, fruit, and comfort'.[59] To this end, both Bacon and Descartes describe an explicit and rigorous experimental 'method' for the reliable acquisition of sound, scientific knowledge.[60] Armed with this method, modern philosophy not only proceeds to the reconstruction of what has passed for knowledge of the external world of nature, it also sets out to rebuild morality, political authority and social order on new and certifiably rational foundations. For this rationalizing spirit, tradition and religion no longer provide sufficient reasons to live one's life in a particular way. Beliefs, values and practices inherited from the past must be subjected to the new trial of scientific rationality.

The associations and continuities between the instrumental rationality of modern philosophy and ancient Epicureanism are apparent in the philosophy of Thomas Hobbes (1588–1679). In his most famous work, *Leviathan* (1651), Hobbes sets out a conception of knowledge that is overtly anti-Aristotelian and anti-scholastic, empiricist and nominalist. In forthright terms, he expounds a radically 'realist' account of rationality (*ratio*) as mere 'reckoning'. Rationality is no more than the human capacity to use symbols, calculate and draw logical inferences: 'For reason, in this sense, is nothing but *reckoning*, that is adding and subtracting, of the consequences of general names agreed upon for the *marking* and *signify-*

ing of our thought.'[61] Hobbes goes on to formulate a conception of 'man' whose fundamental assumptions are boldly hedonist. Just as the new mechanics has identified motion and matter as the two fundamental objects of scientific investigation in nature, a parallel concept of 'voluntary' motion is the basis for a similarly scientific understanding of the actions of human beings. The source of motivation energizing this voluntary motion is 'endeavour', which has two basic forms of 'desire' and 'aversion'. Far from being the expression of some higher faculty of reason or the spark of a divinely created soul, 'will' is no more than 'the last appetite in deliberating'.[62] Will is a causal force without cognitive import.

Crucially, on Hobbes's radically nominalist assumptions, moral evaluations of 'good', 'evil', 'vile' or 'inconsiderable' are not regarded as objective values that should ideally determine our will. Rather, such evaluations are just reflections or projections of that will, deriving from our basic attitudes of desire and aversion.[63] The hedonist implication is that the only basis of moral value is happiness or 'felicity', which Hobbes defines as just the 'continual progress' of desire.[64] If happiness is simply the unimpeded 'progress of desire' or, in effect, getting whatever we want, then we inevitably value power as the means to the fulfilment of that desire. Power is the principal means to pleasure: 'So that in the first place, I put for a general inclination of all mankind, a perpetual and restless desire of power after power, that ceaseth only in death.'[65] Moral philosophy still studies the 'laws of nature', but these are no longer considered as God's commandments. There are no binding moral values or laws in nature, before they are instituted by society or the state. There is no sin before laws and lawmakers.[66] A society's morality or 'manners' are simply the product of custom and the prudential calculations of rational individuals, who are motivated only by the desire for pleasure and for power as a means to the fulfilment of desire.[67] Moral laws are merely what rational men calculate to be 'the means of peaceable, sociable, and comfortable living'.[68]

Although Hobbes does not found morality on an absolute or idealist conception of reason, the instrumental deliberations of rationality deliver surprisingly similar moral and political conclusions. In fact, Hobbes's principles were thought to have destructive implications for traditional morality – copies of *Leviathan* were burnt at Oxford. But the radical implications of Hobbes's philosophy are quickly overridden by his well-known argument for the sovereign authority of the state or 'Leviathan'. Left unchecked in a 'state of nature', the endeavour of pleasure- and power-seeking individuals would inevitably bring about a destructive condition of 'perpetual war', in which 'the life of man' would famously be 'solitary, poor, nasty, brutish, and short'.[69] The only solution to the lawlessness of the state of nature is a universal agreement or 'covenant', whereby each person transfers all his rights to self-defence and the pursuit of desire to a sovereign authority or 'commonwealth'.[70] The absolute requirement of social order justifies the absolute authority of this sovereign in almost all matters, including the religious confession of its subjects. The natural rights of the individual are relinquished, except where 'the law is silent' or cannot speak. The positive law instituted by the sovereign assumes all the legitimacy and punitive force formerly assigned to natural law or divine injunction.[71]

Nor does Hobbes support any hedonist challenge to the restrictive sexual morality of seventeenth-century England. His nominalism is reflected in the unsentimental definitions of lust, love and jealousy quoted above: '*Love* of persons for pleasing the sense only, *natural lust*. *Love* of the same, acquired from rumination, that is, imagination of pleasure past, *luxury*. Love of one singularly, with desire to be singularly loved, *the passion of love*. The same, with fear that the love is not mutual, *jealousy*.'[72] Otherwise, Hobbes recognizes lust as one of the passions which, along with ignorance and bad reasoning, are principal sources of crime.[73] Accordingly, the state has the duty to enforce common conventions concerning marriage, monogamy and family inheritance, which serve the common good. His most explicit comments on the subject of marriage occur in the third and longest part of *Leviathan* on the 'Christian Commonwealth'. Hobbes's overriding concern is to defend the absolute authority of the state over matters of religious confession, in order to avoid destructive wars of religion. His criticisms of asceticism here are directed firmly against the Catholic Church, which seemed to threaten that authority. Those 'that pretend chastity, and continence, for the ground of denying marriage to the clergy' really follow the dubious 'design of the Popes, and priests of after times, to make themselves the clergy, that is to say, sole heirs of the kingdom of God in this world'.[74]

Leviathan's emphasis on the supremacy of civil considerations of peace and social order over religious dogma nonetheless marks a step towards the slow separation of state and Church culminating in the modern, secular state. Hobbes's political thought encouraged the slow liberation of law from religious and traditional morality. A theoretical gap is opened between the 'sins' castigated by the Church and the 'crimes' that the sovereign state finds it necessary to prosecute. In *theory*, the secularization of the state allows for a politics and an administration more pragmatically attuned to the interests of the community. The emphasis on the social rather than traditionally moral and religious necessity of the patriarchal family and marriage would eventually allow a more permissive view of sexuality.

In *practice*, however, the birth of the modern state was accompanied by a hardening of attitudes to gender and sexuality. Although Hobbes's assumptions about gender are not obviously patriarchal, his conclusions acknowledge male supremacy as an established fact. Starting from more blatantly patriarchal assumptions, male political theorists like Locke and Rousseau further entrench the traditional patriarchal exclusion of women from politics, even though they do so not on the traditional ground of biblical authority but on the more 'modern', 'rational' and so more durable basis of 'modern patriarchy'.[75] For the dominant 'malestream' of political thought, the irrational and disruptive sensual tendencies of women's 'nature' render them unsuitable for the coolly rational pursuit of self-interest on which modern economics and politics are based.[76] As for the issue of *sexual* difference, it is rarely if ever mentioned by modern political theorists or philosophers, despite their nominally hedonist premises.

In part, the moral conservatism of early modern thought in the West can be attributed to the continuing strength of humanism. Although the revival of classical culture worked to produce, if not tolerance, then at least somewhat broader sexual knowledge, humanism provided no basis for a *systematic* challenge to traditional prejudice. Even during the Enlightenment, with its self-consciously rational approach to the investigation of 'man', most thinkers continued to appeal to humanist discursive forms. 'Rational discourse' on moral questions rarely ventures beyond casual empirical observation combined with extensive allusion to authoritative classical precedents. This approach was, of course, by no means immune to the persistence of inherited prejudice. The Enlightenment's often shallow dismissal of religion as irrational superstition did not help either. The easy vilification of religion as the enemy of rationality provided cover for otherwise unconvincing arguments. It is not surprising that 'enlightened' pronouncements on morality often did little more than reproduce the 'reasonable' beliefs of educated and privileged men.

The French thinker François-Marie Arouet, better known as Voltaire (1694–1778), exemplifies this kind of conservatism.[77] During his long, productive and eventful life, Voltaire was certainly an unrelenting critic of the Roman Catholic Church. He scorned the Church's superstitious beliefs, its inordinate power and corrupt institutions. He even underwent considerable personal risks to defend some of its victims (notably Calas). But Voltaire's philosophical and moral thought was neither profound nor characterized by any rigorously rational method. Rationality, in his hands, is not always easily distinguished from common sense and even conservative prejudice. This attitude is typified by Voltaire's famous remark: 'If God did not exist, it would be necessary to invent Him.' The implication is that a secular alternative must be found for religion's role in underpinning social stability and the established order.[78] It is not surprising, therefore, that Voltaire's opinions on 'The Love Called "Socratic"' (1764), written for the *Philosophical Dictionary*, are quite conventional, despite the occasionally anti-clericalist tone of the piece.[79]

At the heart of Voltaire's article is the apparent contradiction between normative and secular conceptions of nature. The contradiction between the normative 'Nature' of tradition and the morally neutral 'nature' of science is apparent in the question that begins the article: 'How can it be that a vice, one which would destroy the human race if it became general, an infamous assault upon Nature, can nevertheless be so natural?'[80] He proceeds to offer a number of speciously scientific explanations. Pederasty is the product not of corruption but of immature instincts. Boys who experience sexual desire without finding its 'natural object' turn to another young boy, who may 'resemble a beautiful girl for the space of two or three years'.[81] Such aberrations are more likely to happen in warmer climates, where 'the blood runs hotter' and, since fewer clothes are worn, 'the occasion arises more frequently'.[82] At the same time, Voltaire continues to draw extensively on historical and cultural comparisons and classical learning. He pays considerable attention to what he sees as the misinterpretation of classical texts, suggesting that approving references to pederasty have been exaggerated and taken out of context.

Adopting a position with a long pedigree in western culture, Voltaire claims that references to 'love' between men really refer to an asexual or 'Platonic' friendship. Ancient pederasty is more correctly understood as an exclusively pedagogic relationship, even if one liable to abuse. He is particularly at pains to deny that ancient legislation ever favoured homosexuality – that 'there has ever been an organized nation which has made laws against morals'.[83] Referring to Sextus Empiricus' claim that the laws 'recommended' pederasty, Voltaire makes the irrefutable (and since much repeated) point that such a law 'would make the human race disappear if it were followed to the letter'.[84] Conveniently ignoring the considerable evidence of sexual toleration in the ancient world, he plays on the unsurprising fact that classical legislators never attempted to *enforce* sexual relations between men. In the process, Voltaire's initial assumption that toleration of pederasty really threatens the continuation of the 'human race' is left unproven, resting on the precarious assumption – made only minimally plausible by his own remarks on the 'fresh complexion' and 'sweet eyes' of young boys – that without social and legal prohibitions, homosexuality would become the universal preference.

A much more rigorous but still conservative strand of Enlightenment thought is represented by the Scottish philosopher David Hume (1711–76). Hume sketches with great clarity and conviction the main contours of the modern scientific conception of rationality. He can be described as an Enlightenment *rationalist*, because he rejects any claims to knowledge that are based on religious dogma, tradition, emotion or intuition. But his *sceptical* rationalism is directed against the *dogmatic* rationalism of some modern philosophy, which has more in common with Platonism. Like Plato, dogmatic philosophical rationalists use the example of logic and mathematics to argue that the most important instances of human knowledge are inborn or innate. Although this rationalism is not necessarily associated with Christian belief, its imputation of innate knowledge suggests a view of 'man' that is more easily reconciled with religion.[85]

By contrast, Hume's model of knowledge is more closely aligned to the emerging natural sciences than to mathematics and logic. His *empiricist* epistemology accounts for human knowledge as the product of sensory experience and experiment rather than innate knowledge. The 'impressions' we receive from our senses are the ultimate source of the 'ideas' or concepts that form the basic elements of our substantive knowledge of the external world. Knowledge of reality depends on conscientious observation of the kind made systematic in the natural sciences. Beyond this, we can organize and elaborate our substantive knowledge of 'matters of fact' by manipulating the formal 'relations of ideas' that form the basis of logical and mathematical truths. In sum, all genuine knowledge can be analysed as a combination of 'induction' from 'matters of fact' and logical 'deduction' from 'relations of ideas'.[86]

Hume's empiricism has deeply sceptical implications. He even questions the validity of scientific knowledge of relations of cause and effect. Our knowledge of causal relations, which is surely fundamental to natural science, must also rely exclusively on sensory experience. We cannot legitimately claim to know more than is supported by the empirical evidence. But the only evidence we have is of the 'constant conjunction' of paired events, which we are psychologically inclined to regard, without logical justification, as 'cause' and 'effect'.[87] The process of 'induction' from the constant conjunction of certain events in the *past* to their likely conjunction in the *future* can never be strictly justified. According to Bertrand Russell's well-known comparison, we are really in no better position than the chicken which, waking and being fed every single day of its life, comes to believe that this habit corresponds to a law of nature. The chicken may be disappointed, but it is not entitled to complain when one day its neck is wrung, 'showing that more refined views as to the uniformity of nature would have been useful to the chicken'.[88]

Although Hume does not suggest that there is any more reliable alternative to scientific method, his philosophy *does* seem to have radical implications beyond the sphere of the natural sciences. Hume proposes to apply scientific method to the 'science of man', or what we now call human and social sciences.[89] A science of man would address questions of psychology as well as moral, ethical and aesthetic values with the same methods of empirical observation, induction and logical analysis that are employed so successfully in the natural sciences. By implication, both religion and humanism will lose their long-held and sometimes rival claims to authority on such matters. Hume's approach certainly has radical implications for his understanding of conventional morality. Morality and justice should be recognized for what they are – not something implanted in us by divine Providence, but a form of socially embodied knowledge. Morality is simply a way of encouraging whatever is most useful to society. So, for example, the right of private property and the corresponding condemnation of theft are just effective ways of encouraging industry and thrift. The social institutions of justice and morality can be traced to their practical effects, whether historical or anticipated. Moral judgements are ultimately founded on feelings of pleasure and pain, and related attitudes of approval and disapproval, sympathy and pity, in the societies in which they occur.[90]

Hume's scepticism about religion and traditional morality does permit some radical conclusions. He is, for example, prepared to defend suicide as a potentially rational response to a life of suffering and unhappiness.[91] But overall, he is not motivated by any ambitious desire to transform society as a whole. Rather, like Hobbes, Hume is concerned to ensure stability and good order in society by avoiding the disruptive consequences of religious and political fanaticism. His sceptical rationalism issues in a moderate, reasonable if sometimes surprisingly tolerant conservatism. His radical conception of morality is deployed to largely conservative ends. Thus he upholds the mutually related institutions of private property and marriage – 'an engagement entered into by mutual consent' which 'has for its end the propagation of the species', so 'it must be susceptible of all the variety of conditions, which consent establishes, provided they be not contrary to this end'.[92] He considers a variety of alternative institutions, including polygamy and free divorce, but in the end argues against them on grounds of utility.

A major argument against these alternatives to marriage is their likely damage to love and friendship, which Hume understands in terms strongly reminiscent of Aristotle and, indeed, Epicurus: 'Destroy love and friendship; what remains in the world worth accepting?'[93] He reserves unqualified praise for friendship, which is a 'calm and sedate affection, conducted by reason and cemented by habit'. Friendship contrasts with the fickleness of love, which is a 'restless and impatient passion, full of caprices and variations: arising in a moment from a feature, from an air, from nothing, and suddenly extinguishing after the same manner'.[94] Love can be preserved within the social institution of marriage only with difficulty. The instability of love is allied with the vagaries of sexual pleasure, whereas the institution of marriage must answer to the social necessities of procreation, the rearing of children and transmission of property.[95] Hume advances a radical position for his time (and leaves behind the homosocial assumptions of the humanist tradition) when he proposes friendship between equals as a more stable basis for marriage. Marriage is too often marred by the rivalry between men and women, who each vie for dominion over the other rather than settling for harmonious equality and friendship.[96]

Hume's scientific rationalism is certainly incompatible with Christianity's normative conception of nature, which provides the intellectual basis for the condemnation of non-reproductive sex. But the hedonist and even libertine conclusions that might be drawn from a secular view of nature are far from Hume's cautiously balanced, tolerant and humane attitude to pleasure and sex. Hume rejects any philosophically derived extremism, whether involving an Epicurean 'indulgence of a licentious Mirth and Gaiety' and 'dissolute prodigality', or a Stoic denial of normal human feelings and emotions.[97] In the context of his defence of suicide, he does venture a potentially far-reaching but obscure defence of pleasures denied to us by religion and the fear of eternal punishment. Human beings are naturally timid in the face of the prospect of death, and 'when the menaces of superstition are joined to this natural timidity, no wonder it quite deprives men of all power over their lives; since even many pleasures and enjoyments, to which we are carried by a strong propensity, are torn from us by this inhuman tyrant.'[98] He does not tell us what pleasures he has in mind.

Hume's more explicit discussion of sexual love adopts a similarly relaxed but conservative attitude. In his more theoretical *Treatise of Human Nature*, he endeavours to provide a rigorous explanation of why sexual desire, or the 'bodily appetite for generation', usually arises as a reaction to beauty and gives rise to a 'tender concern and affection'.[99] In his more popular and discursive essay 'Of Love and Marriage', he resorts, in more typically humanist fashion, to commenting on Plato's *Symposium*. Hume recalls Aristophanes' mythical explanation of love as the longing for reunion of the male and female parts of an originally androgynous whole. Of course, Aristophanes' myth has long been a *locus classicus* of attempts to rehabilitate same-sex love in the western tradition. But in contrast to Ficino, Hume notably fails to mention, let alone discuss, the originally all-male and all-female wholes, whose longing to reunite would explain homosexual love.[100]

Elsewhere, without expressing explicit approval, Hume conveys a tolerant attitude to homosexual love. This tendency is demonstrated in his *History of England*, which was for a long time regarded as his most important work. Here he relates the story of King Edward II's 'strong affection' for his favourites Gaveston and Spenser. The sexual nature of these affections is made obvious but is never explicit in Hume's account. He tells how Gaveston, who 'was endowed with the utmost elegance of shape and person' and 'noted for a fine mien and easy carriage', easily captured the affection of Edward, a man 'whose heart was strongly disposed to friendship and confidence'.[101] Likewise Spenser, who succeeded the murdered Gaveston as the king's 'minion', 'possessed all the exterior accomplishments of person and address, which were fitted to engage the weak mind of Edward'.[102] Hume even evinces sympathy for the tragic fate of a king who was deprived 'of the company and society of a person whom, by an unusual infatuation, he valued above all the world, and above every consideration of interest and tranquillity'.[103] He condemns the 'treasonous' and 'unnatural' conspiracy of Edward's queen Isabella and the nobility, blaming the 'turbulence of the great' and the 'madness of the people' for the cruel death of an 'innocent and inoffensive' king.[104]

4 Progressive Rationality and Sexual Reform

The hedonist potential of rationality is brought out forcefully and unequivocally in the work of Jeremy Bentham (1748–1832). Bentham's utilitarianism elaborates and systematizes the approach to morality outlined by Hume. It is an approach which, by the eighteenth century, was widely shared amongst radical intellectuals, who were inclined to scientific materialism, empiricism and atheism or agnosticism. Like Hume's, Bentham's attempt to found morality on rational and enlightened principles takes human well-being, pleasure or what Bentham calls 'utility' as its ultimate standard of moral value. But without Hume's conservative moderation, Bentham unambiguously rehabilitates pleasure as a legitimate human preoccupation and, indeed, as the ultimate point of all human activity. His writings display the critical force of Enlightenment rationalism at its most vigorous, uninhibited and destructive of moral dogma and superstition.

At the same time, Bentham's utilitarian morality still assumes that it is possible to reconcile hedonism with the collective interest of society. It is not simply one's individual pleasure that should be taken as the standard for moral judgement but the pleasures of all people. According to the fundamental 'principle of utility', the goal of human action should be the greatest happiness (pleasure, satisfaction or utility) of the greatest number. Any pleasure is acceptable, as long as its enjoyment does not result in a greater overall quantity of suffering for other people or for society as a whole. Utilitarianism is also *consequentialist* in the sense that it is consideration of the consequences of particular dispositions, actions and institutions that provides the ultimate basis of moral judgement. Apart from these consequences, there can be no meaningful question or standard of the rightness of actions. Religious commandments, traditional moral rules and intuitions must all be judged according to their consequences for the overall utility of society.[105]

In contrast to many of his contemporaries and predecessors, Bentham was eager to apply his utilitarian principles in the cause of radicalism. He wrote extensively on questions of legal and institutional reform. He was also an advocate on behalf of a number of 'oppressed' groups of his time, including slaves, women, Jews, the indigent, indigenous people and even animals.[106] Even more impressively, Bentham was willing to draw the radical implications of his utilitarian principles for sexual morality and legislation. At the hysterical height of homophobic persecution in Georgian England, when the punishment for sodomy was death, he sets out something quite close to the moral and jurisprudential basis of recent liberal legislative reform in the area of sexuality. Over a number of decades at the turn of the nineteenth century, Bentham produced an extensive series of drafts and notes (some 300 folio pages) on 'sexual nonconformity'. Unfortunately, but perhaps not surprisingly, these notes remained unpublished until quite recently.[107] Indeed, it was only after much inner struggle – sometimes visible in the emotional distortion of an already tortuous handwriting – that he overcame his understandable fears of persecution to the point of setting down on paper his anger at the unnecessary suffering of sexual nonconformists.

Throughout his discussion, Bentham elaborates the straightforward but bold utilitarian argument that since 'pederasty' gives obvious pleasure to its willing practitioners, there can be no moral ground for its condemnation, provided that it does not cause greater suffering to others. After the earliest manuscripts, he soon abandons the camouflage of conventionally derogatory references to an 'abominable vice' and 'miserable taste' for more neutral references to an 'improlific appetite'.[108] He assembles a considerable array of arguments to the effect that sexual relations between people of the same sex are harmless and may even be useful. His surprisingly frank discussion displays a wide-ranging knowledge of ancient Greek and Roman sources as well as recent English literature, relevant legal cases, contemporary scandals and anthropological comparisons.

In the spirit of progressive legal reformism, Bentham opposes any legal enforcement of sexual morality. His views are striking for their precocity, anticipating arguments put forward in the 1957 Wolfenden Report in Britain, which advocated limited legal toleration of homosexuality and prostitution on similar grounds.[109] Almost two centuries earlier, Bentham advances the now familiar liberal position that harmless sexual activities should be regarded as private and self-regarding matters beyond the legitimate concern of the law. The law should be concerned only with preventing harm. It only brings itself into disrepute and ridicule when it seeks to regulate sexual activity: 'If there be one idea more ridiculous than another, it is that of a legislator who, when a man and a woman are agreed about a business of this sort, thrusts himself in between them, examining situations, regulating times and prescribing modes and postures.'[110] Foreshadowing other arguments of the 'law and morality' debates of the 1960s, Bentham points out the practical difficulty of enforcing laws against consensual and private acts, for which material evidence (at least before genetic testing) is inevitably scarce. The dangers of malicious prosecution and blackmail are also obviously considerable.[111]

In fact, Bentham goes considerably further than liberal arguments for legal toleration of sexual nonconformity. The liberal position denies only that private morality is a sufficient ground for legal prosecution. It leaves ample room for the persistence and expression of illiberal prejudice. Bentham urges against such prejudice that, provided they result in more pleasure than pain overall, all sexual activities should be regarded not only as legally tolerable but as morally acceptable as well. The general population's prejudice or 'antipathy' against sexual nonconformity, which reflects differences merely 'in point of taste and opinion', is no reason to punish an otherwise harmless activity. If it were accepted as a legitimate ground for punishment, antipathy would justify the prohibition of many perfectly proper activities at significant cost to freedom. Rather, we should seek to transform prejudice by means of utilitarian discussion and enlightened education.[112]

In his later writings, Bentham goes so far as to propose an 'all comprehensive liberty' in matters of sexuality. Sexual pleasure is particularly beneficial: 'Sexual appetite is more conducive to happiness than any other sensual appetite.'[113] Sexual pleasure does not depend on wealth, so it is more equitably available to all.[114] Turning conventional opinion against itself, he suggests that greater sexual freedom would be likely to remove one of the causes of pederasty. Young men are driven to 'improper' sexual outlets by the excessive constraint of their sexual desires. In this context, Bentham wisely draws attention to the corrupting effects of feather beds, those 'implements of indulgence and incentives to the venereal appetite with which the antients were unacquainted'.[115] His newly acquired Malthusian views, which pointed to the inevitable tendency of a population to exceed the resources required to sustain it, provide further evidence for the positive usefulness of the 'improlific appetite'.[116]

Bentham's radicalism contrasts with the conservatism of other major figures of the Enlightenment. He explicitly rebuts the conventionally homophobic views rehearsed by Montesquieu and Voltaire. In response to Montesquieu's apparently pragmatic argument against pederasty – 'It is necessary to proscribe it, since it does no more than give to one sex the weaknesses of the other and prepare for an infamous old age with a shameful youth' – Bentham cites the ancient Greeks and Romans as evidence that passive sodomy neither feminizes its devotees nor diminishes the manly strength of the nation.[117] Montesquieu's fear that the more widespread practice of pederasty might unduly deprive women of their 'venereal pleasures' is equally without foundation. Informed largely by the mores of ancient Greece, Bentham assumes that homosexuality usually takes the form of a transient, pederastic relationship between an older and a younger man. He points out that such relationships are not incompatible with either heterosexual intercourse or marriage at another time. In any case, the sexual enjoyment of women is surely more restricted by customary demands of modesty, whether these are inspired by religion or patriarchal social institutions, than by the neglect of pederasts.[118] Voltaire's similarly specious fear that the human race would disappear if homosexuality were to become the universal rule is more deserving of ridicule than debate: 'The apprehension of a deficiency of population for want of the regular intercourse between the sexes in the way of marriage is altogether upon a par with an apprehension of the like result from a general disposition in mankind to starve themselves.'[119]

Bentham's utilitarian defence of pederasty is supported by an extensive critique and commentary on religion, which draws on Enlightenment currents of anti-clericalism and 'freethinking'.[120] He objects to any morality that superstitiously sacrifices human pleasure on the altar of a spiteful God. The secular conception of nature of scientific rationalism specifically undermines the central pillar of Christian homophobia, which deems pederasty *unnatural* because it violates the divinely ordained goal of reproduction. Apart from the fact that pederasty is less common than the more 'prolific appetite' for procreative intercourse, '[a]ll the difference would be that the one was both natural and necessary where as [*sic*] the other was natural but not necessary. If the mere circumstance of its not being necessary were sufficient to warrant the terming it unnatural it might as well be said that the taste a man has for music is unnatural.'[121] At the same time, Bentham attacks Christianity on its own terms, rebutting standardly homophobic interpretations of the Old Testament. As noted in the previous chapter, the biblical story of the destruction of the 'cities of the plain' can more literally be understood as a lesson against inhospitality rather than sodomy.

In any case, the exceptional act of vengeful Providence which destroyed Sodom and Gomorrah cannot be intended to establish an everlasting moral law. When God commanded Abraham to kill his son Isaac, He presumably did not intend to provide a general justification of infanticide.[122] The Church's commitment to reproduction surely rests on shaky ground too when it encourages the sexual abstinence of its own clergy. As ever, Bentham is in favour of jurisprudential consistency: 'If then merely out of regard to population it were right that paederasts should be burnt alive monks ought to be roasted alive by a slow fire.'[123] As noted in the previous chapter, Bentham traces Christian sexual attitudes to St Paul rather than Jesus, and maintains that '[a]sceticism is not Christianity but Paulism.'[124] In his notes for *Not Paul but Jesus* (written between 1816 and 1818), Bentham claims that Jesus was tolerant towards 'eccentric pleasures of the bed' and even claims evidence for his 'partaking' in them.[125] Unfortunately, the book was published only pseudonymously and with the chapters on sexuality excised.[126]

In the context of a society that routinely killed, mutilated, imprisoned and persecuted sexual dissidents, it is obviously regrettable that Bentham's views were not published in his time. Still, the radical implications of these views were not lost on his contemporaries. Even without the publication of his writings on sexuality, Bentham was accused of dragging humanity back to the mire of bestial enjoyment. The truth in these accusations is that his argument for hedonism was too simple. His exclusively *quantitative* hedonism reduces the moral evaluation of human activity to a mechanical calculus of amounts of pleasure. This calculus has no way of recognizing the multiple levels of subjective and intersubjective meaning, the gradations of value characterizing particular forms of sexual activity. A Benthamite hedonist apparently has no reason to regard a sexual life confined to lonely masturbation or fetishism as in any way inferior to a life of social and multifarious activity.

The absence of any *qualitative* discrimination between pleasures is displayed in some of Bentham's comments on forms of sexuality other than pederasty. As it happens, he condemns masturbation as '[o]f all irregularities of the venereal appetite, that which is the most incontestably pernicious'. But he does so only on the dubious evidence of contemporary medical opinion, which regarded it as 'often of the most serious consequence to the health and lasting happiness of those who are led to practise it'.[127] The qualitative blindness of Bentham's utilitarianism is even more apparent in his surprising calm at the prospect of bestiality: 'Accidents of this sort will sometimes happen; for distress will force a man upon strange expedients.' He seems to have at least some right on his side when he maintains that bestiality is a practice so strange that even the strongest urgings from 'all the sovereigns in Europe' would be unlikely to make this activity popular enough to cause any serious 'political mischief'.[128]

It is possible to defend Bentham's purely quantitative standard of morality and even his assessment of bestiality.[129] But in the context of Victorian England, which increasingly fell under the moralistic sway of the middle classes, it is not surprising that a more respectable version of utilitarianism was soon formulated by the self-professed utilitarian John Stuart Mill (1806–73). Although deeply influenced by Bentham and by his father James Mill, a loyal follower of Bentham, J. S. Mill rebelled against the excessive simplicity and one-dimensionality of doctrinaire utilitarianism. In the biographical essay he wrote shortly after Bentham's death, he praises Bentham's 'precision of thought' on moral and political philosophy and his reforming onslaught on practical abuses of the law. But in the aftermath of his own recent encounter with Romanticism and the ideas of Coleridge, he also laments Bentham's deficiency of imagination and empathy, the narrowness of his views of religion and conscience and, above all, his lack of judgement of pleasures.[130]

Mill's modified version of utilitarianism proposes an important addition to Bentham's one-dimensional conception of pleasure. He hopes that a qualitative distinction between 'higher' and 'lower' pleasures will be able to save utilitarianism from accusations of swinish hedonism. The rehabilitation of pleasure and happiness as legitimate objects of human concern need not imply an indifference to the variable quality of pleasures. Some pleasures are better than others, even if they may be harder to come by: 'It is better to be a human being dissatisfied than a pig satisfied; better to be Socrates dissatisfied than a fool satisfied. And if the fool, or the pig, are of a different opinion, it is because they only know their own side of the question. The other party to the comparison knows both sides.'[131] According to his version of what Rawls calls his Aristotelian principle, Mill argues that those who have experienced a variety of pleasures will always tend to prefer the more sophisticated or 'higher' pleasures to 'lower' ones.[132]

But this solution is problematic in a number of ways. In the first place, Mill's approach requires us to make sense of comparisons between different categories of experience according to a single qualitative scale of value. Even contrasts between higher and lower pleasures *within* a particular dimension of experience such as mathematics, poetry or sex are far from straightforward. But it is still less obvious how comparisons *between* such dimensions of experience might be made. How should we judge the quality of the pleasures associated with an episode of Tantric sex as compared to those of writing a mediocre poem or performing an elementary calculation? Whilst the criterion of quality rhetorically counters accusations of swinish hedonism, it offers no more than a single, abstract scale of comparison for what are inevitably complex moral judgements. We may agree that some discrimination on the basis of the quality of experience is essential, but we are no closer to understanding what 'quality' concretely means, either within or between different orders of experience.[133]

A second, more fundamental problem is that Mill's approach saves Bentham from swinish hedonism only at the risk of rehabilitating an unnecessarily ascetic sexual morality. His examples of 'higher' pleasures conform, albeit on different metaphysical grounds, to ascetic idealism's traditional deprecation of the body in the name of 'reason' or the soul. Predictably, Mill refers to the superior pleasures of the 'higher faculties' as compared to 'those of which the animal nature, disjoined from the higher faculties, is suspectible [*sic*]'. Even whilst admitting that the choice between higher and lower pleasures might involve choosing, not between bodily and mental pleasures, but between two kinds of bodily pleasure, his example still refers in conventionally ascetic terms to the sacrifice of 'sensual indulgences' for the sake of long-term health.[134] His appeal to quality as a standard of pleasure might, in theory, be compatible with a challenging and discriminating account of sexual experience. But it is more congenial to a conventionally ascetic dismissal of sexual pleasures as intrinsically inferior.

Mill's own application of his utilitarian principles is correspondingly cautious. He is well known for his forthright and influential defence of women's equality, which was partly inspired by his wife Harriet Taylor.[135] But he never wrote explicitly and extensively on the topic of sex or sexuality. He comes closest to doing so with some general and abstract remarks on the moral neutrality of a consistently secular conception of 'Nature'. Once religious conceptions have been put aside, nature can only mean one of two things: '. . . it either denotes the entire system of things, with the aggregate of all their properties, or it denotes things as they would be, apart from human intervention.' It is worth quoting Mill's precise summation of the moral implications of these two conceptions:

> In the first of these senses, the doctrine that man ought to follow nature is unmeaning; since man has no power to do anything else than follow nature; all his actions are done through, and in obedience to some one or many of nature's physical or mental laws.
>
> In the other sense of the term, the doctrine that man ought to follow nature, or in other words, ought to make the spontaneous course of things the model of his voluntary actions, is equally irrational and immoral.
>
> Irrational, because all human action whatever, consists in altering, and all useful action in improving, the spontaneous course of nature:
>
> Immoral, because the course of natural phenomena being replete with everything which when committed by human beings is most worthy of abhorrence, any one who endeavoured in his actions to imitate the natural course of things would be universally seen and acknowledged to be the wickedest of men.[136]

If anything, it is criminal actions that come most easily and naturally to 'man'. It is the acquisition of virtue that involves 'a work of labour and difficulty' in overcoming the host of 'natural inclinations' tempting us to vice.[137] 'Natural' should, if anything, be treated as a term of condemnation.

This conclusion follows a brief and elusive discussion of the condemnatory force habitually attached to the term 'unnatural'. Mill considers one significant qualification to his general rule, which would otherwise remove all stigma from sexually unnatural acts. Though he never explicitly mentions sex, this qualification offers an apparent concession to readers who might otherwise be shocked by the sexual interpretation of his views. The tortuous nature of his remarks here might be thought to reveal an unwillingness to take sides:

> But if an action, or an inclination, has been decided on other grounds to be blameable, it may be a circumstance in aggravation that it is unnatural, that is, repugnant to some strong feeling usually found in human beings; since the bad propensity, whatever it be, has afforded evidence of being both strong and deeply rooted, by having overcome that repugnance. This presumption of course fails if the individual never had the repugnance: and the argument, therefore, is not fit to be urged unless the feeling which is violated by the act, is not only justifiable and reasonable, but is one which it is blameable to be without.[138]

At best, he appears to want to have it both ways. And if this equivocation were not enough, Mill reiterates Bentham's condemnation of people's tendency to judge the actions of others according to their own 'antipathy'. The unfortunate result has been that 'differences of opinion, and even differences of taste, have been objects of as intense moral abhorrence as the most atrocious crimes.'[139]

Perhaps the most unstable feature of utilitarianism results from its attempt to combine a hedonist view of individual human motivation with moral altruism. Utilitarianism has the apparent advantage over other systems of morality that its fundamental principle is grounded in how people actually behave. Not only are pleasure and happiness the ultimate grounds of morality, but they are also, at least on the utilitarian interpretation, the ends that we always pursue. But for this hedonist principle to deliver something recognizable as a system of morality requires a further crucial assumption. This is that individuals will recognize the value of universal happiness or the common good and will make that, rather than their own selfish gratification, the object of their endeavours. The latter assumption is, to say the least, questionable. Mill attempts to bridge the gap between selfish and altruistic hedonism with the following famous piece of reasoning:

> No reason can be given why the general happiness is desirable, except that each person, so far as he believes it to be attainable, desires his own happiness. This, however, being a fact, we have not only all the proof which the case admits of, but all which it is possible to require, that happiness is a good: that each person's happiness is a good to that

> person, and the general happiness, therefore, a good to the aggregate of all persons.[140]

The inference, from the possibly universal tendency to pursue one's *own* happiness to a general disposition to pursue the happiness of *all*, is plainly and notoriously invalid.

In practice, utilitarianism has relied on two further steps to bridge the gap between selfish hedonism and altruistic morality. In the first place, satisfaction or utility is given an *economic* interpretation. The argument is fairly straightforward. Only individuals themselves are able to determine their own preferences. But we can be sure that economic resources (money or wealth) will help people to increase their levels of well-being or satisfaction, whatever preferences they happen to have. So the goal of maximizing overall satisfaction is best pursued indirectly by way of the economic goal of maximizing the aggregate wealth of society. Utilitarianism can then rely, secondly, on a basic assumption of classical economics. According to this theory, the individual pursuit of economic self-interest leads automatically, by means of what Adam Smith called the 'invisible hand' of the market, to the greater wealth of the nation as a whole. This means, perhaps, that there is no need to worry about individual selfishness, which will contribute to the common good despite itself. The universal pursuit of self-interest will produce the greatest happiness of the greatest number. But utilitarianism in this version has little useful to say about individual morality, let alone sexuality.[141]

5 Libertinism at the Limit of Rationality

The hedonism of instrumental rationality is expressed in more enticing and sexually illuminating form in the writings of Julien Offray de La Mettrie (1709–51), who was perhaps the eighteenth century's most notorious philosopher of materialism. Such was the outrage occasioned by his philosophical opinions that he was forced to flee from Paris to Leiden, and from there to the court of Frederick the Great in Prussia. Trained as a medical doctor, he combined the empiricist epistemology of Locke with the anti-clericalism of the Enlightenment. But La Mettrie went much further in rejecting not only the dogmas of revealed religion but also the abstract deism of his fellow French *philosophes*.[142] The radicalism of La Mettrie's views derives from his rejection of philosophical dualism, so often the source of the ascetic devaluation of the body. La Mettrie denies the existence of a metaphysically distinct order of mind and provides an exclusively materialist account of the 'soul', which is seen as just the result of the complex organization of matter in the human brain and nervous system. Once it is recognized that matter is not dumb and inert, as opponents of materialism tend to see it, but 'active' and 'sensitive', there is no obstacle to a purely material explanation of human behaviour and no need to posit the existence of an immaterial and immortal soul.

Nor does La Mettrie hesitate to draw the moral implications of his uncompromising metaphysical views. If there is no human soul, then there is no fundamental metaphysical divide between human beings and other animals. 'Man' differs from other animals (and even from plants) only in the degree of complexity of the organization of matter that makes up his body. So Descartes was right to think that animals are merely complex machines without a soul, and wrong only in believing that human beings are any different. An immediate consequence is to undercut any hope of immortality: 'Death is the end of everything; after it, I repeat, an abyss, an eternal nothingness; all's said, everything's done . . . the game is over.'[143] This was obviously a devastating blow for any morality reliant on the motivating force of eternal salvation or damnation.

The finality of death leaves us with the further problem of how we can live, how we *should* live in the face of the inescapable prospect of our extinction. La Mettrie develops his answer in terms of the ancient dispute between Epicureans and Stoics. Attacking what he sees as the sombre and life-denying precepts of Stoicism, he ridicules the arrogance of philosophers who regard the life of the soul or intellect as the only worthwhile one. The Stoic's attempt to become indifferent to both desire and suffering, in order to be invulnerable to all the vicissitudes of life, is really no more than a refusal to live. To have contempt for this life to the extent of recommending suicide, as some ancient philosophers have done, is to propose throwing away everything for the sake of an illusion. And surely there can be no divine injunction or natural law against enjoyment.[144] It is the hostility of philosophy and religion to pleasure, rather than its active pursuit, that should be regarded as unnatural and even as a kind of crime.[145] The denial of pleasure constitutes the real insult to nature and ingratitude towards the Creator: '. . . to deny the gifts of Nature is to be unworthy of life.'[146] With a melancholy and wit reminiscent of Montaigne, La Mettrie deplores 'the fate of humanity for being, so to speak, in such bad hands as its own'.[147]

Since this life is the only one we have, we should rather follow the Epicureans in seeking to live this life to the full, 'for I don't see how we can have anything better to do than to live'.[148] This means that we should enthusiastically identify with our bodily existence: 'All soul, they abstract from the body; all body, we shall abstract from our soul.'[149] We should not renounce bodily pleasures for the sake of dubious demands made on behalf of the soul and the unfounded promise of an after-life. But like Epicurus and Lucretius, La Mettrie is not an undiscriminating advocate of pleasure. He insists on some important distinctions between different kinds of pleasure. Pleasant sensations are distinguished, in the first place, according to their duration. Whereas *plaisir* ('pleasure') is only of short duration, *volupté* ('voluptuousness' or 'delight') lasts longer and *bonheur* ('happiness') is permanent.[150] In fact, Bentham makes similar distinctions according to the 'intensity' and 'duration' of pleasures, distinctions that are clearly compatible with a straightforwardly quantitative approach.[151]

But La Mettrie further distinguishes between *plaisir* and *volupté* in *qualitative* terms, according to their various connections to body and mind. *Volupté* involves the imagination and inventiveness of the mind, whereas *plaisir* is exclusively physical in origin: '. . . delight is to the soul what pleasure is to the body.'[152] Genuine *volupté* requires both intelligence (*esprit*) and artistry (*art*): 'Such is true delight; the spirit and not the instinct of pleasure, the art of using it wisely, to manage it with reason, and to taste it with feeling.'[153] As a result, La Mettrie's hedonism is less obviously vulnerable to charges of animalistic indulgence or of endorsing the standpoint of the 'satisfied pig'. The refined and esoteric practices of the resourceful *roué* could not be more different from the unthinking sexual routines of animals.

La Mettrie also published tracts openly defending sexual pleasure and eroticism. He even dares to mention in favourable terms sexual practices long condemned as unnatural.[154] With considerable boldness – the excised words are not difficult to guess – La Mettrie refers to the prevalence of homosexual love affairs in the ancient world and even claims (perhaps dubiously) that Aristotle favoured pederasty as a measure against excessive population: 'Aristotle favoured [pederasty] to restrain the multitude of citizens without worrying about the commandment "[go forth and] multiply". In those days one had a G[anymede] more publicly than today we have a mistress; that is proven by reading the ancients, who freely celebrate unclean works, which make up half the world.'[155] Consistently with his intellectualized understandingé of *volupté*, La Mettrie distinguishes between 'voluptuous literature' that is 'obscene' and 'dissolute' and that which represents a 'purified sensuality' – in effect a distinction between pornographic and erotic literature. Of the 'voluptuous' writers of antiquity, he has particular praise for Petronius, who 'shows us every kind of *volupté*' with considerable delicacy.[156]

At times, La Mettrie's assault on traditional morality verges on *immoralism*. As with Bentham's utilitarianism, the clear implication of his philosophical position is that no human pleasure, considered apart from its consequences, is intrinsically immoral. But La Mettrie sometimes rhetorically assumes the language of his adversaries in a way that seems to endorse immoral or criminal actions. If some pleasures are criminal, as both Christian moralists and conservative philosophers allege, then perhaps it is the unfortunate lot of human beings to be natural criminals: 'Certainly if the joys we extract from nature are crimes, then the pleasure, the very happiness of men is criminal. "Oh! Miserable are they whose joys are crimes!"'[157] Contrary to the spirit of La Mettrie's atheism and materialism, the suggestion that human beings are condemned to a sinful existence is reinforced by his admission that nature includes the evil inclinations of beings who, like tigers, cannot be blamed for their ferocious instincts.[158] If innocent sexual pleasures are 'natural', then so are the unquestionably criminal instincts of murderers and rapists. As J. S. Mill's discussion of the moral uses of the concept of nature also makes clear, it is dangerous to seek to derive moral lessons from a secularized conception of nature, when nature may harbour decidedly malevolent inclinations.[159]

The risks of an exaggerated reaction to an oppressive sexual moralism are even more clearly realized in the avowed immoralism of Donatien Alphonse François, Marquis de Sade (1740–1814). Sexually mistreated in his youth, Sade was later implicated in a number of violent sexual episodes and was to spend much of his life imprisoned in the lunatic asylum of Charenton.[160] Sade takes scientific rationalism's secular conception of nature to its most radical conclusion and beyond. His writings both depict and, through the mouths of his various characters, openly advocate not only sodomy, adultery and incest but even theft, rape, torture and murder. Sade is not content with simply denying the teachings of religion and traditional morality, he delights in flouting them. Although he is an avowed materialist, his vision of nature does not remain within the confines of a strictly scientific world-view, which conceives nature as a morally indifferent mechanism. Rather, nature does have an intrinsic *telos* or purpose, albeit one that is malevolent rather than benign. Nature's endless movement of creation and destruction, death and rebirth is not merely indifferent to human purposes but openly hostile to them.[161]

Sade's bleak picture of nature has direct implications for human life and morality. If God does not exist, then both human and non-human nature must be accepted for what they are, rather than being forced into the normative framework of Christianity. If human beings are born without obligations to a transcendent deity, then there can be no moral objection to the uninhibited pursuit of pleasure. Sensual pleasures are meagre compensation for an existence marred by suffering, sickness and death. The pursuit of *volupté* is our only compensation for an otherwise baneful existence: '. . . it is only by extending the sphere of his tastes and fantasies, it is only by sacrificing everything to pleasure, that the unfortunate individual who goes by the name of man and who is thrown, despite himself, into this sad universe, can success in strewing a few roses over the thorns of life.'[162] Sensual pleasures are the 'roses' that compensate for the 'thorns' inflicted by a malevolent and destructive nature. It makes sense, therefore, that our best guides are the desires and impulses implanted in us by nature rather than the artificial constructions of 'virtue': '. . . virtue is just an illusion whose cult consists in endless sacrifices, in permanent rebellion against the inspirations of one's temperament. Can such actions be natural? Does Nature recommend what offends it?'[163] We should not sacrifice natural pleasures for the sake of an illusory cult of virtue.

What is more, Sade thinks that we should pursue even our apparently evil impulses, because these too are 'implanted' in us by nature. In contrast to the respectable social hedonism proposed by Bentham and Mill, Sade espouses an aggressively egotistical morality of pleasure. The goal of the Sadeian calculus is not the maximization of the overall or aggregate pleasure of humanity. Rather, the self-conscious libertine seeks to maximize his (or her) pleasure at whatever cost to other individuals. In his pursuit of sensual pleasures of every kind, the victim's lack of enjoyment, suffering and even death are matters of principled indifference to the Sadeian hero. Indeed, Sade himself evidently prefers pleasures that involve the maximum of suffering on the part of others. Violence, theft and murder are everyday features of the natural world of animals, straightforward reflections of nature's endless cycle of creation and destruction.

For Sade, the immoral inclinations implanted by nature are particularly in evidence in the area of sexuality. More daring and explicit than La Mettrie, he actively ridicules Christianity's procreative view of sexuality. According to Mme de Saint-Ange in Sade's philosophical novel *Philosophy in the Bedroom* (*Philosophie dans le boudoir*), procreation is something nature does not so much require as 'tolerate'.[164] It follows that contraception, abortion and sodomy (whether heterosexual or homosexual) cannot be condemned as 'perverting' the natural goal of sexuality. Since the only criterion for judging any activity should be pleasure, the only sexual activities that deserve to be condemned are those that are not enjoyed. If anything, non-procreative forms of sex are even preferable, because they allow sexual activity to be enjoyed without fear of any consequences. So women can enjoy anal intercourse without fear of pregnancy and its arduous responsibilities.[165] The apparent purposelessness, from a human or divine point of view, of 'disorderly' sexual desires is just further evidence of their origin in nature. We obey nature by following rather than suppressing such inclinations.[166] If anyone should be blamed, it is not the man with such desires but nature itself: '. . . is man master of his tastes? Those with unusual ones should be pitied not insulted: their wrong is Nature's doing; they are no more responsible for arriving in the world with different tastes than we are for being born either crippled or well-formed.'[167]

The result is a startling combination of seemingly progressive and highly unpalatable opinions. Sade unsentimentally flouts moralistic views of the sanctity of marriage and family relationships. Like the ancient Greeks, he regards love as no more than a form of madness caused by the sight of beautiful objects.[168] Neither men nor women should sacrifice their freedom or pleasures to the wish of parents that they get married. They should not enter into the folly of a long-term commitment that will inevitably outlast their mutual sexual enjoyment. The marriage contract is an illegitimate restriction on the endless and protean search for sexual pleasure. So adultery should not be regarded as a crime either. Chastity is a futile and unnatural imposition.[169] Parents do not have any rights over their offspring beyond the period of their dependence, and children should feel no duties towards parents, who did not consult them before bringing them into this world.[170]

A woman's rights over her own body and sexuality are asserted against the conventional claims of marriage. But this occurs in the context of a justification of rape, which, for Sade, is the straightforward expression of women's permanent availability for the satisfaction of men's desires.[171] A husband has no right to impose lifelong fidelity on his wife, but only because that would preclude her constant and 'instantaneous' availability to other men. In the remarkable 'address to revolutionaries', he even proposes that the state should provide sexual facilities or 'houses of pleasure' for both men and women. These facilities are designed to provide safe outlets for the 'despotic' desires of both men and women in the interest of the stability of the republic. But once again, Sade has no regard for the wishes of the involuntary objects of these desires. In case the nihilistic implications of his philosophy could be mistaken, in the same section he justifies theft, incest and murder. How can murder be a crime, when destruction is the universal law of nature?[172]

Still, it is possible to appreciate Sade as something other than the personification of absolute evil. He can be seen as an acute observer of human sexual behaviour and a precursor of the scientific sexology of the nineteenth century. Much of *Philosophy in the Bedroom* can be read as a somewhat eccentric sex-education manual. It includes explanations of scientific and vernacular sexual terms, the rudiments of sexual biology and a reasonably extensive survey of the varieties of the sexual act. Sade's discussion is sometimes surprisingly modern. Although he rehearses the misogynist view, common at least since Aristotle, that the male is the only 'creative principle' in procreation, he also finds room for a discussion of female ejaculation and various methods of contraception.[173] The 'shocking' perversions exhaustively (and exhaustingly) described in his pornographic works turn out to be persistent if not always common diversions of the sexual instinct. The detailed sexual taxonomy of *120 Days of Sodom* covers much the same ground as Krafft-Ebing's *Psychopathia Sexualis*, published a century later. No doubt Sade takes more than a clinical interest in his sexual descriptions. But similarly ulterior motives would be attributed (and not always without justification) to later pioneers of scientific sexology such as Krafft-Ebing, Hirschfeld and Havelock Ellis.[174]

Further uncertainty results from the central role of imagination in Sade's work. As a dedicated pornographer, Sade's scenes of extravagant cruelty are arguably intended to inspire nothing more shocking than masturbation. Certainly, whether by necessity or circumstance, his own energies were devoted almost entirely to the fictional depiction rather than real enactment of his erotic obsessions. As Simone de Beauvoir suggests, 'It was not murder that fulfilled Sade's erotic nature; it was literature.'[175] It is just that Sade's erotic imagination – and, he supposes, the imagination of his audience – thrives above all on the defiance of conventional morality. Indeed, Sade clearly depends on conventional morality more than he likes to pretend. His eroticism could not exist without the social conventions he sets out to defy. Sade's perverse eroticism is a kind of blasphemy, which depends on the existence of the ideals it flouts.[176] It is hard to deny that his predominant interest and discursive aim is pornographic. At times he explicitly invites this interpretation as, for example, when he claims to write only for those who cannot be corrupted because they are 'capable of understanding me'.[177] For Sade, it is not violence but *imagination* that is the indispensable 'spur' of pleasure.[178]

Overall, the development of hedonism and libertinism reflects the inherent limitations of the second constellation of rationality and the self. On the positive side, instrumental rationality no longer supports the sacrifice of sexual pleasure to ascetic ideals of reason, virtue or God. Pleasure is rehabilitated and unnecessary sexual prohibitions are able to be challenged. But the tradition of instrumental rationality nevertheless retains a feature shared with the western tradition's more idealist conception of reason. Like reason, rationality is still treated as a separate faculty essentially external to the self and its inclinations. Certainly, the utilitarianism of Bentham or the libertinism of La Mettrie and Sade casts rationality in the role of defender rather than prosecutor of bodily pleasures and inclinations. But as an instrument serving these inclinations, rationality is unable to judge or discriminate between particular pleasures, inclinations or forms of sexual activity. These can only be assessed in quantitative terms. Other consequences being equal, utilitarianism and hedonism have no rational basis to distinguish between the pleasures of pushpin and poetry or, for that matter, between a loving relationship, Tantric sex and necrophilia. Reason and rationality may, in their different configurations, either castigate or champion bodily pleasure and sexual impulses. But in either form, they offer only a limited basis for a fully human understanding of desire, sexuality and love.

3

Passion beyond Reason

The inspired Diotima revealed only half of love to her Socrates. Love is not only a silent longing for the infinite; it is also the holy enjoyment of a beautiful present. It is not only a mixture, a transition from the mortal to the immortal, it is rather the complete unity of both.[1]

1 Mystical and Courtly Love

A third and looser constellation of reason, self and sexuality eclipses to varying degrees and in various ways the primacy accorded to reason or rationality in the intellectual tradition of the West. This constellation, one of whose subspecies is Romanticism, displaces both idealist and realist forms of rationalism, shifting moral and ontological emphasis towards love and passion. It has two principal sources. One source is a negative reaction against the tradition of sexual realism and hedonism (considered in chapter 2), which tends to treat love and passion simply as desires or impulses to be served by rationality. For the broadly Romantic constellation that emerges from this reaction, love and related emotions are elevated above the level of mere urge or impulse, and the moral distance between love and sexuality is correspondingly increased. This reaction can be explored through the ideas of Jean-Jacques Rousseau and Mary Wollstonecraft.[2]

A second and more direct source of a broadly Romantic constellation results from the gradual emancipation of love from the gravitational pull of transcendent reason and rationalist conceptions of God. Through this development, an order of truth and value is established which is neither derived from nor straightforwardly reducible to reason. Passionate love is elevated beyond reason to a position of moral and existential pre-eminence for the self. The idealization of love in a way that ultimately favours its association with passion as opposed to reason is first and most unambiguously present in the context of religion. Of course, as we have seen, Christianity in the West followed Platonic and Platonist philosophy in understanding both God and love in the terms of reason. Genuine love or eros draws us ever higher towards what is eternal, rational and divine. Sexual desire is correspondingly devalued.[3] But the monotheistic religions of Judaism, Christianity and Islam are exceptional in this regard. Animist and polytheistic religions – *pre*-monotheistic from the perspective of a supposedly more advanced monotheism, 'pagan' or 'heathen' in the eyes of a supposedly more civilized Christendom – offer a contrary model, which elevates passionate love and even sexuality above any conception of reason or mere rationality.[4]

The overriding concern of many traditional societies with the productivity of the land is expressed in fertility rites and cults – some of which, like Easter, are preserved in modified form within Christianity. For societies recognizing the sexual basis of reproduction, these rites include worship of the phallus and semen as well as symbols of female fertility. Not infrequently, priests or ordinary worshippers perform sexual acts deemed to have spiritual significance.[5] The ecstatic frenzy induced by some cultic practices, which may or may not involve actual orgasm, is interpreted in religious terms as overcoming the individual's limited, selfish perspective on the world and consequently as an effective way of achieving a direct encounter with the sacred or divine. The religious meanings and functions of sexual activity are preserved in some Eastern religions such as Hinduism. In Tantric sex, for example, spiritual beatitude is sought through sexual acts strictly choreographed to avoid the actual emission of semen.

The sexual dimension of religion was a commonplace of ancient Greek and Roman polytheism. The Greek and Roman cults of Dionysus and Bacchus involved orgiastic and ecstatic rituals that were thought to transport practitioners beyond the confines of the earthly realm. The cult of Dionysus inspired Nietzsche to identify the 'Dionysian' as a basic principle of unruly creativity complementing the more familiar principles of order and harmony associated with the god Apollo.[6] Indeed, the sexual licentiousness of ancient pagan rites was a prime target of the ascetic Christianity of the early Church. The austere sexual morality promoted by early Church fathers like St Augustine was asserted in explicit opposition to the sexual depravity of pagans – in the case of Augustine, against his own formerly pagan life. But even early Christianity was not immune to spiritual interpretations of sex. Ostensibly Christian heresies such as Gnosticism treated sexual activity as potentially having religious significance.[7] The early Church fathers' intense hostility to orgiastic rites and even their more general asceticism can be understood in this context. Both positions served to establish a clear moral line of demarcation between paganism and Christianity, making it less likely that those Christians still attracted to pagan practices would defect. Indeed, on occasions during its subsequent history, the Church found it necessary to resist religious tendencies that threatened to open the door to sexual or quasi-sexual surrogates for religious experience.

Christian mysticism represents a variety of religious experience that serves to revive the association between religion and passion and, correspondingly, to loosen the connection between God and reason. Christian mysticism combines a suspicion of reason with a passionate and, at times, ostensibly sexual understanding of spiritual experience. In contrast to Augustine's resolutely activist Christianity of 'will', mysticism emphasizes the need to accept passively God's beneficence and truth. In contrast to the intellectual theology of Aquinas, mysticism manifests a Christianity of passion, favouring 'heart' or soul over intellect. Dissatisfied with the theological attempt to apprehend the divine, mysticism seeks a direct spiritual experience, a personal encounter and even ongoing communion with God. There is less emphasis on a conception of God as the abstract and eternal embodiment of reason and goodness and more emphasis on the personality of God. According to Irving Singer's definition, the 'mysticism of the West is an effort to achieve oneness with a divinity more or less conceived to be a person'.[8]

Mysticism's view of religious experience is justified by a relatively small development in the Platonist doctrine which, unamended, forms the philosophical bedrock of Christian theology. An important intermediary between Platonism and Christian mysticism was the pagan philosopher Plotinus (AD *c.*205–70), who espouses a form of rationalism at the limit of reason.[9] Plotinus elaborates Plato's metaphysics into a complex hierarchy of levels of being which, crucially, includes a level of being *superior* to the rational and intelligible realm of Platonic Forms. The intelligible roots of the soul and the ultimate cause of the universe are described by Plotinus as the 'One' or the 'Good'. The One, an entity that Christian Neoplatonists readily identified with God, is understood not as equivalent to reason but as the ultimate source and foundation of reason and intellect. By implication, the soul's salvation, which involves access to the 'One' or at least an approach towards it, must take the soul *beyond* reason.

Philosophical enlightenment is conceived as a kind of 'rapture' or 'ravishment' that overcomes the merely intellectual aspects of the self.[10]

It is but a short step to the tradition of Christian mysticism. The writings of fellow Carmelites St Teresa of Ávila (1515–82) and St John of the Cross (1542–91) demonstrate a deep suspicion of rationalism combined with passionate longing for an almost erotic communion with God.[11] According to Teresa's highly individual account, the genuinely religious life depends not on the intellectual sophistication of theology but on a disciplined practice of prayer which, at its furthest reaches, may lead to a mystical experience of immediate union with God. At the same time, there is much that is orthodox in the writings of Teresa – indeed, it is doubtful whether she would otherwise have survived the Spanish Inquisition. Teresa's mystical doctrines are founded on the familiar Christian theme of the worthlessness of ordinary human life, which in the absence of God is no better than 'a prisoner's life'.[12] The soul's ascent to higher things is only possible with its wholehearted realization of the worthlessness of 'everything here below'. Whilst recognizing the goodness and beauty of God's creation, we must turn 'resolutely from all worldly things'. We must 'withdraw from the satisfactions and pleasures of the world', including, of course, sexual pleasures and, for the clergy, the domestic pleasures of marriage and family.[13]

St Teresa is, however, less preoccupied with the perils of worldly sexuality than her fellow mystic, St John of the Cross. It is worth quoting his eloquent harangue against sensual pleasures, particularly those of touch, which lead ineluctably to effeminacy and a catalogue of other sins and weaknesses:

> Enjoyment in the touch of soft objects foments more numerous and pernicious kinds of harm, and by it the senses more quickly pervert the spirit and extinguish its strength and vigor. The consequence is the abominable vice of effeminacy or incentives toward it in proportion to this kind of joy. This joy foments lust; it makes the spirit cowardly and timid and the senses flattering, honey-mouthed, disposed toward sin and causing harm. It pours vain gladness and mirth into the heart, engenders license of the tongue and freedom of the eyes, and ravishes and stupefies the other senses according to the intensity of the appetite. It confounds the judgment, nurturing it on spiritual incipience and stupidity, and morally engenders cowardice and inconstancy.[14]

For St John, sensory enjoyments are also inseparable from an ungodly and socially divisive vanity. Even the sense of smell can lead us seriously astray. For 'Joy in sweet fragrance foments disgust for the poor (which is contrary to Christ's doctrine), aversion for servants, unsubmissiveness of heart in humble things, and spiritual insensitivity, at least in the measure of the appetite.'[15]

The further step to mysticism occurs once the worthlessness of this world and unredeemed humanity is extended to human intellectual abilities. St Teresa regards human reason and, by implication, theology as miserably inadequate instruments for the comprehension of God's 'grandeurs': 'So, Sisters, we don't have to look for reasons to understand the hidden things of God. Since we believe He is powerful, clearly we must believe that a worm with as limited power as ours will not understand His grandeurs.'[16] Of course, St Teresa's emphasis on the inadequacy of human intellectual powers is not itself unorthodox. Augustine, too, had little confidence in humanity's unaided intelligence or virtue, attributing his own spiritual and intellectual achievements entirely to the grace of God.[17] But Augustine nevertheless believed that by God's grace we may nevertheless will with goodness and right reason. For St Teresa, by contrast, the corruption of all worldly things and human faculties requires that the will be overcome or transcended, rather than simply corrected. As it begins its long and painful ascent towards divinity, the soul renounces all will and desire: 'The soul no longer wants to desire, nor would it want to have free will – and this is what I beg the Lord . . . From here on the soul desires nothing for itself; it wants its actions to be in complete conformity with His glory and His will.'[18] The soul is unable to rely on intellect or reason in any way: 'Here there is no more to do than surrender our intellects and reflect that they are of no avail when it comes to understanding the grandeurs of God.'[19] St Teresa emphasizes that the purely intellectual apprehension of God offered by theology is completely inadequate in the absence of the soul's only reliable recourse, which is through the efficacy of divine love.

St Teresa's disparagement of human will and intellect contrasts with her positive evaluation of the power of the prayerful and loving soul. Only the soul's path of loving prayer offers any sure hope of genuine spiritual experience and truths unattainable by mere intellect.[20] The 'agile soul' is more suited than the 'slovenly intellect' to the passionate but, sadly, usually transient union with Jesus that can be achieved through prayer. The intellect arrives too late and can never recover the essence of the spiritual experience: 'The intellect loses sight at that time, for the union never lasts long, but is brief.'[21] Teresa is even bold enough to associate what she sees as the Church's neglect of the power of love and prayer with its low opinion of the capacities of women. Speaking of the Virgin Mary, she combines praise of the soul and simple faith with criticism of the intellectual arrogance of male theologians:

> She did not act as do some learned men (whom the Lord does not lead by this mode of prayer and who haven't begun a life of prayer), for they want to be so rational about things and so precise in their understanding that it doesn't seem anyone else but they with their learning can understand the grandeurs of God. If only they would learn something from the humility of the most Blessed Virgin.[22]

Not surprisingly, though never incarcerated by the Inquisition, St Teresa experienced considerable difficulties at the hands of her male superiors in the Church and even in her own order of Carmelites.[23]

The radical renunciation of will and intellect is reflected in the passionate language and sometimes sexual imagery of St Teresa's writings. Mystical union is described as an ecstatic and almost death-like experience.[24] The mystic experiences the 'holy inebriation' of doing God's will and a profound but temporary forgetfulness of self.[25] The irresistible 'rapture' of union with the divine is experienced as an overpowering 'transport' or 'flight of the spirit'.[26] Teresa's description of the swooning mystical union with God has sexual overtones. Drawing on a long line of Christian exegesis, she turns to the biblical Song of Songs for its allegorical portrayal of the blissful union of the individual soul or 'bride' with her 'Bridegroom' or 'Spouse'. The earthly pleasures that must be sacrificed for the sake of the soul's salvation are, it seems, compensated by spiritual 'delights' that are just as intense. The 'bride' understands how it is 'possible for a soul in love with its Spouse to experience all these favors, swoons, deaths, afflictions, delights, and joys in relation to Him'.[27] The soul is overpowered by a spiritual force that is recognizably (if only metaphorically) erotic: 'The soul is moved with a delightful desire to enjoy Him, and thereby it is prepared to make intense acts of love and praise of our Lord.'[28]

At times, St Teresa's descriptions of mystical experience even intimate a masochistic enjoyment of pain for the sake of spiritual salvation. The ultimately worthless pleasures of the body are contrasted with the soul's delightfully painful ascent to the level of spirit. Pain results from the 'desire the body and the soul have of not being separated'. This desire must be overcome by the higher, more spiritual part of the soul, which prefers pain.[29] But the 'pain of love' suffered by the aspiring soul is at the same time 'delightful':

> You can't exaggerate or describe the way in which God wounds the soul and the extreme pain this wound produces, for it causes the soul to forget itself. Yet this pain is so delightful that there is no pleasure in life that gives greater happiness. The soul would always want, as I said, to be dying of this sickness. . . .
>
> . . . The pain was so great that it made me moan, and the sweetness this greatest pain caused me was so superabundant that there is no desire capable of taking it away; nor is the soul content with less than God. The pain is not bodily but spiritual, although the body doesn't fail to share in some of it, and even a great deal. The loving exchange that takes place between the soul and God is so sweet that I beg Him in His goodness to give a taste of his love to anyone who thinks I am lying.[30]

Indeed, the soul's longing for pain is one of the main proofs of the divine rather than diabolic inspiration of its mystical visions.[31]

According to St Teresa, of course, the potent sexual imagery of the Song of Songs is intended to illuminate a deeper spiritual meaning. 'Let Him kiss me with the kiss of His mouth' should be understood as a request for peace and friendship.[32] 'Your breasts are better than wine' is meant to convey the swooning of the bride in 'great pleasure and happiness', because she is supported by God, her Bridegroom.[33] The apparently sexual connotations can be tolerated only, it seems, because St Teresa's heightened spirituality has shifted moral and metaphysical emphasis so far from any more worldly interpretation. What remains bold, however, is her conviction that the passionately erotic discourse of the Song of Songs provides a more reliable guide to the religious life than the dry intellectual reasonings of theology. In the face of criticisms and suspicion from her superiors in the Church, she has no doubt that her 'daring' approach offers a better course than a religious practice devoid of love and prayer.[34] The spiritual salvation of the soul is not helped by the rational, intellectual discourses of theology and philosophy. Love rather than reason offers the privileged route to spiritual salvation.

The separation of love from its Platonic and Christian connection with reason and the divine also takes a rather different form – one closer to contemporary understandings of Romanticism – in the tradition of courtly love, which contributes to the 'humanization' of Platonic eros and Christian *agape*.[35] As with mysticism, there is a shift away from rationalist conceptions of love towards the contemporary understanding of passionate love. In contrast to Christian mysticism, on the other hand, the abstract and exclusively other-worldly understanding of love is abandoned. Love is no longer projected on to another super-human or divine realm but regarded as something within human grasp. In this tradition, love is not confined within the realm of religious aspirations or associated exclusively with God but conceived in decidedly this-worldly terms as a relationship between human beings. But love is still strongly idealized – it is still thought to provide a path to some higher reality or truth for the individual. Human relationships are infused with something like the intensity and aura characteristic of the divine.

Indeed, according to Denis de Rougemont, the idealization of human passion that culminates in Romanticism can be traced to the heretical religious doctrines of the Cathars in twelfth-century France. The love poetry of the Troubadours, in which the ideas of courtly love first assumed clear form, can be read as a disguised expression of Cathar heresies, which can themselves be traced to the radical dualism and other-worldly asceticism of Manicheanism.[36] According to this hypothesis, the worship of the beloved in the poetry of the Troubadours is derived from worship of the 'Lady', a term used by Cathars to refer to their own 'Church of Love' and later recuperated for the orthodox Church in the Catholic cult of the Virgin Mary.[37] Whatever its origins, courtly love's worship of the beloved certainly exhibits a religious intensity and fervour. The tradition of courtly love elevates love into the absolute goal of life, a passion so absolute that it negates all other commitments and ties, including duties to society, family and even one's spouse. The characteristic relationships of courtly love are extra-marital, often between lovers from different and conventionally incompatible social positions. At the same time, courtly love is typically unconsummated. Passionate love is expressed most purely and most powerfully in the willingness of the lover to suffer chastely even 'unto death' for the sake of his beloved.

The more mundane conception of courtly love finds classical expression in the twelfth-century *Art of Courtly Love* of Andreas Capellanus, about whom little else is known. Capellanus combines a pragmatic interest in the physical enjoyments and dangers of love with a more idealized, almost Platonic, view. His definition of love is explicitly sexual: 'Love is a certain inborn suffering derived from the sight of and excessive meditation upon the beauty of the opposite sex, which causes each one to wish above all things the embraces of the other and by common desire to carry out all of love's precepts in the other's embrace.'[38] At the same time, love is seen as intrinsically ennobling:

> Love causes a rough and uncouth man to be distinguished for his handsomeness; it can endow a man even of the humblest birth with nobi-

> lity of character; it blesses the proud with humility; and the man in love becomes accustomed to performing many services gracefully for everyone. O what a wonderful thing is love, which makes a man shine with so many virtues and teaches everyone, no matter who he is, so many good traits of character! [39]

Love may even make a man chaste, if only in the sense that, once in love, he is less likely to want sexual relations with another woman. Capellanus also recommends that in matters of love we should place greater emphasis on character and virtue than on beauty and other merely external accomplishments.[40] At the same time, Christian strictures against sensual indulgence and vice are taken for granted, whether sincerely or merely expediently. The concluding chapters of Capellanus' treatise go against the courtly sentiments of earlier ones, assembling a collection of more or less unconvincing arguments against love. These include familiar biblical condemnations of fornication and lust as well as a misogynist catalogue of the supposed vices of women.[41] Unsurprisingly, homosexual relations are roundly condemned: '. . . for we see that two persons of the same sex are not at all fitted for giving each other the exchanges of love or for practicing the acts natural to it.'[42]

2 Romantic Critique of Rationality

The courtly tradition's idealized conception of human love contributed to the thought of Jean-Jacques Rousseau (1712–78), who can be regarded as one of the originators of Romanticism. He is unusual among philosophers (after Plato) for his extensive concern with the place of love, passion and sexuality in a modern society. Not unrelatedly, Rousseau is perhaps the first major philosopher in the western canon since Plato to express philosophical ideas as much in literary as in discursive form – some of his most influential ideas are presented in his novels. His autobiographical *Confessions* were also a *succès de scandale*, with their intimate revelations of his often troubled affairs with women as well as sexual episodes that include masturbation and flagellation – a life that contrasts with the asexual reputation of most philosophers.

Rousseau's philosophical concern with love and sexuality emerges from his critical reaction to the Enlightenment, even though his thought is at the same time unmistakably one of the products of that social and intellectual movement. He was certainly influenced by the Enlightenment's sceptical and anti-clerical spirit. He is hostile to any metaphysical system, dogmatic morality or religious superstition barring the way to greater human fulfilment. His combination of republican and radically democratic ideas makes him one of the chief intellectual sources of the French Revolution. He radicalizes the characteristically Enlightenment value of human freedom in a way that has been taken to inspire everything from radical libertarianism and participatory democracy to totalitarianism.[43] At the same time, Rousseau's thought derives most directly from his antagonism to some of the Enlightenment's central convictions. He is highly critical of the 'civilized' commercial society of his time and corresponding ideas of progress and advancement. Above all, he is opposed to prevailing currents of materialism, hedonism and libertinism. Against these currents, he affirms a strenuous moral idealism that is based not on reason but on the value of love. In effect, both the western tradition's infatuation with reason and the Enlightenment's materialist rationalism must be corrected and supplemented by a revaluation of the place of passion and love in human life.[44]

Perhaps the best way to approach Rousseau's doctrine of passion is through his critical diagnosis of the 'advanced' civilization of his time. For most *philosophes*, rational improvement and progress were inseparable from the increasing sophistication, productivity and wealth of commercial society. Rousseau, on the other hand, was both sceptical of the supposed benefits of modern civilization and fearful of the Enlightenment's individualist, materialist and hedonist assumptions. He shares with progressive Enlightenment thinkers the belief that humanity is not naturally evil and has at least the potential for good. But he does not think that it is enough simply to remove the fetters of religion, conventional morality and political despotism in order to release humanity's innate potential for happiness. The problem is that humanity is being *corrupted* by the very features of modern civilization welcomed by the partisans of Enlightenment – the division of labour, social and economic progress and the profusion of increasingly sophisticated tastes and pleasures.

Rousseau's speculative history of civilization, contained in his *Discourse on the Origin of Inequality* (1755) and also informing his philosophical novel *Émile, or Education* (1762), turns the Enlightenment's optimistic narrative of progress on its head. In effect, the momentary lapse of Adam and Eve is extended over the entire period of human history and pre-history. As in the biblical story of the Fall, human beings are held responsible for their own misery: 'God makes all things good; man meddles with them and they become evil.'[45] But humanity's decline from a state of natural goodness and innocence occurs for very different reasons and over a much longer time-scale. Rousseau supposes that 'man' originally lived an isolated life governed only by a few immediate needs and his own healthy instincts. In the 'state of nature', humanity was naturally healthy and vigorous, had little foresight and consequently no fear of death. Human beings had no command of language, because in their isolated state they had no need of it. For the same reason they lived without morality. They lived without 'moral relations or determinate obligations one with another' so that 'men in a state of nature . . . could not be either good or bad, virtuous or vicious.'[46] Neither calculating human rationality nor the restraints of morality played any significant role in the state of nature.

The essential instruments of survival for 'savage man' were his natural instincts and passions, which, being implanted in us by nature or God, were not originally destructive or immoral. Far from being destructively selfish, human beings were guided by healthy passions and a harmless 'love of self' (*amour de soi*), which ensured all that was necessary for survival.[47] The destructive selfishness of humanity is thus not so much the starting-point as a by-product of history. As population increases and more intensive forms of agriculture and commerce emerge, human beings are forced into closer and more frequent contact with one another. With settled agriculture also come private property, the division of labour and, for the first time, economic, social and political inequalities. This more social existence in turn encourages the development of language, which brings with it some advantages – language facilitates foresight, memory and the transmission of knowledge and culture between generations. But the advance of civilization also brings significant disadvantages.

Above all, civilization corrupts the originally healthy passions of natural 'man'. People living in closer proximity begin to compare themselves with one another according to 'ideas of beauty and merit'. Innocent 'love of self' is replaced with *amour propre* (closer to selfishness), the competitive and ultimately destructive concern with one's position relative to others. Civilized man is either arrogant or envious and resentful according to his idea of his status. As a result, his originally modest wants begin to expand without limit: 'Self-love, which concerns itself only with ourselves, is content to satisfy our own needs; but selfishness, which is always comparing self with others, is never satisfied and never can be.'[48] Having many needs, civilized man inevitably comes into conflict with his fellows. *Amour propre* causes each person to demand that others love him more than they love themselves, which 'causes all the mutual damage men inflict one on another'.[49] It is only with civilization that, as Rousseau strikingly puts it, human beings *become* 'essentially bad'.[50]

Paradoxically, this account of the corruption of humanity also sets the scene for its redemption. Although the transition to civilized society has corrupted the natural innocence of 'savage man', humanity may yet be able to escape to an ultimately higher state. This transition involves the exchange of innocence for *morality* and, relatedly, of one kind of freedom for another. In the state of nature, human beings have an unimpeded 'natural' (or 'negative') liberty to follow their natural inclinations and passions unrestricted by either social norms or the interference of other people.[51] With the transition to civilized society, this natural or negative liberty is inevitably compromised. But what the individual loses in natural liberty is potentially compensated by the gain of a different kind of liberty, what Rousseau calls 'civil' or 'moral liberty'. In society the individual has the opportunity to become a responsible moral agent and so escape from being a mere creature of impulse like other animals. Moral liberty 'alone makes him truly master of himself; for the mere impulse of appetite is slavery, while obedience to a law which we prescribe to ourselves is liberty'.[52]

The key to the progression from the innocence of 'savage man' to the higher morality and freedom of 'civilized man' is provided by humanity's *erotic* nature. Of course, Rousseau does not doubt that our sexual passions have been corrupted by civilization. In common with man's other natural passions, civilization corrupts the originally idyllic forms of sexual and family relationship.[53] *Amour propre* infects sexual relations at least as virulently as any other area of human life. Sexual needs too are exaggerated and distorted by our pride and concern with status. Rousseau was critical of the unbridled libertinism he witnessed in cities like Paris, which feeds the disruptive passions of 'jealousy', 'discord' and 'impetuous fury'.[54] He attacked the effeminacy of civilized man as compared to the rugged masculinity and 'virtue' of at least some of the ancients. He notes that after the heroic age of Homer, Greece fell into a 'dissoluteness of manners', 'always learned, always voluptuous, and always a slave'.[55] Even Rome declined from martial glories and republican virtue into 'luxury, profligacy' and 'effeminacy of manners'.[56]

For Rousseau, the only possible path to a well-ordered society and healthy individuals is through a fundamental re-ordering of our passions. Love is the passion that, without our knowing it, has worked to overcome some of the deleterious effect of civilization and offers some prospect of a more adequate form of society. Although it can also inspire less desirable qualities, love potentially has a moralizing effect: 'True love, whatever you may say, will always be held in honour by mankind; for although its impulses lead us astray, although it does not bar the door of the heart to certain detestable qualities, although it even gives rise to these, yet it always presupposes certain worthy characteristics, without which we should be incapable of love.'[57] Love can effect changes in us that we would never arrive at through reason or rational calculation. Love, Rousseau implies, has reasons and perceives realities that our limited understanding of reason cannot recognize: 'This choice, which is supposed to be contrary to reason, really springs from reason. We say Love is blind because his eyes are better than ours, and he perceives relations which we cannot discern.'[58] The transformative power of love to raise the individual to the level of *moral* liberty comes from its ability to limit our otherwise boundless sexual desires: 'Love does not spring from nature, far from it; it is the curb and law of her desires; it is love that makes one sex indifferent to the other, the loved one alone excepted.'[59]

However, because our natural passions have been so deeply corrupted by society, the moralizing force of love depends on outside intervention. In the first place, we must educate children to prevent their otherwise inevitable corruption. The topic of education is explicitly addressed in Rousseau's *Émile*, which describes the method employed by an idealized guardian and teacher, Jean-Jacques, to mould his still uncorrupted child, Émile. Only the careful manipulation of the circumstances of Émile's education can assure the ascendancy of love as a bulwark against the corrupt 'progress' of civilization. We cannot simply wait for love to develop spontaneously. Émile's passionate and sexual impulses will not be controlled spontaneously by the child's rudimentary rationality. Although the child's early 'instinctive' and 'mechanical' attachments provide the kernel for genuine love, these instincts must be carefully manipulated if Émile's primitive love of self is to be transformed into love for another person.[60] His knowledge of sex and experience of sexual satisfaction must be delayed. His unruly and self-centred sexual impulses must be redirected towards the moral relationship of monogamous love.[61]

Rousseau's philosophy is further elaborated in his epistolary novel *Julie, or the New Eloise* (1761), in which he fleshes out a conception of Romantic love that would inspire a generation of writers and philosophers. In the novel, Julie forms a passionate attachment to her young tutor, Saint-Preux. They consummate the relationship but are ultimately forced apart by the intervention of Julie's outraged father. A central message is that Romantic relationships should be freely chosen without interference from patriarchs concerned only with property and dynastic connections. Conventional marriage, in other words, cannot be relied upon to provide the necessary moralizing force. But neither is Romantic love something to be followed at all costs. Although Saint-Preux is unconditionally committed to his love, Julie masters her passion and relinquishes any thoughts of marrying Saint-Preux out of duty to her father. Love must be regulated and restrained, albeit not in the way proposed by conventional morality. Only then can love be that 'chaste bond' celebrated by Julie:

> I am possibly mistaken, but it seems to me that true love is the most chaste of all bonds. It is true love, it is its divine fire which can purify our natural inclinations by concentrating them in a single object. It is true love which shelters us from temptations and which makes the opposite sex no longer important, except for the beloved one.[62]

At the same time, *Julie* foreshadows more pessimistic and even tragic themes. After her heroic renunciation, Julie finds only sober friendship and good works with the worthy Wolmar. Both she and Saint-Preux meet with early deaths. Rousseau seems to imply that Romantic passion is more securely based in imagination and hope than in reality. Romantic love is fragile and, at worst, illusory. Émile, too, is warned that the promise of a happily married life is one all too likely to be disappointed: 'You have tasted greater joys through hope than you will ever enjoy in reality. The imagination which adorns what we long for, deserts its possession.'[63] Ultimately, Rousseau is more concerned to exploit the moralizing force of passionate love than with the loving relationship itself. It is this force that provides an essential condition of both life and philosophy. As Lord Bomston says of his perhaps excessively passionate friend, Saint-Preux: 'Such a love as his is not so much a weakness as a strength badly exerted . . . for the highest reason is only attained through the same power of the soul which gives rise to great passions, and we serve philosophy worthily only with the same ardor that we feel for a mistress.'[64] Rousseau's idealization of love between human beings thus retains something of the 'divine fire' of ancient Greek eros.

Given the central place of love in Rousseau's moral, social and political thought, it is unfortunate that his ideas of sexuality and love are conceived in such decidedly patriarchal terms. In *Émile*, he sets out the complementary but nonetheless hierarchical relationship between Émile and his idealized partner, Sophie – a name that alludes to the Greek word for wisdom, *sophia*. Julie provides a statement of the complementarity of the sexes that Rousseau would presumably endorse: 'The attack and the defense, the audacity of men, the modesty of women – these are by no means conventions, as your philosophers think, but natural institutions which are easily accounted for and from which all the other moral distinctions are readily inferred.'[65] Men, it seems, are naturally drawn to reasoning and philosophy, women to novels and the potentially redemptive moral force of love.

Although Rousseau's sexist attitudes were not unusual for his time, his 'male aristocracy' provoked an acerbic reaction from someone who was otherwise one of his passionate admirers, Mary Wollstonecraft (1759–97). In effect, Wollstonecraft pursues Rousseau's arguments about the corrupting influence of power and inequality with greater consistency and comprehensiveness than he does himself. She famously insists that women should be educated in the same way as men in order to develop their strength, reason and virtue, and not be encouraged to be weak, dependent and frivolous. Wollstonecraft's *Vindication of the Rights of Woman* (1792) gathers together her many insights and observations and, above all, a host of passionate arguments for a more suitable position and education for women. But although Wollstonecraft is remembered mainly as an early advocate of feminism, she is also an insightful early critic of Romanticism.

According to Wollstonecraft's useful summing up, Rousseau claims to 'prove that woman ought to be weak and passive, because she has less bodily strength than man; and hence infers that she was formed to please and to be subject to him, and that it is her duty to render herself *agreeable* to her master – this being the grand end of her existence'.[66] The proper role of woman is that of wife and mother, subordinated to her husband and excluded from public life. At the same time, Rousseau 'gallantly' insists that a man depends on 'the will of the woman', so that although 'master in appearance' he is really dependent on her. But this evidently does nothing to mitigate his patriarchal conclusions. The supposed *sexual* dependence of men becomes just another reason for women's subordination. Women are to be educated according to their sexually defined role or, in other words, to serve the emotional and sexual needs of men:

> For this reason the education of the women should be always relative to the men. To please, to be useful to us, to make us love and esteem them, to educate us when young, and take care of us when grown up, to advise, to console us, to render our lives easy and agreeable – these are the duties of women at all times, and what they should be taught in their infancy.[67]

As Wollstonecraft painstakingly and repeatedly points out, this means an education for superficial attractiveness rather than virtue, for the power of guile and deceit rather than genuine strength or understanding.

So, despite his own objections to libertinism, Rousseau's philosophy is really just a more sophisticated 'philosophy of lasciviousness', which derives the proper place and education of women solely from a *sexual* view of their proper relations with men.[68] By the same token, Wollstonecraft's contrary position, that women and men alike should be educated in strength, virtue and understanding, corresponds to a much lower estimation of the place of sex in human life. The unrestrained pursuit of physical pleasure diverts women and men from the more important values of wisdom, respectability, virtue.[69] Sensuality inflames passions that may ultimately be corrosive of morality: 'Most of the evils of life arise from a desire of present enjoyment that outruns itself.'[70] The sexually inspired education of women is, as ever, a particularly poisonous 'source of female vices and follies'.[71] Although sexual attraction plays an important role in inspiring relationships between men and women, passionate love should and (as even Rousseau recognized) usually does quickly give way to the calmer intercourse of friendship: 'Love, from its very nature, must be transitory. . . . The most holy band of society is friendship.'[72]

Wollstonecraft's suspicion of sex also translates into conventional condemnation of homosexuality. Giving an eighteenth-century orientalist twist to an explanation familiar since antiquity, she explains that effeminacy and homosexuality are natural outcomes of unbridled sensuality (at least in warmer climates):

> The depravity of the appetite which brings the sexes together, has had a still more fatal effect. Nature must ever be the standard of taste, the gauge of appetite – yet how grossly is nature insulted by the voluptuary. . . .
>
> So voluptuous, indeed, often grows the lustful prowler, that he refines on female softness. Something more soft than women is then sought for; till, in Italy and Portugal, men attend the levees of equivocal beings, to sigh for more than female languor.[73]

She is also concerned about the vices learned in boarding-schools, advocating co-educational day-schools as a much safer setting for young boys and girls.[74] Not that Wollstonecraft should be simply dismissed as a prude. Her suspicion of sex diminished as she acquired greater sexual experience (or, indeed, *some* sexual experience) later in her life.[75] In any case, the 'lasciviousness' she fears most is not so much unrestrained sexual desire as its Romantic exaggeration. She even suggests that Rousseau's distorted views on women may have resulted from the effects of sexual frustration on his excessive 'sensibility':

> Even his virtues also led him farther astray; for, born with a warm constitution and lively fancy, nature carried him toward the other sex with such eager fondness that he soon became lascivious. Had he given way to these desires, the fire would have extinguished itself in a natural manner, but virtue, and a romantic kind of delicacy, made him practice self-denial; yet when fear, delicacy, or virtue restrained him, he debauched his imagination, and reflecting on the sensations to which fancy gave force, he traced them in the most glowing colours, and sunk them deep into his soul.[76]

This view of the pathological consequences of denying healthy sexual release almost seems worthy of an eighteenth-century libertine.

But for Wollstonecraft, such straightforward hedonism would be acceptable only if we were not immortal.[77] If there were no God, then the 'prudent voluptuary' and our natural 'appetites' would be our best guides. There would then be as little point in arduous intellectual activity as in purified Romantic pursuits. It is only Wollstonecraft's rationalist faith in the prospect of an after-life that justifies the subordination of pleasure and passion to reason and virtue. But within this hierarchy of value, crucially, love also has a central place. As for Plato, love for another person is valued as a vehicle that brings us closer to virtue, which must first appear to us in human form as the 'beloved object'. It is only in this context, too, that the mistakes induced by passionate love may be useful, because they enlarge our experience and mind, preparing us for a higher form of existence after death.[78]

Wollstonecraft's critique of Rousseau certainly demonstrates that a social philosophy premised on the sexual complementarity of women and men is intrinsically patriarchal. As such, it is inconsistent with the egalitarian intentions that he otherwise espoused. Unfortunately, her critique was largely ignored by the subsequent Romantic tradition, which typically placed considerable emphasis on the complementary and unequal capacities of women and men. But beyond that, her position also suggests that, in the absence of religious faith, Romanticism may represent an inherently *unstable* amalgam of idealized love and sexual desire. Only religious faith, it seems, can make sense of the strenuous idealism of the Romantic conception of love. Without faith, Romanticism is always liable to revert to an exaggerated, 'licentious' or 'voluptuary' hedonism. Or, worse, the pursuit of love ends in either fantasy or despair.

3 Romantic Philosophy as Religion of Love

Rousseau's writings exerted considerable influence over a range of thinkers and artists broadly associated with Romanticism. Although embracing a number of different themes and positions, taken as a whole this artistic movement questioned the supposedly timeless formal demands of classicism, exploring new artistic forms. Romantics pioneered a different aesthetic, emphasizing feeling, creativity and originality rather than order, harmony and perfection. Romantic art and poetry found solace and communion but also metaphysical awe in a nature experienced as both beautiful and sublime.[79] Poets like Wordsworth and Coleridge were more likely to celebrate the sublimity of wild, craggy scenery than the well-ordered nature of formal gardens and classical landscapes. Others like Brentano and Tieck in Germany explored myths and fantasy in ways that, with Freudian hindsight, resemble explorations of the unconscious mind. Some Romantics rejected all classical models, finding inspiration in the culture and thought of the Middle Ages. Others, particularly in Germany, rebelled against the rigid and lifeless classicism of the eighteenth-century academy but were drawn to an ancient world reinterpreted in Romantic terms.

Romanticism was not confined to a literary or artistic movement but encompassed politics, historical and hermeneutic studies as well as philosophy. For Romantic philosophy, the order and meaningfulness of nature and life are closely associated with the concept of love. But love is, at first, only indirectly associated with *inter-personal* love, let alone with sexual passion or desire. Romanticism in philosophy begins life as a form of metaphysical idealism. In other words, nature is understood to reflect a deeper, underlying reality and meaning that is not reducible to the mechanical relationships of matter. But in contrast to Platonic idealism, this reality is understood in terms of love rather than reason. It is only indirectly, albeit with a certain inevitability, that the personal love of one human being for another is validated as a potentially worthy manifestation of the underlying meaning of reality and life. Love is understood first of all in a general and metaphysical sense as the key to overcoming the division and conflict that seems to characterize materialist conceptions of the world.[80] Evidently, it is not sexual desire but love that is proposed as the central metaphysical concept in this way, although the emphasis on passionate love has a tendency to rehabilitate sexual desire in the long run.

A major and characteristic figure of Romantic philosophy is the German critic, novelist and philosopher Friedrich von Schlegel (1772–1829). Although he is best known today for his aesthetics and literary criticism, he is of particular interest for his comprehensive and systematic formulation of a philosophically Romantic approach to love and sexuality. The Romantic and lyrical Hellenism of the eighteenth century in Germany, which had been influenced by Winckelmann's writings on ancient Greek art, permeates much of Schlegel's literary and critical work.[81] The ancient Greek *polis* provides a model of unity, harmony and a beguilingly aesthetic existence, which contrasted with the busy commercial society of the eighteenth century. In common with many German intellectuals at the end of that century, Schlegel reacted against the dominant currents of the French Enlightenment, particularly its rationalism, materialism, atheism and hedonism. Like Rousseau, he was critical of the apparent divisions and alienation of 'modern' society that were particularly in evidence in cities like Paris and London. But in his search for an alternative model of life and society, Schlegel was also attracted by the apparent unity and harmony of life in medieval Christendom, which had been dissolved by the Enlightenment in the name of a sterile academic conception of scientific and philosophical truth.

Schlegel's philosophy is one of a number of currents of German idealism that emerged in reaction to Kant's thought.[82] Kant's unsatisfactory dualism between the causally determined world of appearance and the 'noumenal' realm of 'things-in-themselves' could easily be read as a kind of reluctant materialism. Philosophical idealists, on the other hand, came to the conclusion that the underlying reality of things-in-themselves must be understood as essentially ideal or spiritual rather than material. Although the metaphysical arguments are complex, the essential point is that idealism insists that the world and human life must be understood as potentially meaningful.[83] Not unrelatedly – and of particular importance for Schlegel – idealism also provides a philosophically respectable basis for religious faith in the face of Enlightenment materialism and atheism. Schlegel seeks to formulate a metaphysical conception of nature which, in contrast to the materialist metaphysics and atheist tendencies of the French Enlightenment, preserves a place for God and for religious belief. In the words of J. B. Robertson, he attempts to revive 'the lofty physics of remote antiquity, when nature was regarded only as the splendid and almost transparent veil of the spiritual world'.[84]

In opposition to the mainstream of German idealism, Schlegel is distinctively *Romantic* in his further suspicion of abstract and systematic approaches to philosophy. Idealist philosophers like Schelling and, in a different way, Hegel are relentless rationalists, despite their criticism of the limitations of the Enlightenment's limited conception of rationality. By contrast, Schlegel formulates an approach to philosophy and life which foreshadows existentialist themes more fully developed by Kierkegaard. Schlegel even refers to the 'key-word of existence'.[85] It is necessary to go beyond 'school form' and the purely 'mathematical view of the world' inaugurated with modern philosophy's promotion of the natural sciences over history and the humanities.[86] The abstractions of academic philosophy and natural science can only be properly understood in the context of 'the living unity of the full consciousness'.[87] Divorced from this meaning-giving context, even though they give us a limited technical mastery over natural processes, these abstractions are really useless to *life* – they do not tell us how we should live, they do not give meaning to our lives. The real and most important subject matter of philosophy is 'inwardness' or 'subjectivity': it is 'the sublime conception of our inner life, struggling to unravel the mystery of its own being'.[88]

The architecture of Schlegel's metaphysics is presented dogmatically and has had little influence on subsequent philosophy. It is characteristically Romantic in the way it fixes the supposedly complementary natures of men and women in metaphysical categories. Rousseau's chivalrous chauvinism is translated into the gendered dualism of intellectual and spiritual dimensions of human life. 'Mind', Schlegel supposes, predominates in men and incorporates 'will' and 'understanding' (*Verstand*) or, in effect, rationality in the instrumental sense of the Enlightenment and science. 'Soul', which is more developed in women than men, is the location of imagination or 'fancy' and 'reason' (*Vernunft*), which for German philosophy is the idea of a more adequate, less divisive and reductive manifestation of human intellectual powers. *Vernunft* is a more synthetic, speculative faculty that accounts for the possibility of insights beyond the limited domain of analytical Understanding.[89] Soul is also the faculty particularly associated with love in a transcendent sense: 'The soul is nothing less than the faculty of love in man. For this reason, also, the loving soul . . . is the clear mirror in which we gaze upon the secrets of divine love . . .'[90] Schlegel's attempt to re-balance life and philosophy involves shifting emphasis back from the masculine world of mind and rationality to the feminine soul. An adequate conception of life and society cannot be derived from either rationality or reason alone. The limited faculty of understanding must be complemented by soul.

But the soul is only able to perform its restorative function if the original harmony of its own twin faculties of reason and imagination is restored. And love is the only force that can re-establish this harmony, overcoming the potentially pathological influence of 'fancy' by reconciling it with 'reason':

> In love both halves of the soul are united. For, taken separately and apart, reason is only one half of the soul, and fancy the other. In love alone do both concur, and the soul is there present totally and perfectly. In it both halves, which otherwise are ever apart, being again united, restore a perfect state of the consciousness.[91]

Schlegel associates love here with Christian notions of divine love, but he also alludes to Plato's *Symposium*, which had recently been re-translated into German by his friend, the theologian Friedrich Schleiermacher (1768–1834). The inter-personal and even erotic love between humans exists on a continuum with the abstract cosmic love idealized by Plato.

But Schlegel proposes a quite different attitude to this continuum, marking out new ground with his emphasis on the complementarity and equal value of our spiritual and bodily natures. We should not strive simply to 'ascend' towards the abstract, ideal pole of Goodness, Truth or divinity, as recommended by the Priestess Diotima, Socrates' teacher in the *Symposium*. Rather, we should seek to maintain the two poles of our physical and spiritual aspects in a permanent and creative tension. There is nothing intrinsically wrong with love's sensual or sexual manifestations, as long as they are not exaggerated or distorted by over-excited 'fancy' or imagination.[92] Schlegel shares Rousseau's belief that human passions are originally benign but easily corrupted by hedonism:

> . . . the true source of the evil – the irresistible energy and the false magic of this passion – lies in an over-excited, deluded, or poisoned fancy. The natural instinct itself, in so far as it is inborn and agreeable to nature, is obnoxious to no reproach. The blame lies altogether in the want of principle, or that weakness of character which half-voluntarily concedes to the mere instinct an unlimited authority, or at least is incapable of exercising over it a due control.[93]

Genuine sensuality is recognized by the fact that it persists beyond the moment of sexual consummation, whereas unhealthy passions immediately die away.[94]

Love between the sexes is accorded a positive value as well, because it promises to correct the one-sided development of either sex in isolation. Women with their preponderance of 'soul' complement the coldly rational intellectuality of man's 'mind' or 'understanding'. In Schlegel's later works, this version of love as the 'pursuit of the whole' culminates in a sober endorsement of marriage and the bourgeois family.[95] But equally paradigmatic is the mother's love for her child, which similarly transcends self-interested rationality: '. . . no one can call this love irrational, although it must be judged by an entirely different standard from that of reason.'[96] The power of love is the unifying principle that harmonizes family, society and cosmos:

> By all noble natures among civilized nations in their best and purest times, this instinct has, by means of various moral relations, been spontaneously associated with a higher element. . . . And it is in truth the moral sanctuary of earthly existence, on which God's first and earliest blessing still rests. It is, moreover, the foundation on which is built the happiness and the moral welfare of races and nations. This soul-connecting link of love, which constitutes the family union, is the source from which emanate the strong and beautiful ties of a mother's love, of filial duty, and of fraternal affection, between brethren and kindred, which together make up the invisible soul, and, as it were, the inner vital fluid of the nerves of human society.[97]

Romanticism in this form underwrites existing social relations and conventional sexual morality. The essential complementarity of sexual characteristics even establishes a novel line in homophobia. If love is valuable because it unites otherwise incomplete male and female individuals, then homosexual relationships presumably exaggerate the one-sidedness of men and women.[98]

Schlegel's views on love and sexuality received much less conservative expression in his philosophical novel *Lucinde* (1799). This work, which was violently attacked by his scandalized contemporaries, was defended by his friend Schleiermacher in a now famous series of 'intimate letters'. The 'religion of love' formulated in this early novel anticipates many of the themes of Schlegel's later philosophical writings, but there is little sign of the conservative Catholicism of his maturity. Instead, love is placed firmly in the context of Diotima's pronouncements in the *Symposium*, with the significant qualification that love must be understood as a spiritual and sensual whole. As we noted in the epigraph to this chapter, the sensual, sexual element must not be sacrificed: 'The inspired Diotima revealed only half of love to her Socrates. Love is not only a silent longing for the infinite; it is also the holy enjoyment of a beautiful present. It is not only a mixture, a transition from the mortal to the immortal, it is rather the complete unity of both.'[99] The need to combine the spiritual with the physical and sensual is perhaps the central theme of the novel. Through his various characters, Schlegel openly takes up arms against the 'prudery' and 'prejudice' of his contemporaries.[100]

Schlegel's allusions to sexuality are so provocative that, in Martha Helfer's words, *Lucinde* 'was considered to be not only shockingly personal and obscene, if not downright pornographic, but an aesthetic abomination to boot'.[101] Descriptions of sexual experience are only superficially veiled by poetic and metaphorical language. At the same time, Schlegel is always concerned to distinguish genuine sensuality (*Empfindung des Fleisches*) from mere 'libertinism'. As Schleiermacher approvingly notes, the crucial point is Schlegel's rejection of the dichotomy between ascetic spirituality and gross libertinism. We must find an alternative to either regarding sensuality as no more than a 'necessary evil that we must endure out of obedience to the will of God and Nature', or adopting an 'unspiritual and unworthy libertinism which boasts of having refined and humanized an animal urge to the level of gastronomy'.[102] In contrast to the sensual gastronomy of the libertine, genuine sensuality can only be learned through simultaneous participation in the higher, transcendent emotions of love: 'A libertine may understand how to untie a belt with a certain taste. But only love can teach a young man that higher artistry of lust, through which alone masculine potency reaches the level of beauty.'[103] Love depends on a synthesis of sensuality, passion and affection.

Once again, the complementarity of the sexes is an important theme. Genuine sensuality is seen as the 'innate gift of women', who must teach it to men within a loving and monogamous relationship.[104] The complementary qualities of men and women are explored through the initially stormy and complex relationship between Julius and his eventual true love, Lucinde.[105] The distinctive nature of woman has the innocence and spontaneity of children like Little Wilhelmine, who is playful and free of prudish prejudices.[106] Only women remain 'natural beings', preserving the 'childlike sense' necessary for life.[107] Women feel more intensely and more truly than men. They are largely unaffected by the understanding's analytical divisions and abstractions, which are so destructive of feeling. As Julius writes to Lucinde, 'You feel everything wholly and infinitely, you know of no separation, your being is one and indivisible.'[108] But whereas in his later writings, the complementarity of the sexes provides a straightforward justification of marriage, Schlegel comes close in *Lucinde* to a celebration of androgyny. He praises passivity as naturally feminine but also as something that men need to combine with their natural activity and strength of will. Men should acquire passivity in a way that retains the benefits of masculine activity, a 'deliberate, wilful, one-sided' passivity.[109] His enthusiastic description of the inevitable pains of love comes close to masochism.[110]

Schlegel's toying with aspects of an androgynous masculinity even permits contemplation of homosexuality. At one point, love is described as a harmonious 'warmth' (*Wärme*), which is a colloquial German expression for homosexuality.[111] The novel describes Julius's passionate friendships – his 'hot love' – with other men, who, for a time, take the place of women in his emotional life: '. . . he embraced young men who resembled him in some way with a fervent love and a truly raging friendship.'[112] He hints that these relationships might have involved a physical, even a sexual, dimension: 'It can easily be imagined that he, who regarded everything as permissible to him and who did not mind looking ridiculous, had a different kind of propriety in mind from that which generally applied.'[113] This occurs, it should be added, in a work that explicitly emphasizes the importance of sensitivity towards double meanings, allegories and indirect speech.[114]

As Schleiermacher immediately recognizes, though, the young Schlegel's broad-minded appreciation of sexuality is not incompatible with his higher moral ambitions. In the end, the mundane physical details (or 'recipes') of sex are not important. It is the inseparable unity of love and sex that represents the only possible purpose of human life. When Julius finally recognizes his true love for Lucinde, all doubts about the direction of his life disappear.[115] The unity of two souls in eternal matrimony is able to give meaning to our life, because it transcends earthly time and existence in 'the one true, indivisible, nameless, infinite world'.[116] Fatefully for the subsequent history of Romanticism, true love must therefore be indifferent to, or even welcome, death. The meaning of one's life is tied to a relationship that transcends mere physical existence. Drawing a shocking corollary, Julius remarks at one point that the only thing wrong with the Indian practice of suttee is that the woman does not die willingly.[117]

In other words, Schlegel's religion of love has an other-worldliness comparable to that of some conventional religions. Relatedly, his critique of the modern world is too readily inclined to withdraw from an unsympathetic reality into the subjective world of emotion and imagination. He shares the Romantics' hostility to the industrializing urban society of eighteenth- and nineteenth-century Europe. Julius feels trapped by the exclusively active, masculine culture of 'industry and usefulness', the 'empty restless activity' that leads only to boredom and apathy. He praises 'idleness' instead as the only attitude conducive to sensitivity and genuine emotion.[118] Schlegel believes that only a less frenetic attitude to life permits devotion to the arts and the ideal of beauty, and so is consistent with 'a more liberal and comprehensive culture of the mind'.[119] But as Schleiermacher recognized, Romantic criticism of cultural barrenness and crass materialism risks encouraging an other-worldly disengagement from this world.[120] In the more conservative works of his maturity, Schlegel avoids this risk, but only at the cost of his earlier radicalism. In effect, he trades 'Romantic agony' for the certainties of marriage, Catholicism and the authoritarian state.[121]

4 Death, Fantasy and Indifferent Nature

Schlegel's Romantic synthesis of sensual and spiritual, self and other, masculine and feminine, humanity and universe, represents an uneasy and unstable amalgam of religious and philosophical themes. The order of society and universe, the earthly fulfilment of lovers and the conformity of love with reason and soul with mind are all underwritten by the Christian guarantee of God's benevolence. The plausibility of Schlegel's synthesis depends on a combination of philosophical idealism and Christian faith that was essentially dogmatic, and neither philosophical idealism nor Romanticism proved philosophically sustainable or attractive in the long run.[122] Once the essential contribution of religion is lost, Romanticism's distinctive constellation of reason, love and sexuality falls apart. Without the guarantee of faith, the presupposed harmony of passionate love with rationality and the social order is no longer plausible. It becomes far more risky to equate the meaning of individual existence with passionate love. Romantics who did not, like Schlegel, retreat into conventional religion faced a number of alternative paths. In the further development and decay of the Romantic synthesis, the fragile balance between eros and reason, passion and social order, sexual desire and marriage, gives way to a range of derived forms and by-products – Romanticisms and post-Romanticisms of excess, fantasy, cynicism and pessimism.

One outcome of this process of development and decay is a form of Romantic extremism. Passionate love is still regarded as the sole basis for a meaningful life. But without the real prospects of a happy marriage and eternal life provided by orthodox Christian faith, this form of Romanticism readily tends to excess. In reality, the relationship of lovers is always vulnerable to frustration either by a hostile society or as a result of the waywardness of human emotion. Romantic extremism responds by showing its willingness to sacrifice reason, social order and, if necessary, life itself for the sake of its absolute commitment to love 'even unto death'. The impossibility of love in *this* world becomes the reason for its pursuit in *another*. A preoccupation with death was, indeed, a recurrent feature of Romantic thought. Rousseau's Julie accepts the impossibility of love's this-worldly fulfilment, and neither she nor the passionate Saint-Preux survives for long after her decision. Schlegel's Julius is drawn to the idea that the most perfect fulfilment of love must be in death.[123] The possibility that it might be right for disappointed lovers to choose suicide was famously contemplated in Goethe's immensely popular epistolary novel, *The Sorrows of Young Werther* (1774). Not only do the disappointed Werther and his lover commit suicide, but the publication of this work provoked a host of young lovers to imitate their course of action.[124]

The equation of love with death reaches its apogee and quintessential expression in Wagner's operatic treatment of the medieval romance of *Tristan und Isolde*. In that work, Romantic extremism and pessimism are elaborated into a fateful philosophy of life. Throughout the opera love is associated with the welcoming powers of darkness, night and death and opposed to the unwelcome forces of life and light. The unbearable light of day symbolizes the lovers' duties and commitments in this world, the moral demands placed upon them by their social obligations. Needless to say, the lovers are irresistibly drawn to the realm of darkness and death, which alone promises the fulfilment of their love. The concluding *Liebestod* ('love-death') expresses the ecstatic, almost orgasmic, fulfilment of Isolde's passion, which is possible only at the moment of her death. Of course, the potentially disorderly and destructive consequences of passionate love are an old theme in western culture. Shakespeare's *Romeo and Juliet* and Racine's *Phèdre* are just two of its classic expressions. But in both cases, the opposition between passionate love and the requirements of society is understood to be tragic. The conflict is resolved but love is not fulfilled by the death of the protagonists. In *Tristan und Isolde*, on the other hand, there is no suggestion that death is not the drama's most appropriate and satisfying dénouement.

An alternative outcome of Romantic other-worldliness is the retreat into fantasy or imagination. Romanticism has flourished longest and with greatest impact in artistic and imaginative form. Even the philosophical Romanticism of Rousseau and Schlegel was sometimes expressed in novels as well as in theoretical tracts. But a Romanticism of fantasy represents, beyond this, a choice to find not only a means of expression but also a kind of existence in works of imagination. Where the expectations of passionate intensity fostered by Romanticism are not able to be fulfilled, Romantic art then provides not so much a model as a partial *substitute* for mundane existence.[125] At least since the eighteenth century, the novel has been accused of distracting its vulnerable, usually female, readers from real life. The individual is encouraged to withdraw into an inner world of imaginary satisfaction or wish-fulfilment, even if at the same time marriage and other conventional social commitments are maintained.

From this perspective, too, the contrast between the tragic and Romantic portrayal of the conflict between reason and passion is no longer absolute. Death, for a Romanticism of fantasy, is a dramatic motif rather than a serious ethical proposition. It is no coincidence that the most powerful expressions of the Romantic preoccupation with love-unto-death are literary and artistic. These works are surely not meant literally as recommendations of suicide. They are better understood as expressions of an imaginative withdrawal from ordinary life. The preoccupation with death in *Tristan und Isolde* is no more to be taken at its word than are the obsessive cruelties of Sade. After all, Wagner did not commit suicide for the sake of his lover, Mathilde Wesendonck. In that sense, the works of Romantic extremism are closer to tragedies like *Romeo and Juliet* and *Phèdre* after all. Although these plays portray death as defeat rather than victory, at the same time they present an intriguing and even enticing portrayal of the life of passion. The power of these tragedies depends on our empathy with the uncontrollable passions of the protagonists, even if we are not expected to share them.

A Romanticism of fantasy itself readily decays into less demanding and more formulaic recipes for imaginative escape. With the increasing commodification of cultural products, the elusive and sometimes destructive adventures of passion have been further recycled into the easily digested, constantly available products of art as amusement or entertainment. As Collingwood puts it, this kind of art – which 'at its crudest and most brutal is called pornography' – makes 'an appeal to the sexual emotions of the audience, not in order to stimulate these emotions for actual commerce between the sexes, but in order to provide them with make-believe objects and thus divert them from their practical goal in the interests of amusement'.[126] What Rougemont calls the 'profanation of passion' is certainly a marked feature of contemporary culture. The intrinsic limitlessness of the Romantic wish for passionate fulfilment, which so often brings it into conflict with society and reality, is more easily reconciled with the manufactured satisfactions of consumerism and what Frankfurt School theorists like Horkheimer and Adorno call the 'culture industry'.[127] From the perspective of their critical Marxism, popular music, film and fiction weave their escapist web in the interests of commercial profit and ideological 'affirmation' of the existing capitalist order. Certainly, Romantic philosophy's after-life in the standardized entertainments of a commodified culture industry represents the definitive defeat of its original critique of the values of modern commercial society. This resolution of Romanticism's religion of love – probably its most prominent manifestation today – brings it to the boundary of the kind of materialistic hedonism to which Romantics like Rousseau and Schlegel were so opposed.

The incompatibility of passionate love with reason and reality inspires an antithetical reaction in the essentially *anti*-Romantic pessimism of the German philosopher Arthur Schopenhauer (1788–1860). Schopenhauer recognizes the centrality of love to the meaning of human lives and happiness. He does not doubt that people find it difficult to live without love and may even be willing to die for its sake. But he examines these Romantic assumptions from the perspective of his pessimism about human life and cynicism about love and sexuality. Like the Romantics, he devotes considerable attention to what he calls the 'metaphysics of sexual love', a topic otherwise either ignored entirely or accorded only a minor role by philosophers in the western tradition after Plato. But Schopenhauer is intent on demystifying passionate, sexual love as a delusion foisted upon us by an indifferent cosmos.

Although there can be no doubt that passionate love is important for our lives, it is equally obvious that love is not a reliable means to happiness in this world. That the unconditional pursuit of passionate love is not really in our best interests is proven by the considerable suffering and even death that so often results. Schopenhauer's assessment could be supported by the rapidly growing body of Romantic art and literature, particularly their more realistic and extremist variants, as well as by contemporary anecdotes and case histories of frustrated love and the desperate measures it inspired. As a classical scholar, he could also appeal to salutary lessons from the 'sexual realism' of classical authors like Ovid and Lucretius, who tirelessly warned of the manifold follies of love.[128] According to Schopenhauer, the suffering associated with the pursuit of passionate love derives from the incorrect assumption, fundamental to Romantic conceptions, that only the unique object of our desire, our one-and-only 'true love', is able to give us sexual satisfaction and life-long happiness. But sexual satisfaction really has nothing to do with the presumed qualities of beauty, youth or charm that play such a large role in the Romantic appeal of sexual partners. The idea that life-long monogamous marriage is a reliable recipe for everlasting happiness is similarly implausible. Schopenhauer's philosophy is designed to dispel such harmful Romantic delusions.

The metaphysical basis for Schopenhauer's account of sexual love is developed most fully and systematically in the two volumes of *The World as Will and Representation* (1818, 1844). Schopenhauer's metaphysics represents another reaction to Kant's unsatisfactory dichotomy between the 'phenomenal' world of appearances and the 'noumenal' world of things-in-themselves. Kant had argued that our empirical or scientific knowledge is confined to the world of appearances and that we can never have reliable empirical knowledge of things-in-themselves. At the same time, he thought that the freedom of the rational self and hence morality were only possible on the basis of certain assumptions about the noumenal realm.[129] Schopenhauer believes that we can indeed know the real nature of the self and cosmos underlying the superficial phenomena of our experience. Partly inspired by his explorations of the religious cosmologies of Hinduism and Buddhism, he claims that the ultimate metaphysical reality underlying the world of appearances is blind, purposeless, impersonal 'Will' (*Wille*). This cosmic force manifests itself throughout the natural world as 'vital force' or 'will-to-life'. Evidence for it is provided principally by the insight human beings have into their own fundamental nature as willing beings. In fact, Will is manifest in the life-force of all animals, what Spinoza characterizes as an underlying and universal *conatus*, the striving of all natural entities to 'persist in their own being'.[130]

One very important manifestation of this will-to-life is the sex instinct, which Schopenhauer describes as 'the focus of the will, its concentration and highest expression'.[131] It is the blind, cosmic force of Will in the form of sexual instinct that is ultimately responsible for our subjectively compelling feelings of love and desire: 'For all amorousness is rooted in the sexual impulse alone, is in fact absolutely only a more closely determined, specialized, and indeed, in the strictest sense, individualized sexual impulse, however ethereally it may deport itself.'[132] Although the lover may think he is pursuing the unique object of his desire and the essential condition of his own deepest happiness, experience – and the excesses of Romanticism – prove otherwise. The inconveniences of sexual love are considerable:

> Next to the love of life, it shows itself here as the strongest and most active of all motives, and incessantly lays claim to half the powers and thoughts of the younger portion of mankind. It is the ultimate goal of almost all human effort; it has an unfavourable influence on the most

> important affairs, interrupts every hour the most serious occupations. . . . Every day it brews and hatches the worst and most perplexing quarrels and disputes, destroys the most valuable relationships, and breaks the strongest bonds. It demands the sacrifice sometimes of life or health, sometimes of wealth, position, and happiness. Indeed, it robs of all conscience those who were previously honourable and upright, and makes traitors of those who have hitherto been loyal and faithful. Accordingly, it appears on the whole as a malevolent demon, striving to pervert, to confuse, and to overthrow everything.[133]

In fact, though consciously in thrall to Romantic love, we are really the deluded slaves of the reproductive interests of the species, which are themselves expressions of the blind striving of Will: '. . . nature can attain her end only by implanting in the individual a certain *delusion*, and by virtue of this, that which in truth is merely a good thing for the species seems to him to be a good thing for himself, so that he serves the species, whereas he is under the delusion that he is serving himself.'[134] Schopenhauer's account of sexual love foreshadows sociobiology's view of the overriding explanatory importance of the evolutionary interests of the species (our 'selfish genes') as compared to subjective and cultural factors. He even anticipates the sociobiological explanation that men are promiscuous because they can easily father a hundred offspring in a year, whilst women are more faithful because they can only have one.[135] Our attraction to the unique object of desire really reflects nature's goal of bringing about the ideal combination of parents for the best offspring: 'The true end of the whole love-story, though the parties concerned are unaware of it, is that this particular child may be begotten.'[136] If we were to act in our *own* interests, we would not pursue Romantic love at the cost of inevitable suffering and even death. Rather, we would seek sexual gratification in the most direct and uncomplicated of ways. The 'essential thing' turns out to be 'not perhaps mutual affection, but possession, in other words, physical enjoyment'. This is confirmed by the fact that 'when those who are deeply in love cannot obtain mutual affection, they are easily satisfied with possession' and sometimes even with 'forced marriages', prostitution and rape.[137]

Crucially, Schopenhauer's conception of nature as cosmic Will is a radically secularized one. So although he understands love and sexuality in terms of the natural goal of procreation, he neither rationalizes nor sanctifies nature in the way of western and Christian traditions of natural law.[138] At the same time, he does not see reality as merely neutral or indifferent to human purposes. The amoral machinations of nature as Will reveal something more akin to a malevolent force than divine Providence. Nature is the source not of reason and truth, but of irrational and ultimately futile passions foisted on a deluded and suffering humanity. Schopenhauer's pessimism about Romantic love is thus just one manifestation of his far-reaching pessimism about human existence. Nor does human reason really offer any kind of solution or escape. Our rationality only makes us more aware of the prevalence of human suffering in general and the inevitability of our own unhappiness in particular. Instead, as Buddhism recommends, we should seek to detach ourselves from the delusions of the self or ego, for the sake of the peace and tranquillity that come from escaping the endless cycle of becoming, suffering and death. Since the natural world is the expression of a malevolent cosmic Will bringing only suffering, it is our duty to resist its continuation by avoiding further reproduction of our species.[139]

Schopenhauer's radically secular conception of nature and antagonism to cosmic Will might suggest a more favourable attitude to 'perversely' non-reproductive forms of sexuality such as homosexuality. As with Manicheanism and in the thought of Sade, the malevolence of nature argues against *reproductive* sexuality in particular as a wrong-headed affirmation of earthly life.[140] Presumably not wishing to cause unnecessary offence to his prudish contemporaries, Schopenhauer refers in conventionally derogatory terms to pederasty as this 'disgusting depravity of the sexual instinct'. But he is at pains to point out what was always obvious to the ancient Greeks, that pederasty must be regarded as natural: '. . . the universal nature and persistent ineradicability of the thing show that it arises in some way from human nature itself.'[141]

At the same time, Schopenhauer is aware that the prevalence of non-procreative sexual acts, which make no obvious contribution to the reproduction of the species or the ulterior designs of Will, contradicts his theory of sexual love. So why does homosexuality persist? He puts forward an explanation which, whilst purportedly scientific, owes more to his humanist education. What he has gleaned about ancient Greek pederasty from his reading of classical authors leads him to conclude that homosexuality is almost always a relationship between adolescents and older men. According to Aristotle, such apparently sterile relationships do indirectly serve the reproductive goal of nature, since the offspring of men who are 'too young' or 'too old' are invariably 'inferior, feeble, defective, and undersized'.[142] Pederasty is nature's ingenious way of preserving the health of the species by diverting the sexual attentions of poor breeders to relatively harmless outlets. Schopenhauer is, of course, aware that this explanation does not account for the many homosexual relationships between men of sound reproductive age. Still, to see homosexuality as the product of a fundamentally amoral nature represented a potent challenge to the axiomatic homophobia of Christian morality.

For Schopenhauer, only aesthetic experience and philosophy offer us the possibility of an apprehension of the 'true nature of things' liberated from the painful compulsions of Will: 'For this reason the result of every purely objective, and so of every artistic, apprehension of things is an expression more of the true nature of life and of existence, more an answer to the question, "What is life?"' In contrast to the ancient Greeks, Schopenhauer clearly distinguishes between the driven compulsiveness of sexual desire and the aesthetic contemplation of beauty. But if art offers the calm of detached contemplation, only philosophy can ultimately provide a clear and permanent answer to the question of life: 'But all the arts speak only the naïve and childlike language of *perception*, not the abstract and serious language of *reflection*; their answer is thus a fleeting image, not a permanent universal knowledge.'[143] Although not a philosophical idealist in the conventional sense, Schopenhauer thus endorses a kind of cultural and intellectual idealism after all. Physical existence and sensual inclinations should be left behind for the sake of the higher and less driven pursuits of mind.

5 Freud and the Sexual Unconscious

The uneasy co-existence of Romanticism and scientific rationalism is played out in a parallel way through the thought of Sigmund Freud (1856–1939). Both Schopenhauer and Freud recognize the subjective importance of love and sexuality for our lives. But they treat this fundamental tenet of Romanticism not as ultimate truth but as the starting-point for philosophical and psychological investigation. Born in Moravia, Freud lived for most of his life in Vienna, where he founded the approach to the study of mental life and illness that came to be known as psychoanalysis. There are clear affinities between Schopenhauer's fundamental idea that the human will is the plaything of forces beyond its control or ken and the central insight of Freudian psychoanalysis that the conscious will is often misled by the mind's unconscious sexual motivations.[144] Freud also ultimately recommends a 'sublimation' of instinctual energies for the sake of 'civilization', which is not unlike Schopenhauer's ideal of aesthetic and intellectual contemplation.

Central to Freud's approach is his theory of the 'unconscious'. Like Schopenhauer, Freud emphasizes the gap between the conscious aims and ideals of adult individuals and their underlying causes. In a variety of ways, the *conscious* self or subject is revealed as little more than a self-deceptive and often misguided superstructure of the mind. By the same token, the self's much vaunted rationality is better understood as just one component of the largely *unconscious* processes that really determine the contents of the conscious mind. The apparently rational deliberations and decisions of the individual subject are more often the invention of plausible reasons for motivations with a quite different but, for consciousness, inadmissible and indeed unknown rationale. Not reason or rationality, but *rationalization* is the most characteristic cognitive function of the Freudian mind.

Psychoanalytic theory results from Freud's development of these fundamental ideas to explain a wide range of mental phenomena from 'Freudian' slips to psychological illness and even madness. Neurosis and psychosis are traced to childhood experiences of psychological shock or 'trauma', which result in the 'repression' of wishes or memories that are unacceptable to the conscious mind. The persistence of the mind's unconscious 'defence mechanisms' perpetuates the exclusion of this material from consciousness. The symptoms of mental illness in later life are the result of these psychic devices which, by then, no longer serve any useful defensive purpose. Freud also seeks to explain slips of the tongue, lapses of memory and even jokes in terms of the otherwise obscure workings of the unconscious mind.[145] What seem at first to be unintended or chance mental events are revealed as the deliberate products of the unconscious. We forget an appointment because we don't really want to keep it. An accidental verbal slip communicates something we consciously do not wish to say. Freud similarly explains phenomena like hypnosis and his own therapeutic techniques of 'free association' and 'dream analysis' as evidence that our unconscious mind has aims and intentions that our conscious mind normally never knows.

Less palatable to the bourgeoisie of *fin de siècle* Vienna was Freud's belief, also shared with Schopenhauer, that the unconscious mind is particularly interested in *sex*. The pathologies of Freud's patients typically relate to failures or anomalies in love and sex. More fundamentally, his case studies invariably trace neurotic symptoms and psychoses to experiences of a sexual nature. Even more shockingly for his contemporaries, these traumatic events are found to occur during his patients' early childhood. The traumatic childhood scenes uncovered by the psychoanalyst typically involve experiences of sexual frustration and even abuse. If these memories are evidence of real rather than merely imagined abuse – and Freud equivocated on this crucial issue – then the implications were deeply unsettling. It followed not only that the sexual abuse of children by adults was far more common than previously suspected – a fact since amply confirmed – but also that children were not the asexual innocents of Victorian imagining. In addition to the evidence of adult symptoms, dreams and associations, Freud claimed that children exhibit essentially sexual instincts in the pleasure they take from 'erogenous' zones of the body, such as the mouth, anus and genitals as well as in the intensity of their loving attachments to their mother and father. Through 'Oedipus' and 'Electra' complexes, the fate of these attachments plays a crucial role in the subsequent mental life of the individual.[146]

Although Freud attracted particular odium for his views on childhood sexuality, his shocked contemporaries did not necessarily realize that his extension of sexuality to the early lives of children also changed its meaning. Crucial to Freud's revised conception of sexuality is his distinction between 'sexual aim' and 'sexual object', which helps to undermine the conventional assumption that sex must involve behaviour of a reproductive and genital kind. 'Let us', he says, 'call the person from whom sexual attraction proceeds the *sexual object* and the act towards which the instinct tends the *sexual aim*.'[147] As had already been shown by such conscientious observers of the startling variety of sexual activity as the Marquis de Sade and Richard von Krafft-Ebing, seemingly sexual behaviour involves an endless variety of 'aims' – active, passive, penetrative and non-penetrative, pleasurable and painful – employing almost every part of the body (not just the genitals), in conjunction with a limitless variety of 'sexual objects' – of the same, opposite or intermediate sex, human, animal and inanimate, living, mutilated or dead, adult, adolescent and infant. So although Freud attributes sexuality to children, this does not mean that the child's 'sexual' urges are supposed to resemble those of an adult. The diffuse, libidinous longings and pleasurable sensations of the child may form the bedrock and origin of adult sexuality, but otherwise they have little in common with it.

Freud's theory of sexuality potentially explodes the dogmatic conviction, fundamental to Christian sexual morality and even (until well into the twentieth century) western science, that sexuality is by nature essentially reproductive and hence genital and heterosexual. His extended concept of sexuality implies a radical theory of non-reproductive 'sexual aberrations' as a universal potential of human individuals. Sexual 'perversion' is really no more than the expression of impulses that are more or less prominent at different stages in the life of the individual and have been more or less prevalent in different cultures and historical times. Both historical and anthropological evidence confirms, as Freud notes, that homosexuality, or 'inversion', has been tolerated or even celebrated in many societies, including, of course, ancient Greece. This is only to be expected on Freudian assumptions, because sexual aberrations are already anticipated in the 'polymorphous perversity' of the child's sensuous desires. These desires are eventually – and only with difficulty – compressed by society into the limiting mould of 'normal', 'adult' reproductive sexuality.

This issue obviously caused Freud considerable difficulty. His eventual position is stated in a lengthy footnote added in 1915 to the first of his three 'Essays on Sexuality'. Both the length of this footnote and the number of revisions it underwent in different editions attest to his anxiety and caution:

> . . . psychoanalysis considers that a choice of an object independently of its sex – freedom to range equally over male and female objects – as it is found in childhood, in primitive states of society and early periods of history, is the original basis from which, as a result of restriction in one direction or the other, both the normal and the inverted types develop.[148]

The radical implication of postulating an original bisexuality or even polymorphous perversity is, as Freud recognizes, that heterosexuality stands as much in need of explanation as any other manifestation of the sexual instinct. There is nothing intrinsically natural about heterosexual desire nor anything intrinsically *un*natural about homosexuality and other varieties of the sexual instinct. For a traditional sexual morality built on the absolute assumption that only reproductive, heterosexual intercourse is 'according to nature' and, for believers, according to God's will, this was disturbing indeed.

However, two factors serve to blunt the radicalism of Freud's theory. In the first place, although Freud postulates an original polymorphous perversity of sexual desire, his theory of sexuality nevertheless goes on to posit a normal path of sexual development or 'maturation'. At puberty the sexual aim is normally subordinated to the reproductive function, at the same time as oral and anal 'erotogenic zones' are 'subordinated to the primacy of the genital zone'.[149] In other words, perverse sexuality is cast as a kind of arrested development: 'In inverted types, a predominance of archaic constitutions and primitive psychical mechanisms is regularly to be found.'[150] As Jerome Neu tersely puts it, 'Perverse sexuality is, ultimately, infantile sexuality.'[151] By implication, societies like ancient Greece where homosexuality was tolerated should be seen as merely 'archaic' or 'primitive' as well. Western civilization's compulsory heterosexuality is endorsed as the product of normal development.

A second factor qualifying Freud's radicalism is his theory of 'sublimation'. Although often accused of dragging civilization down to the level of animal sexuality, in fact he emphasizes our ability to 'sublimate' our sex drives or 'libido'. A fundamental feature of human psychology is the ability to divert our libidinous sexual energies to more socially useful purposes. Freud suggests that the redirection of this energy to social, artistic and intellectual activities was essential for the initial emergence of civilization. What is more, further progress will require even greater instinctual renunciation in the future.[152] Accordingly, the aim of psychoanalysis is not, as some of Freud's critics may have feared, to release sexual energies into disinhibited sexual activity. Therapy aims only to dissolve the fixation of libidinal energies in unproductive neurotic fixations and symptoms which cripple the individual and prevent her contributing more effectively to society. In the end, Freud advocates the necessary sublimation of sexual instincts in a kind of Platonic ascent to the good, the beautiful and the socially useful. His psychosexual biography of the artist Leonardo da Vinci shows how a troubled sexuality can ultimately contribute to great cultural achievements. His back-handed defence of the sexual perversions is thus that 'by being suppressed or by being diverted to higher, asexual aims – by being "sublimated" – [they] are destined to provide the energy for a great number of our cultural achievements.'[153] Sexual instincts may be at the root of the products of civilization, but it is the further development of civilization rather than any radical liberation of these instincts that Freud wishes to promote. It is in this sense that he can with some justice claim that 'the enlarged sexuality of psychoanalysis coincides with the Eros of the divine Plato.'[154]

The subsequent history and development of Freudian psychoanalysis and its various offshoots has served to emphasize one or other of the implicit possibilities of the original theory. The radical potential of Freud's theories is developed by a number of thinkers including Wilhelm Reich and Herbert Marcuse.[155] Freudian psychoanalysts in Britain and the USA, on the other hand, were more inclined to prescribe treatment for what were still regarded as undesirable sexual perversions like homosexuality. Ironically, Freud's expansion of the scope of *psychological* as opposed to previously popular biological explanation of anomalous sexualities contributed to the popularity of ineffective or, at worst, punitive 'cures'. Psychoanalysis in this form also contributed to an expansion of sexual guilt. Sexual 'dysfunctions' were typically explained as products of unsuccessfully resolved Oedipus (or Electra) complexes. A boy's (or girl's) excessive attachment to his mother (or her father) was held responsible for the individual's subsequent 'failure' to make an appropriate sexual 'object choice'.[156] So the guilt of a son or daughter who could not achieve that final psychosexual development was compounded by the guilt of parents whose excessive or possessive love had trapped their child in a state of sexual immaturity. It was only slowly and hesitantly that a more neutral attitude emerged within the psychoanalytic community.[157]

A striking example of the contradictory potential of Freudian assumptions can be found in the educational writings of A. S. Neill (1883–1973). Following earlier experiments in Germany and Austria, Neill eventually founded a co-educational 'free' school in England which, after moving to Suffolk in 1927, became famous as 'Summerhill'. Deeply influenced by Freud's ideas, Neill advocates a permissive and child-centred education, aiming to avoid, above all, any repression of the child's sexuality. The 'self-regulated' child will, Neill supposes, develop into a 'normal', healthy adolescent lacking any morbid or prurient interest in sex. Unfortunately, Neill's faith in the goodness of an unrepressed human nature and sexuality does not preclude homophobia. He assumes that the healthy child will also lack any 'perverted tendencies':

> I do not know what early repressions lead to homosexuality, but it seems quite certain that they must have originated in very early childhood. Summerhill nowadays does not take children under five, and therefore we have often had to deal with children who were wrongly handled in the nursery. Nevertheless, over a period of forty years, the school has not turned out a single homosexual. The reason is that freedom breeds healthy children.[158]

The free and healthy child will, it seems, naturally conform to traditional standards of sexual morality and maturity. Even more disturbingly, the harmony between conventional standards of sexual morality and 'freedom' turns out to be orchestrated by other means. Neill does not appear worried when the 'spontaneous' harmony between freedom, health and conventional morality is reinforced by the similarly 'spontaneous' actions of the children: 'Some years ago, a new boy fresh from a public school tried to introduce sodomy. He was unsuccessful. Incidentally, he was surprised and alarmed when he discovered that the whole school knew about his efforts.'[159] Presumably the other children had retained enough from their time in the nursery to know how to treat the deviant in their midst.

Overall, the various currents of Romanticism and post-Romanticism are important for establishing the central and irreducible place of erotic experience in our lives. Love and sexuality have a significance that is not captured by the previously considered traditions of reason and sexuality. The idealism of reason acknowledges the value of love between human beings only as the manifestation of a force that promises to transcend the limitations of this world and, in the end, transcend merely personal relationships as well. Love reflects and is drawn towards the divine and must ultimately shun the level of merely physical, sexual relations. The hedonism of rationality, on the other hand, devalues inter-personal love from the opposite direction as an unnecessary diversion from less complicated sensual pleasures. Love is regarded as madness or a disease that can be cured by copious orgasms.[160]

Only for the array of Romantic and post-Romantic approaches considered here is the significance of sexual love for the life of individuals recognized in unqualified, if various, terms. Love may still aspire to the ideal or divine. But love is only love as long as it retains its connection with the personality and individuality of a human being. For most currents of Romantic and post-Romantic thought, love must retain its connection with the individual's sexuality as well. Of course, it might be objected that Romantic and post-Romantic intellectual and cultural currents do not so much *recognize* as *institute* this pre-eminence of erotic experience. The particular significance of erotic experience for *our* lives may hold to that degree and in that form only for people formed by the cultural and intellectual traditions of the West – traditions that have been deeply influenced by Romanticism in the broadest sense. This would be a decisive objection, however, only for a philosophy committed to transcendent or universal conceptions of reason, love and sexuality. The instability of Romantic philosophy nevertheless means that the 'existential' significance of erotic experience cannot be taken as a simple given for subsequent thought. Rather, this significance poses a crucial and unavoidable question for philosophy.

4

Perspectives on Reason and Sexuality

> Our sexual being cannot be compartmentalized into one corner of our existence, but it itself reflects postures taken up in other dimensions of our lives. From this point of view, thematizing the erotic significance of philosophy no more reduces philosophy to sexuality than it reduces it to existence. Rather, philosophy is understood as the articulation and self-interpretation of human experience, which is inalienably the experience of sexual beings.
>
> R. M. Schott[1]

1 Holism of Human Experience

The limitations of idealist, realist and Romantic constellations of reason, self and sexuality are brought into relief when set against a more holistic account of human reason, experience and the self. A beguiling portrait of the *whole* of human experience, including sexual experience, and a powerful argument against one-sided distortions of that experience can be found in the remarkable essays of Michel de Montaigne (1533–92). Montaigne develops the perspective of Renaissance humanism with considerable originality and flair, drawing on a remarkable range of classical anecdote, ancient wisdom and poetry. He cites contemporary narratives and observations, travellers' tales and other descriptions of supposedly less 'civilized' peoples. Most surprisingly, he pays considerable and very relaxed attention to the facts and experience of sex.

Although Montaigne demonstrates considerable independence of Christian orthodoxy and the authority of the Church, he is a humanist who deflates rather than fosters the pretensions of human being. He is, in particular, sceptical of the claims made on behalf of human reason and contemptuous of the exaggerated pretensions of both philosophy and theology. In his 'Apology for Raymond Sebond', Montaigne develops his own brand of radical scepticism in terms of three categories of philosopher. The first category of 'dogmatists' are those who claim to have reliable moral knowledge and confidently urge us to live accordingly. This category includes Aristotle (rather unflatteringly described as 'the Prince of the Dogmatists') and also Epicureans and Stoics.[2] Somewhat more attractive to Montaigne is the second category of philosophers, the 'traditional sceptics'. This category includes Plato and Socrates, at least when they can be taken to argue 'that Truth cannot be grasped by human means'. As Socrates famously remarked, all we can know is that we know nothing.[3] But even these sceptics are really just dogmatists, albeit in negative guise. Traditional scepticism still lays claim to definite knowledge, even if it is only the knowledge that we know nothing. Closest to Montaigne's own position is the more radical scepticism of the followers of Pyrrho of Elis (*c.*360–*c.*270 BC). Pyrrhonian scepticism regards even dogmatic claims of ignorance as unjustified: 'Ignorance which is aware of itself, judges itself, condemns itself, is not complete ignorance: complete ignorance does not even know itself.'[4]

Despite, or rather because of, its slender cognitive pretensions, Pyrrhonian scepticism turns out to be the most effective remedy for the many human ills and sufferings caused by dogmatic philosophy and religion, which only add more unnecessary sufferings to those inseparable from the human condition. All the sophistications of philosophy and theology – these products of our supposedly superior human intellectual capacities – are really worse than useless. For the Stoic philosophy of the ancients, for example, the only remedy for unbearable suffering is suicide: 'a haven is always near: swim out of your body as from a leaky boat', for 'only a fool is bound to his body, not by love of life but by fear of death.'[5] Montaigne relates with scarcely restrained horror the stories of a number of people who chose to follow this dubious advice.[6] An equally virulent species of dogmatism is, of course, associated with religion, which was responsible for devastating wars and persecutions during Montaigne's lifetime.

The general sense of superiority felt by Montaigne's 'civilized' European contemporaries is similarly deflated. Judgements that another society is primitive or barbarous are supported by little more than chauvinism, for 'every man calls barbarous anything he is not accustomed to.'[7] Montaigne gathers numerous examples of apparently superior beliefs and practices from different cultures and times. The *Essays* are typically humanist in their rehearsal of classical anecdotes and other evidence of ancient virtue and wisdom. But even supposedly 'barbaric' peoples should not be regarded as inferior simply because they do not conform to our moral and cultural standards. In many ways they are better than us for being more natural. They are less distorted by the 'artifice' of our excessively sophisticated customs.[8] Even cannibalism is no worse and may even be preferable to some of our own 'civilized' practices.[9]

Our habitual arrogance towards animals is also seen as misplaced. Human beings are more like other animals than they are different, and our assumption of superiority is no better than prejudice: 'Beasts are born, reproduce, feed, move, live and die in ways so closely related to our own that, if we seek to lower their motivations or to raise our own status above theirs, that cannot arise from any reasoned argument on our part.'[10] Philosophy and theology make matters worse when they turn our distance from nature into an article of faith and basis of morality: '. . . in its excesses philosophy enslaves our native freedom and with untimely subtleties makes us stray from that beautiful and easy path that Nature has traced for us.'[11] We would do better to behave more like the other animals, who 'obey the rules of Nature better than we do and remain more moderately within her prescribed limits'.[12] Animals are often surprisingly intelligent and certainly more reliably loyal and loving than human beings.

Much of the damage caused by dogmatism and human arrogance derives from the ingrained prejudice of the philosophical and religious tradition in favour of the mind or soul and against the body. This prejudice of what we have called idealist rationalism leads to asceticism, which, more than anything, demonstrates the dangerous power of the mind. Philosophy and theology show their hostility to life when they unnecessarily persecute rather than augment our pleasures: 'Human wisdom is stupidly clever when used to diminish the number and sweetness of such pleasures as do belong to us.'[13] Perversity and arrogance lead us to condemn our own pleasures as sinful: 'What a monstrosity of an animal, who strikes terror in himself, whose pleasures are a burden to him and who thinks himself a curse.'[14]

In fact, the body should not be consigned to a metaphysically and morally inferior category but be recognized as an equal partner of the soul. The physical and spiritual sides of our nature are inseparable. So it is ridiculous to inflict punishments on the body for the sake of the soul's salvation. The 'body' surely has responsibilities to the 'soul', but it is equally self-evident that the soul has responsibilities towards the body. The latter include, at the very least, the duty to provide for the body's needs and ensure that its pleasures outnumber its pains: 'May we not say that there is nothing in us during this earthly prison either purely corporeal or purely spiritual and that it is injurious to tear a living man apart; and that it seems reasonable that we should adopt towards the enjoyment of pleasure at least as favourable an attitude as we do towards pain?'[15]

The soul should follow nature by attending to the body, not perversely denying all its pleasures. But it would be equally wrong for the mind to artificially augment the pleasures of the body in pursuit of a dogmatic hedonism.[16] Montaigne's radical scepticism inspires moderation with regard to our natural inclinations rather than excess: 'In short, there is no pleasure, however proper, which does not become a matter of reproach when excessive and intemperate.'[17] Moderation will not be achieved by following the ascetic principles of dogmatic philosophy and religion, which have only made us more obsessively preoccupied with pleasure. We simply need to avoid the unnecessary sophistications of civilized life and abandon the self-conscious pursuit of pleasure, which drive us beyond the harmless demands of natural inclination:

> Desires are either natural and necessary, like eating and drinking; natural and not necessary, such as mating with a female; or else neither natural nor necessary, like virtually all human ones, which are entirely superfluous and artificial. . . . The choiceness of our wines owes nothing to Nature's teachings, any more than do the refinements we load on to our sexual appetites.[18]

Montaigne agrees with the Epicureans that the secret of a happy life is avoidance of all but the simplest and most necessary, natural pleasures.

At the same time, Montaigne recognizes that we cannot simply imitate the unthinking behaviour of animals. Human beings have a distinctive emotional and social life, which means that for us it is natural to live according to law and custom. Montaigne assumes a reasonable compromise between natural inclination, personal emotion and social custom. People 'find it appropriate to yield to natural inclinations, to the thrusts and constraints of their emotions, to established laws and customs and to the traditional arts'. Montaigne's sceptical moderation provides no basis for violent conflict with society and its norms: 'Where morals are concerned, they conform to the common mould.'[19]

Despite this profession of conservatism, Montaigne engages in a surprisingly bold discussion of sexuality, though, in order to avoid causing too great an offence to his contemporaries, he leaves more shocking and explicit remarks in Latin. He comments, often with humour, on a wide range of topics, including impotence, priapic cults, the size of the penis and codpieces, rape, necrophilia and the healthy effects of sex as a form of exercise and recreation.[20] Unlike his pious contemporaries, Montaigne believes that there are much worse vices than lasciviousness. According to his moderate hedonism, we should accept the innocuousness of our 'genital activities' and learn to overcome the embarrassment and shame associated with them. Such emotions are just further unnecessary and painful by-products of our pretentious mind. They are, in addition, largely hypocritical, since the mind never ceases to *think* about sex even if we do not allow ourselves to *talk* openly about it: 'Does that mean that the less we breathe a word about sex the more right we have to allow it to fill our thoughts?'[21] Reticence about sex contrasts strikingly, in this regard, with our attitude to violence and crime: 'The genital activities of mankind are so natural, so necessary and so right: what have they done to make us never dare to mention them without embarrassment and to exclude them from serious orderly conversation? We are not afraid to utter the words *kill*, *thieve* or *betray*; but those others we only dare to mutter through our teeth.'[22] It is equally strange that killing is done openly for glory, whereas making a human being is done secretly and shamefully.[23]

It even seems that there must be something perverted or contradictory about human nature, which leads us to be so afraid of something so natural as sex. Our nature offers us inconsistent advice, inclining us both to sexual activity and to shame at that activity: 'On the one hand Nature incites us to it, having attached to this desire the most noble, useful and agreeable of her labours: on the other hand she lets us condemn it as immoderate and flee it as indecorous, lets us blush at it and recommend abstaining from it.'[24] Once again the paradox is traced to the arrogance of human beings, who find it difficult to reconcile the absurd physicality of sex with their elevated metaphysical status. For that very reason Montaigne praises sex as an invaluable tool, 'bringing the mad and the wise, men and beasts, to the same level'.[25] Impotence is particularly salutary in this respect. In stark contrast to Augustine's proud dismay at the vagaries of his penis, Montaigne welcomes the fact that sex so often puts us in our place.[26]

Montaigne's tolerant and matter-of-fact attitude to sex is combined with a down-to-earth and demystifying view of sexual love: '...

sexual love is nothing but the thirst for the enjoyment of that pleasure within the object of our desire, and . . . Venus is nothing but the pleasure of unloading our balls.' But Montaigne also mentions the Stoic definition of love as 'the striving to establish friendship on the external signs of beauty'.[27] Rather than being bewitched by romantic ideals of passionate love, marriage partners should aim for a form of loving friendship. Sexual passion and marriage involve quite different enjoyments and accomplishments. It follows that if sexual passion is pursued adulterously, this need not be fatal to the more settled, less dramatic emotions of the marital state.[28] In any case, the prohibition of adultery only makes sexual 'transgression' more desirable and so more likely. If one's spouse commits adultery, it is probably better not to find out. Jealousy is an unnecessary and destructive emotion that should be discouraged.[29] Montaigne pragmatically acknowledges that marriage has less to do with 'beauty and amorous desire' and more to do with family, descendants and property.[30]

Montaigne's views on marriage are also informed by his belief that the differences between men and women are matters of custom rather than nature: '. . . save for education and custom the difference between them is not great.'[31] Some of the problems of marriage derive from the unfortunate way women are educated for love and romance rather than the enduring demands of marriage and friendship.[32] If their fundamental similarity were recognized rather than being obscured by harmful education and social conventions, men and women would be more likely to achieve the genuine reciprocity of loving friendship which is the essential 'currency' of marriage.[33] At the same time, Montaigne notes what he sees as some inevitable consequences of biology. He deduces the necessary sexual passivity of women from an obvious difference of anatomy, 'for whereas Nature has so arranged it that men's desires should declare themselves by a visible projection, theirs are hidden and internal and she has furnished them with organs unsuited to making a display and strictly defensive.'[34] Still, Montaigne does not subscribe to the view of women as asexual. Women desire and are capable of more sex than men, so it is absurd that social norms of chastity are imposed more severely upon them.[35]

In contrast to his pragmatic and relaxed views of marriage and sex, Montaigne has an intense and highly idealized view of same-sex friendship. Genuine friendship is a perfect union of two souls, complete and unqualified, virtually exclusive of others. Not surprisingly such friendships are extremely rare.[36] Unlike marriage, friendship is not complicated by considerations of property and inheritance.

Between friends there can be no meaningful division of goods, so that receiving a gift from a friend is really a form of giving.[37] Montaigne's most eloquent praise of friendship describes his passionate relationship with Étienne de la Boétïe. When he loses his friend to an early death from plague, he is inconsolable. He laments his life since 'those four years which it was vouchsafed to me to enjoy in the sweet companionship and fellowship of a man like that . . . [as] but smoke and ashes, a night dark and dreary.'[38] Such is the intensity of Montaigne's love for la Boétïe that their relationship has been thought to be homosexual.[39]

Whatever the value of such speculations, it is clear that Montaigne does not regard sexual relationships between men as either unthinkable or unmentionable. He refers casually and without apparent censure to the homosexual relationships of antiquity. He mentions Socrates' 'arousal' by Cleinias and Plato's alleged affairs.[40] Referring to ancient Greek pederasty, he observes calmly that the age for such loves is the age when boys look like girls.[41] Montaigne admittedly makes some concessions to contemporary mores – he consistently avoids mentioning the sex of male partners and sometimes even appears to condemn pederasty. The later version of the *Essays* makes clear, however, that earlier condemnation is aimed not at the *sex* of partners but at their age and relationship: '[A] And that alternative licence of the Greeks is rightly abhorrent to our manners; [C] moreover since as they practised it it required a great disparity of age and divergence of favours between the lovers, it did not correspond either to that perfect union and congruity which we are seeking here.'[42] He cites Aristotle's similar worries that pederastic relationships often involve 'base traffickings' for riches, presents and offices as well as more useful and noble instruction in philosophy and patriotism.[43] In their 'childlike' immaturity the Greeks were still inordinately influenced by physical beauty rather than the higher moral and intellectual ideals promoted by Plato. In the absence of such ulterior motivation, it seems, there is nothing wrong with pederasty.[44]

Overall Montaigne is critical of the partial and distorting perspectives of ascetic reason, hedonism and passionate love. He espouses instead the perspective of a whole human life informed by nature, emotion, custom and reflection. The whole of his own life is refracted through the sometimes idiosyncratic, anecdotal, episodic and apparently unstructured personal discourse of the *Essays*. A wide-ranging and energetic eclecticism is put to the service of a consciousness remarkably free of self-imposed limitations and constraints. He does *not* set out to provide a general method for morality. The 'ruling form' (or *forme maistresse*) that guides his own judgements is never intended to amount to a system of morality in the conventional sense: 'Montaigne does not claim that his particular ruling form holds for others, and it gives him no guidance for anything outside his private life.'[45] But his reflections point to a previously unrecognized terrain of moral reflection and experience. They manifest an important shift of consciousness, a powerful practical demonstration of the philosophical thinking of a life. In that sense, too, Montaigne's thought represents a shift *to* consciousness. It implies that we should never abdicate our judgement to any strictly external standard, that judgement is inseparable from the reflections of a conscious self. It might be said that Montaigne raises humanism to the level of philosophy.

2 Metaphysical Unity of Body and Self

Benedict de Spinoza (1632–77), a philosopher of Jewish and Portuguese origins who lived in Holland, provides a more systematic alternative to the distorting metaphysical and moral dichotomies of mind and body, idealism and materialism.[46] We have seen that Montaigne is not only opposed to the artificial privileging of either mind or body and the harmful moral doctrines that ensue, but also sceptical of any metaphysical system. By contrast, Spinoza develops a rigorously systematic philosophy designed to resist any sacrifice or reduction of either pole of the dualist dichotomy of mind and body. There is for Spinoza emphatically only one indivisible 'substance', which, in the religiously charged context of seventeenth-century Europe, he provocatively dubs 'God or Nature' (*deus sive natura*). The single substance that is both nature and God exists and is known through its two basic aspects or attributes as, on the one hand, a mental world of mind, ideas or thoughts and, on the other, physical substance extended in space, a material world of things. At the same time, the single substance can be understood either in active-creative or in passive-substantive terms, as creating (*natura naturans*) or created (*natura naturata*). The former is the single substance in its manifestation as God, the latter in its manifestation as nature.[47]

On the face of it, Spinoza's fundamental metaphysics is compatible with both religious and secular or scientific views of the world. Everything is God and God is everything, so there can be no doubting that God exists. But if Spinoza's metaphysics can be understood in a religious way, it evidently has no place for the personal Creator-God of revealed Christianity or Judaism. It is even incompatible with the remote and abstract, divine 'first cause' of later seventeenth- and eighteenth-century deism. Spinoza's 'religion' is immediately recognizable as a form of pantheism which, for his Christian and Jewish contemporaries, was scarcely distinguishable from atheism. A god that is everywhere might as well be nowhere, if it makes no difference to the workings of 'nature'. Even sympathetic followers of Spinoza read him as an advocate of a radical atheism and materialism. As a result, he is a major source of the 'radical Enlightenment' and an important influence on eighteenth-century atheists and hedonists like La Mettrie and Diderot. This influence, however, was based only to a limited extent on direct knowledge of his writings and was instead largely that of the 'public Spinoza' associated with the widely ridiculed and condemned ideological party of 'Spinozists',[48] who, like Marxists in the nineteenth and twentieth centuries, assumed an intellectual and ideological life substantially independent of their progenitor.

In fact, Spinoza's views differ crucially from the position espoused by most materialists and atheists. His 'materialism' always co-exists in a fruitful if uneasy tension with idealism and rationalism. Although he firmly rejected the dualism of his philosophical predecessor and mentor René Descartes (1596–1650), he retained a strongly rationalist conviction that the truth about all things human and natural must be able to be derived deductively from 'clear and distinct' ideas.[49] Spinoza's writings are striking (and even off-putting) for their determinedly mathematical or 'geometrical' method of exposition reminiscent of Euclid. His arguments are developed by way of axioms, definitions and deductively derived propositions and corollaries. But more importantly, he refuses to abandon the insights of rationalism. In particular, his distinctive version of materialism effectively bars the way to any materialist or hedonist reduction of life and morality.

The distinctiveness of Spinoza's position becomes clear when it is compared to the moral and political thought of his near contemporary, Thomas Hobbes, whose view of the self, sexuality and rationality is more predictably empiricist, materialist and hedonist.[50] There is no doubt that certain elements of Spinoza's philosophy are strikingly Hobbesian. It is well known that Spinoza's justification of government (or the 'right of supreme authorities') and his claim that the natural right of 'every individual thing extends as far as its power' are influenced by Hobbes.[51] More fundamentally, Spinoza shares Hobbes's individualist moral ontology. For Spinoza, the essence of every individual thing, whether animate or inanimate, animal or human, is its *conatus* or will: 'Everything, in so far as it is in itself, endeavours to persist in its own being.'[52] Every individual thing strives, in other words, for its own self-preservation. Hobbes, in similar vein, refers to the 'general inclination of all mankind, a perpetual and restless desire of power after power, that ceaseth only in death'.[53]

Spinoza's moral individualism rules out the characteristic claim of rationalism that our common human essence implies a common human purpose and morality. For Spinoza our 'essence' is equivalent to our striving to persist in our own individuality: 'The endeavour, wherewith everything endeavours to persist in its own being, is nothing else but the actual essence of the thing in question.'[54] Aristotle distinguished human beings generically from other species according to their greater capacity to reason, and defines the *summum bonum* for human beings accordingly. No universal standard of behaviour can be derived directly from Spinoza's definition of our *individual* essence. Our will to persist 'in our own being' is not, as it tends to be for rationalists and idealists, simply equivalent to the exercise of reason. It is even arguable that to regard individuality as what we are essentially is tantamount to a denial of any human essence, being rather an assertion of the potential for individual difference. Sartre's existentialist claim that for human beings 'existence precedes essence' has similar implications.[55]

But although Spinoza does not see the exercise of reason as the essential goal of human life, unlike Hobbes he regards rationality as more than merely an instrument to ensure the satisfaction of our given impulses and inclinations. Rationality and understanding are the indispensable means for the fullest development of our individuality and, indeed, freedom. Spinoza believes that all our actions are causally determined, so that freedom of will does not exist in the conventional sense. But he is not satisfied with Hobbes's merely *negative* conception of freedom, which implies that we are free as long as no individual or agency forces us to act in some way. Spinoza identifies an alternative and *positive* conception of freedom, which is concerned with the mental states giving rise to our actions. The important point is that we may not be free even though we are acting according to our own intentions without being overtly coerced by someone else. We are free, according to Spinoza's conception, only to the extent that the emotions and inclinations that inspire our actions are genuinely 'internal' to us. What can then be called 'actions' or 'affections in regard to which we are active or free' are contrasted with 'passions', or occasions when we are passive or unfree in relation to our affections.[56]

The 'internality' of the causes of our actions seems, at first sight, to bear no obvious relationship to our freedom. But crucially, the criterion of internality is at the same time a criterion of *rationality*. It is only emotions or affections that are genuinely 'internal' that we can hope to understand in the strong sense implied by Spinoza's residual rationalism. Hampshire's interpretation is helpful:

> I experience an active emotion, if and only if the idea which is the psychical accompaniment of the 'affection' is logically deducible from the previous idea constituting my mind; only if it is so deducible, can I be said to have an adequate idea of the cause of my emotion. If the idea annexed to the emotion is not deducible from a previous idea in my mind, it follows that the emotion or 'affection' must be the effect of an external cause, and that I am in this sense passive in respect of it.

Because Spinoza's monism implies that ideas are at the same time modifications of my body 'under the attribute of thought', it follows that 'I can only have adequate knowledge of the causes of those of my "affections" which are not the effects of external causes.'[57] So actions that are 'internally caused' and those that can be 'adequately conceived' are really the same. Passive affections, on the other hand, inevitably resist the efforts of the understanding. They cannot be adequately conceived, because their causes are external to the individual. Ruled by such passive affections, the self acts from reasons that are not its own and therefore acts less than rationally and less than freely.

Of course, an individual human being is only a small part of nature and can never be completely independent of external influences. Only the one eternal substance 'God or Nature' is, because it includes everything, necessarily determined only by things internal to itself and, in that sense, absolutely free. Still, Spinoza believes that the extent of the individual's independence from external causes is subject to the exertions of its understanding. Rationality or understanding is not merely a *symptom* of freedom, it is also a *means* of attaining it. The 'improvement of the understanding' is thus also a kind of emancipatory practice or (in Foucault's phrase) a 'practice of freedom': 'An emotion, which is a passion, ceases to be a passion, as soon as we form a clear and distinct idea thereof. . . . An emotion therefore becomes more under our control, and the mind is less passive in respect to it, in proportion as it is more known to us.'[58] Everyone has 'the power of clearly and distinctly understanding himself and his emotions, if not absolutely, at any rate in part, and consequently of bringing it about that he should become less subject to them'.[59] In the process of understanding my affections I achieve at least partial freedom, because through the exercise of my understanding I free myself from subjection to those influences that are merely transient and variable. The *Ethics* looks in detail at the ways in which through understanding we can achieve the maximum degree of freedom in relation to our passions and, in so far as we are inevitably subject to passions, how understanding can liberate us from passive emotions.[60]

But it is here that Spinoza's metaphysical principles place a critical wedge between rationalism and asceticism. His denial of dualism and his assertion of the parallelism of mind and body rule out any superior status for rational or mental pleasures, any hasty demotion of the merely physical. The experience of joy or pleasure is, for Spinoza, simply the mental state accompanying the individual's transition to a state of greater perfection. Crucially, this perfection is understood not as the ascendancy of reason over mere physical impulse but as a single state with both physical and mental aspects of equal intrinsic value. As Moira Gatens puts it: 'Spinoza's monistic view of human being dictates that what increases the power of action of the body also increases the power of the mind. Hence bodily pleasures are as important for the well-being of the individual as is the cultivation of reason.'[61] In Spinoza's words, 'Whatsoever increases or diminishes, helps or hinders the power of activity in our body, the idea thereof increases or diminishes, helps or hinders the power of thought in our mind.' Pleasure and pain are defined accordingly as the mental signs of increasing or diminishing perfection: 'By *pleasure* . . . I shall signify *a passive state wherein the mind passes to a greater perfection.* By *pain* I shall signify *a passive state wherein the mind passes to a lesser perfection.*'[62] Other things being equal, *all* pleasures are good, *all* pains intrinsically bad.

What follows from Spinoza's seemingly austerely metaphysical propositions is an assertion of the value of pleasure that is remarkably forthright in the severely religious moral atmosphere of seventeenth-century Holland:

> No deity, nor anyone else, save the envious, takes pleasure in my infirmity and discomfort, nor sets down to my virtue the tears, sobs, fear, and the like, which are signs of infirmity of spirit; on the contrary, the greater the pleasure wherewith we are affected, the greater the perfection whereto we pass; in other words, the more must we necessarily partake of the divine nature. Therefore to make use of what comes in our way, and to enjoy it as much as possible (not to the point of satiety, for that would not be enjoyment) is the part of a wise man. I say it is the part of a wise man to refresh and recreate himself with moderate and pleasant food and drink, and also with perfumes, with the soft

> beauty of growing plants, with dress, with music, with many sports, with theatres, and the like, such as every man may make use of without injury to his neighbour.[63]

Even physical pleasures are, it seems, signs of our proximity to the 'divine nature'. Hostility to pleasure, on the other hand, derives from the impositions of priests and false religion: 'Superstition . . . seems to account as good all that brings pain, and as bad all that brings pleasure.' Genuine morality is an expression of our own enlightened or rationalized self-interest: '. . . no pleasure can ever be evil, which is regulated by a true regard for our advantage.' So the morality of superstition and fear is no true morality, for 'he, who is led by fear and does good only to avoid evil, is not guided by reason.'[64]

Spinoza's philosophy has radical implications in the area of sexuality. We can only assume that, in Gatens's words, '[t]he sexual relation, in so far as it give rise to joyful feelings, is good.'[65] Spinoza's positive attitude to sex has sometimes been ignored, because he also acknowledges that 'lust' and love are possible sources of 'human bondage'. Although 'all those things which bring pleasure are good', there is always a tendency to excess: '. . . most emotions of pleasure (unless reason and watchfulness be at hand), and consequently the desires arising therefrom, may become excessive.'[66] When not actually equivalent to a species of madness, lust in particular is a persistent source of the passive emotions of jealousy and hatred. Lust is a one-sided desire, which binds the individual to an exclusively physical attraction and dependency: 'Again, meretricious love, that is, the lust of generation arising from bodily beauty, and generally every sort of love, which owns anything save freedom of soul as its cause, readily passes into hate.'[67] As a result, conventional marriage is not only the proper context for the upbringing of children but also a suitable setting for genuine love, which is based on 'freedom of soul' rather than merely 'bodily beauty'.[68]

Spinoza's attitude to sex is nonetheless essentially positive. His awareness of the dangers of lust does not imply a rejection of 'base' sexual attraction for the sake of idealized and purely spiritual relationships of love. In fact, the ontological unity of body and mind translates into the moral equivalence of love and desire, which are both expressions of our underlying *conatus*, our endeavour to persist in our own being. As Alexandre Mathéron shows, Spinoza defines love as 'joy associated with the idea of an external cause', and joy as 'an increase in the power to act'. But the power to act is just the same thing as *conatus*, and '*conatus* so defined is the same as desire'.[69] In contrast to Hobbes's merely hydraulic understanding of sexual desire as the wish to expel something and so as the prelude to mere *release* or *relief*, Spinoza understands sexual desire as intrinsically and positively joyful.[70] Both love and sexual desire become a form of human bondage only when they are partial or obsessive and when, as a result, they are no longer compatible with the rational and free activity of a single and whole individual.

3 Love and Reason within History

A holistic view of human life, reason and sexuality is given further depth and complexity by the philosophy of Georg Wilhelm Friedrich Hegel (1770–1831).[71] At the heart of Hegel's novel approach is recognition of the intrinsically *social* and *historical* nature of human experience. His philosophy is designed to overcome the limitations of the reductive account of rationality pioneered by Locke and developed most elegantly and succinctly by Hume. The tradition of rationality and hedonism, which dominated the eighteenth-century Enlightenment, fails to do justice to the complexity and depth of human as opposed to merely animal experience.[72] Even the more sophisticated philosophy of Immanuel Kant leaves us with irreconcilable divisions between a narrow faculty of rationality and irrational emotion, between unruly natural inclinations and harsh moral duty, between selfish individuals and the universal demands of society.[73] At the same time, Hegel is equally worried by the irrational excesses implicit in the fundamental tenets of Romanticism. In his early theological writings, he had explored the possibility of overcoming the divisions and alienation bequeathed by Enlightenment rationalism through a religion of love, which has affinities with the religious Romanticism of Schlegel. He gestures towards a religion more in tune with life, one based not on theological dogma but on human experience. He speculates on the possibility that *love* might be the transcendent force capable of uniting and reconciling the disparate elements of human experience.[74] But Hegel soon abandoned faith in any explicitly religious or Romantic solution. Rejection of the limitations of rationality should not lead to the abandonment of reason.

In his mature philosophy, Hegel seeks to provide an account of 'reason' (*Vernunft*) which is rich enough to be able to reconcile the divisions of human experience without resorting to dogma, faith or mere emotion. His basic approach is to provide an alternative conception of reason not through any single principle or isolated faculty of rationality, but rather in terms of the complex interrelationship of the various elements or 'moments' that make up human life and consciousness. Crucially, these relationships are not confined to the mind or consciousness of a single individual but encompass the concrete social relations of particular cultures and societies. What is more, these cultural and social relations are understood as products of a long and complex process of historical development. So although Hegel's philosophy is designed to recover some of the valuable truths and moral ideals of the Platonic and Christian traditions, he is in a better position to avoid the ascetic sacrifice of individuality, natural inclination and pleasure that follows from the absolutizing of reason as an essentially *transcendent* faculty.[75] Reason, for Hegel, is neither a separate 'reasoning faculty' nor, as it were, a spark of divinity lodged in the human soul, but something immanent to, and inseparable from, the concrete history of humanity.

This conception of reason finds direct and fruitful application in the area of morality, enabling Hegel to overcome the stark opposition inherited from Kant's moral philosophy between duty and inclination. According to Kant's account of the 'categorical imperative' of morality, the individual self acts rationally, freely and morally only when it ignores, in forming its 'will', all particular desires and inclinations and is determined solely by universal considerations.[76] Kant's universalistic conception of practical reason is evidently unable to engage with the substantive *content* of individual desires or inclinations, which are simply treated as natural or given. In that sense, his moral philosophy has something in common with utilitarianism, to which it is otherwise so radically opposed. Although utilitarianism identifies morality with satisfying rather than subjugating individual wants and preferences, it too has nothing to say about the particular content of the preferences that are factored into the calculation of overall utility.[77] Where Kant seems to exclude particular inclinations from the sphere of morality altogether, utilitarianism bases its moral calculus on the merely external relations between them. Both approaches rule out the possibility of any substantive moral critique or 'rationalization' of wants.

The 'Hegelian turn' is to substitute for the stark opposition between inclination and duty a process of individual and social development. Both Kant and utilitarianism make the mistake of simply presupposing the possibility of rational and autonomous individuals, eliding the fundamental problem of morality, which is how rational individuals come to exist in the first place. The individual with his or her particular interests should not be regarded as something already given, or as existing in abstraction from society. Individuals are formed and only exist within society. Human animals do not become individual human beings without the essentially social contribution made by language, socialization and education. In the process, the properly natural inclinations implied by human biology are socialized and potentially 'moralized' and 'rationalized' as well. As soon as it is born, the infant's 'wants' are interpreted by its parents according to a culturally elaborated system of needs.

By the same token, what is regarded as rational or moral within modern societies is itself something that has been formed and reformed in the very process in which individuals themselves have emerged. The moral requirements of 'society' – in Hegel's terms, particular conceptions of 'ethical life' (or *Sittlichkeit*) – have themselves changed and developed historically in a dialectical interaction with the lives pursued by the people comprising it. In modern society, morality is not something that is simply and absolutely opposed to the individual and his or her interests. In fact, the emphasis we place on the satisfaction of an individual's interests, or in other words modern *individualism*, is itself a product of a distinctive history. It is only after a long and complex process of moral development, which in Hegel's opinion has occurred predominantly if not exclusively in the West, that greater recognition has come to be afforded to the particular subjective perspective, interests and satisfactions of individuals. It is in this sense that Hegel somewhat chauvinistically claims that 'the History of the world is nothing but the development of the Idea of Freedom.'[78]

Hegel's approach provides a distinctive solution to the classic problem of the relation between individual and society and, relatedly, between duty and inclination. This problem can be understood from complementary perspectives as both how individuals can be free without coming into conflict with the community, and how social harmony and order can be maintained without denying freedom to society's individual members. According to Hegel's account, the conflict between socially imposed duty and individual inclinations is not as stark and absolute as Kantian morality implies. The possibility of reconciling personal freedom with the moral requirements of society is expressed in Hegel's concept of 'rational will'. In abstract terms, the individual's will is potentially rationalized through its involvement with social processes; at the same time, society's moral demands take some account of the individual's particular wants and needs. Because rational will preserves the particularity of individuals, albeit at a 'higher' and more socially informed level, it also represents a form of *positive* freedom. As Rousseau's related conception of 'moral' freedom also implied, the individual is potentially free even within the constraints of morality and society.[79] Indeed, the individual could *not* be a free individual *without* the socializing, moralizing and, above all, individualizing force of society. This still does not, of course, rule out the possibility of conflict between individuals and society. Individuals will not always behave morally. But such conflicts occur against the background of a larger historical dialectic, which forms and continually re-forms society, individuals and the particular terms of their mutual engagement.

Hegel's various works explore different aspects and stages in the complex processes of development that he sees as contributing to western modernity and – what he sees as amounting to the same thing – the unfolding of reason. In his first major work, *The Phenomenology of Spirit* (1807), he traces the genealogy of the self-conscious, knowing subject. The self-certainty of this subject was for Descartes the first thing that we can know with certainty and the absolute starting-point for the rational reconstruction of knowledge. By contrast, Hegel shows how the elements of our world of knowledge and experience of the world themselves first emerge from the process of development of consciousness. What is more, this process of development does not occur exclusively within the realm of disinterested cognition or contemplation, as it does for the tradition of 'theory' (Gk *theoria*) from Plato and Aristotle to Kant. The deep connections between the 'world of appearances' and the self first become manifest in the experience of *desire*, which Hegel sees as an essential moment in mind's development.[80] Desire is the mind's attempt to make the world-as-it-is correspond to the world as mind would like it to be. It is in the experience of desire, and above all *frustrated* desire, that consciousness becomes acutely 'aware that the object has its own independence'. External reality must exist as an 'other' to mind for desire to be able to supersede it and so become 'certain of itself' as consciousness.[81] In effect, it is the dynamics of desire and action on the world, satisfaction, frustration and the world's resistance to our wishful thinking that first delivers to consciousness the distinction, taken for granted by much previous philosophy, between a real and an unreal world.

But desire corresponds to only a rudimentary stage in the unfolding of self-conscious mind. Its fuller development depends on its relationship with another consciousness: '*Self-consciousness achieves its satisfaction only in another self-consciousness.*'[82] In the *Phenomenology*, the dialectic of mutual recognition between self-consciousnesses takes the form of a struggle for survival, a dialectic of 'lordship' and 'bondage'. One consciousness seeks absolute recognition from another consciousness in such a way that the latter is reduced to the status of a mere object or thing. Consciousness seeks to enslave its other. But with that, the consciousness seeking recognition achieves only a pyrrhic victory, because it can achieve recognition only through another *consciousness* or subject. No mere object can deliver recognition in that sense. Hegel relates this struggle for recognition to the historical relations between master and slaves or servants. Famously, this account was incorporated into Marx's 'materialist' understanding of history as the development of modes of production through class conflict.[83] What neither Hegel nor Marx explored, however, were the *sexual* manifestations of the struggle for mutual recognition.[84]

Hegel's insistence on the primacy of *self*-consciousness over merely desiring consciousness in the genesis of mind has significant implications for his understanding of sexuality and love. In the first place, it translates into a deprecation, habitual within idealist western philosophy, of the body and merely physical pleasures. But although his remarks are reminiscent of Kant, Hegel does not endorse Kant's jaundiced view of sexual satisfaction. At the level of 'pleasure and necessity', consciousness 'takes hold of life much as a ripe fruit is plucked, which readily offers itself to the hand that takes it'.[85] But the problem with sexual activity is not that it leaves the other person, in the terms of Kant's piquant analogy, like a lemon that has been squeezed dry. It is rather that the desiring consciousness is condemned to a promiscuous search for ever-new objects of desire. It is perhaps advisable here to rely on J. N. Findlay's heroic commentary, as Hegel's text is particularly obscure at this point:

> Pleasure taken in another's person for one's own gratification is essentially self-destroying. The rational categories essential to personality are bypassed, and there is therefore nothing to hold one to an individual object. There is therefore a blind necessity driving one on to seek ever new objects in unending self-frustration. This necessity is nothing but the expression of the sheer emptiness of what is merely individual.[86]

Mere sexual desire and satisfaction must be transcended at the higher level of intersubjective social relations proper to *self*-consciousness.

It is important to note, however, that the higher dialectical level of self-consciousness is not to be reached by extirpating sensual, sexual desires altogether. Religious asceticism is, for Hegel, an example of the futile attempt to *abolish* what should rather be *transcended* – surpassed but nevertheless preserved in a higher and more complex form. In fact, in its very preoccupation with extinguishing all sexual desires, asceticism only reinforces the dependence of the self on its body. Ascetic disgust at our own 'animal functions' only serves to elevate 'matters trifling in themselves' into matters of the 'utmost importance'. The victory of the ascetic over his body is thus self-defeating:

> This enemy, however, renews himself in his defeat, and consciousness, in fixing its attention on him, far from freeing itself from him, really remains for ever in contact with him, and for ever sees itself as defiled; and, since at the same time this object of its efforts, instead of being something essential, is of the meanest character, instead of being a universal, is the merest particular, we have here only a personality confined to its own self and its own petty actions, a personality brooding over itself, as wretched as it is impoverished.[87]

Hegel thus follows the ascetic-idealist tradition only to the extent of placing sex, as an 'animal function' of 'the meanest character', at an early and primitive stage in the evolution of mind. He still insists, at least in theory, that the sensual dimension of human experience has its proper place.

The emphasis on the mutual recognition of subjects or self-consciousnesses does, however, imply that sex should be subordinated to love. Only loving relationships promise a union of minds and a more lasting satisfaction than can be provided by the mutually objectifying and promiscuous coupling of bodies. But although love offers a higher level of self-conscious being than mere sex, the absolute sway of this emotion, encouraged by some currents of Romanticism, is potentially dangerous as well. Romantic love is destructive when it fails to recognize the wider context of social relationships and obligations. In his major work of political philosophy, *The Philosophy of Right* (1821), Hegel sees marriage and the family as the appropriate context for the transcendence of both sexual desire and passionate love. The family is an essential institution within modern society, because it establishes social cohesion and harmony through the medium of personal feelings of attachment and love. But love is not the absolute principle of family life, which must be more securely established. The family is not equivalent to a Romantic union based on merely 'transient, fickle, and purely subjective aspects of love'.[88] Marriage is a 'spiritual bond' whose role is to transcend its unstable origins in mere passion and 'caprice'. Sexual passion is, in these terms, a legitimate but strictly subordinated, 'transcended' aspect of married life that 'sinks to the level of a physical moment, destined to vanish in its very satisfaction'.[89]

By incorporating and transcending the emotional and sexual aspects of individual experience, the family mediates between the individual and the wider society. The family unit is a basic element in the social and economic life of the bourgeois 'civil society' of Hegel's time. The family's capital or property represents its 'real external existence', whilst its role in the education of children constitutes its external and spiritual unity.[90] Hegel similarly incorporates conventional assumptions about the relations between men and women into his account. He accepts the Christian view of marriage as necessarily monogamous and exogamous.[91] The requirement that marriage should be a heterosexual relationship follows from the family's essential contribution to reproduction.[92] The nature and roles of men and women are understood in conventional patriarchal terms to be complementary. Men are especially suited for public and intellectual life and all things 'universal', whereas women should be concerned with affairs of the family and the heart.[93] The man must be the legal head of the family and the only legal owner of its property.[94] Although Hegel is Rousseauian enough to acknowledge that children have certain rights and must not be treated as their parents' slaves or chattels, at the same time he insists that their education must be based on discipline rather than just spontaneous play, if they are to realize their positive freedom as responsible individuals within society.[95]

Overall, Hegel's holistic account of reason as the articulation of all aspects of human life, experience and thought at least moderates the long-standing opposition between reason and sexual pleasure. The notions of positive freedom and rational will offer, at least in theory, a middle way between the ascetic sacrifice and the mindless pursuit of sexual inclinations. But the common accusation that Hegel ultimately sacrifices the individual to the organically conceived totality of the state finds a parallel in his failure to do justice to the real significance of love and sexuality in the life of the individual. In principle, the individual's particular inclinations are preserved and even enhanced in the higher unities of marriage and family life, civil society and the state. In reality, the particular individual's sexual and emotional life is still sacrificed to the requirements of the 'universal'. Hegel's specific views on gender, marriage, the family and sexuality largely reproduce the conventional morality and institutions of nineteenth-century Europe. The individual's sexual and emotional experience is subordinated and, in the end, sacrificed to the educative and economic functions of the family.

Of course, it is possible to conjugate Hegelian conceptions in more radical and socially critical ways.[96] The conservatism of Hegel's own views is, in any case, commonly exaggerated. Far from being some kind of totalitarian advocate of the organic state, Hegel was a lifelong advocate of liberal freedoms and representative institutions.[97] His views on the family are similarly nuanced. But the subsequent history of Hegelian idealism has tended to confirm more conservative readings of his views on love and sexuality. T. H. Green, for example, modulates Hegel's idea of positive freedom in a socially progressive way, laying the moral groundwork for the welfare rights of 'social liberalism'. At the same time, he deploys the same notion of positive freedom in a highly conventional endorsement of ascetic sexual morality. According to Richter, Green claims that 'the root of all immoral behaviour is this same "antagonism of the natural to the spiritual man"', so that '[s]elf-indulgence is the greatest of sins; the highest virtue involves the subordination of fleshly impulse and worldly interest to a good transcending the individual but also present in him.'[98] Although perhaps useful for their criticisms of a crude hedonism, these currents of idealism fail to do justice to the Romantic insight into the 'existential' importance of love and sexuality, which cannot be absorbed without loss into the social and historical totality. Although Hegel's holistic conception of reason shows how the meaning of an individual's emotional and sexual life is informed by the totality of human history and social experience, it does so in a way that ultimately threatens its irreducibly subjective significance.

4 Subjective Existence and the Sexual Self

One philosophical reaction to Hegel's philosophy during the nineteenth century served to rescue the perspective of the existing subject from the theoretical abstractions of his and similar systems. The philosophical writings of Søren Kierkegaard (1813–55) are also a major source of existentialism and phenomenology. In effect, although Kierkegaard judged the approach of Hegel's *Phenomenology of Spirit* to be promising, he believed that Hegel had incorrectly applied this approach to insoluble theoretical problems of epistemology and metaphysics. The 'phenomenological' perspective of the subject's conscious experience could more usefully be applied to other questions, which might be resolved and surely must be addressed, questions concerning human life, its meaning and conduct. The result is a radical challenge to the ideal of objective theoretical knowledge at the heart of both idealist and scientific traditions of rationalism at least since Aristotle. Kierkegaard's emphasis on the perspective of the existing subject also intriguingly illuminates the nature of our sexual and emotional experience.

For Kierkegaard, the perspective of objective theoretical knowledge or 'theory' (*theoria*) is essentially blind to the 'subjective truths' that are of immediate concern for the life of the individual. Although objective theoretical knowledge is useful in an instrumental way, giving human beings greater control over the physical world of nature, it makes no useful contribution to the conduct of a meaningful life. We are easily misled into thinking that it might do so only because the intellectual approach, which attempts to understand life in theoretical terms, gives a deceptive impression of completeness. It seems that it can tell us something about everything, but really it does not begin to tell us what we need to know in order to live. We can understand life intellectually without really *existing* at all. Thus Kierkegaard can say of a character – invented in order to present a view he rejects – that 'he has thought everything possible, and yet he has not existed at all.'[99] Existence can only be known or understood subjectively or from within.

The notion of subjective truth is closely related to the fundamental role of choice in our lives. Kierkegaard emphasizes the absolute necessity for an individual to *choose* a particular kind of life. This choice would not be meaningful if there were some objectively ascertainable moral or ethical theory determining a single right answer. Kierkegaard does think, though, that it is possible to throw some light on possible alternatives. Because he is concerned to elucidate fundamental choices rather than provide an objective theoretical moral system, he does not employ the ordered, systematic and reasoned discourse of conventional philosophy. Instead, he exploits a wide range of discursive forms more suited to illuminate the existential choices facing the individual. In his most well-known work, *Either/Or* (1843), for example, he presents a series of apparently unconnected autobiographical reflections, disconnected aphorisms, essays, speeches, letters, fairy tales and anecdotes, each attributed to a particular fictional character representing one perspective on the life-choices he wishes to portray. In the end, it becomes clear that Kierkegaard regards the life of religious faith as the only choice that is not fatally flawed and inadequate. But on the way to this conclusion, he explores two other basic orientations to existence, the 'aesthetic' and the 'ethical' way of life, which throw light on the role of sex and love in our lives.

Kierkegaard's account of the 'aesthetic' life takes advantage of Hegelian insights to supplement the traditional philosophical and theological objections to sensuality and hedonism.[100] From the perspective of Hegel's historical account of human ethical life, it is apparent that sensuality is not a timeless symptom of fallen and sinful humanity or, from the more sympathetic perspective of hedonism, the proper expression of a morally indifferent nature. The aesthetic life of 'sensuousness' is a particular psychological and cultural phenomenon that has its own distinctive history in the West. The pagan Greeks experienced sensuousness in a significantly different way from modern Europeans, because sensuousness was then still an unquestioned part of life. In Kierkegaard's terms, sensuousness was not then 'posited as a principle':

> In the Greek consciousness, the sensuous was under control in the beautiful personality, or, more rightly stated, it was not controlled; for it was not an enemy to be subjugated, not a dangerous rebel who should be held in check; it was liberated unto life and joy in the beautiful personality. The sensuous was thus not posited as a principle; the principle of soul which constituted the beautiful personality was unthinkable without the sensuous; the erotic based upon the sensuous was for this reason not posited as a principle.[101]

Provocatively, Kierkegaard adds that sensuousness is first posited as a principle only as a result of Christian asceticism: 'Christianity has brought sensuousness into the world.'[102] Here again Kierkegaard relies on Hegel's dialectical insight that 'in positing one thing, we also indirectly posit the other which we exclude.'[103] Pagan sensuousness already existed before Christianity. But by suppressing and excluding sensuousness in the name of 'spirit' and the spiritual life, Christianity made sensuousness exist 'in another sense', that is, as 'principle, as power, as a self-contained system', 'as a determinant of spirit'.[104]

The 'aesthetic existence' pursued by Kierkegaard's 'modern' contemporaries thus has a very different subjective truth from that of the ancients. The pursuit of pleasure is now expected to deliver not just transitory satisfactions but also the subjective meaning and purpose of life itself. The greater 'existential' demands placed on modern sensuousness account for its chronic difficulties. The quintessential expression of modern sensuality is the mythical character of Don Juan, discussed in Kierkegaard's pseudo-academic essay on 'The Immediate Stages of the Erotic or the Musical Erotic'. In fact music is the ideal medium for the spiritual expression of the sensuous principle, according to Kierkegaard. So there can be no better expression of the 'genius of sensuousness' than Mozart's opera *Don Juan*, which conveys the passionate intensity and restlessness of desire in a way that no other medium could achieve: 'When Don Juan is interpreted musically, then I hear in him the whole infinitude of passion, but also its infinite power which nothing can withstand; I hear the wild craving of desire, but also the absolute victory of this desire, against which it would be futile for anyone to offer resistance.'[105] It would seem that the pseudonymous author of this essay – if not Kierkegaard – is more than a little seduced himself.

It is important to Kierkegaard's approach that he portrays the 'sensuous principle' with all the irresistible appeal of a Don Juan. But he portrays sensuousness at its most appealing and subjectively convincing in one part of his work – and through the voice of one 'author' – only to deal it a more crushing blow elsewhere. In the section of *Either/Or* entitled 'Diapsalmata', another 'anonymous' author presents a series of disconnected reflections and musings on his own unsatisfactory aesthetic existence. The aesthetic life is characterized here not by the demonic energy of Don Juan, but by apathy and purposelessness.[106] The ultimate fate of the aesthetic individual who is prey to 'the soul's momentary passion' is melancholy and boredom. Far from being brimful with pleasures and enjoyments, his life is empty and drifting, a collection of disparate and ultimately meaningless episodes. In what might be taken as a description of Kierkegaard's own dissipated youth, the author dwells at tedious – and so perhaps even more effective – length on the ultimate futility of his existence. For one thing, the life of pleasure does not really involve as much pleasure – is not, ironically, as hedonistic – as people suppose: 'Most men pursue pleasure with such breathless haste that they hurry past it.'[107] It is a mistake simply to equate pleasure with some particular mechanical procedure such as eating or sex, as the common-sense understanding of physical pleasures suggests. The enjoyment of pleasure depends on the *spiritual* state of the individual: 'The essence of pleasure does not lie in the thing enjoyed, but in the accompanying consciousness.'[108] Pleasure depends on desire for the thing enjoyed, and this is difficult and eventually impossible to sustain.

Here Kierkegaard significantly enriches the classical case against hedonism. The problem is not, as the classic tradition contends, that desire is limitless and so intrinsically addictive that it inevitably undermines the moral responsibilities and virtue of the citizen. It is rather the impossibility of constantly *renewing* desire that proves fatal for the aesthetic life. The life of pleasure has an irresistible appeal and even its proper place in the young, who are not normally troubled by a lack of desire. Hedonism is, in effect, the philosophy of the youthful and inexperienced. The difficult thing is to maintain interest in pleasure, which is increasingly more attractive in the promise than in reality. The life of pleasure becomes less enticing with the almost inevitable waning of desire and enthusiasm that comes with age:

> My soul is faint and impotent; in vain I prick the spur of pleasure into its flank, its strength is gone, it rises no more to the royal leap. I have lost my illusions. . . . My soul has lost its potentiality. If I were to wish for anything, I should not wish for wealth and power, but for the passionate sense of the potential, for the eye which, ever young and ardent, sees the possible. Pleasure disappoints, possibility never.[109]

Nor is it surprising that the pleasures of the sensuous life are most convincing either in fiction or in the nostalgic recollections of jaded maturity. The endless conquests of a Don Juan or a Casanova are most enticing as either memory or anecdote. But the relentless search for pleasurable diversion produces diminishing returns, gradually turning into a desperate attempt to conceal the irresistible onset of boredom.[110] From the point of view of the aesthetic life, boredom is 'the root of all evil' and boredom is its ultimate fate.[111]

Nor are the problems of the aesthetic life of desire confined to the pursuit of physical pleasure and sexual gratification. When, in response to Christian asceticism, the sensuous life is posited as a 'principle' and 'determinant of spirit', the stage is set for Romanticism. But when sexual passion metamorphoses into the more spiritualized form of Romantic love, the outcome is similarly fraught with difficulties for the subject of the aesthetic life. In the section entitled 'Shadowgraphs', Kierkegaard relates a number of stories of deceived, disappointed or just uncertain love, in order to show that the lover's more 'spiritual' concern with the inner self of the beloved creates its own problems. In love we are no longer satisfied with the merely 'external' circumstances of physical attraction and possession, we are essentially concerned with the other's subjective or inner life: 'For our passion is not mere curiosity, content with the external and the superficial. It is sympathetic dread which searches the reins and the hidden thoughts of the heart.'[112] Where the sensuous orientation of Don Juan requires only the physical compliance of its 'object', Romantic love must be reciprocated in order to be fulfilled. In Hegelian terms, love involves mutual recognition between self-consciousnesses. Love depends on an internal state of the beloved. Because this internal state is not open to immediate inspection and can never be known with certainty, the lover is caught in an endless cycle of doubt and 'reflection'. Kierkegaard relates a number of stories drawn from Romantic literature in order to illustrate the fateful dialectic of reflection – the lover's endless attempts to reach some certainty about the beloved, either that love is reciprocated or that love is impossible and must be abandoned. The lover's uncertainty is exacerbated by the peculiarities of mutual attraction, which is perversely intensified by neglect and most effectively extinguished by devoted infatuation.[113]

In fact, the painful uncertainties of the lover can never be resolved in a purely intellectual or reflective way through the discovery of some elusive truth (that 'he loves me' or 'he loves me not'). The lure of objective truth only diverts the lover from the necessity of choice. The lover's uncertainty can be resolved only by a decisive act of *will* and the consequent progression from an aesthetic to an *ethical* level of existence: 'The process of reflection pursues an endless path, and can come to an end only if the individual arbitrarily breaks it off by bringing something else into play, a resolution of the will, but in so doing the individual brings himself under ethical categories, and loses his aesthetic interest.'[114] It is no coincidence that the Romantic novel typically ends when the lovers marry, supposedly to live happily ever after. With their decision, the lovers exchange an aesthetic life of indecision and purposelessness for the ethical life of commitment and duty. The value of ethical life is set out in the second volume of *Either/Or*, which contains a lengthy letter purportedly written by a judge to his young friend. The judge admonishes him to abandon the superficial and restless pleasures of aesthetic existence in order to make the ethical commitment of Christian marriage, which alone offers the permanence of a life '*sub specie aeternitate*' as well as a sanctioned place within the order of society.[115] In the course of his verbose and sometimes exasperating discourse, the judge takes account of other beneficial effects that can be expected from marriage. Marriage serves the purposes of nature and of the state by propagating the race and educating children.[116] It provides an emotional sanctuary and a 'school for character' that educates partners in the qualities of the other sex.[117]

Marriage, in other words, has all the attributes acknowledged in Hegel's account of the family as a moment in the complex totality of civil society and state. But the judge's proposed 'transcendence' of passionate love is less willing to sacrifice the Romantic moment, more sensitive to the intrinsic contradiction of the marital state. The judge whole-heartedly rejects the pragmatic, bourgeois view of marriage as no more than an arrangement for the purpose of child-rearing, social solidarity and the transmission of property. It is essential for the ethical value of marriage that it is founded and persists on the aesthetic basis of a love that also includes sensuousness and physical attraction.[118] Consequently, as the judge is at pains to emphasize, the ethical choice of marriage presents a fundamental problem of its own. The Romantic 'religion of love' may indeed be doomed to frustration and interminable uncertainty, but the resolute decision for life-long monogamy does not, for its part, magically guarantee the permanence of passionate love as a subsumed moment of the greater ethical totality. The essential question of marriage becomes how the spontaneous, restless and 'pagan' moment of passionate love can be united with the permanent commitment of life-long marriage: '. . . if one will not say that love must be excluded by Christianity, then it must be shown that love can be united with marriage.'[119]

In fact, the judge fails to resolve this question, relying on the dogmatic conviction that Christian marriage almost magically preserves the passionate intensity of 'first love'. But it would be a mistake to assume that the judge represents Kierkegaard's own views. For the judge, the Christian rite of marriage binds lovers in an eternal ethical and aesthetic union, leaving nothing wanting in the search for a fulfilled existence:

> Religion is not so foreign to human nature that a rupture is necessary in order to awaken it. But if the individuals in question are religious, then the power which encounters them in the wedding ceremony is not foreign to them; and as their love unites them in a higher unity, so does the religious lift them to a still higher plane.[120]

This is *not* what Kierkegaard himself believes. For him the religious existence certainly represents a 'higher plane', but it can only be reached by a decisive break from aesthetic and ethical levels of existence. Crucially, for Kierkegaard, the demands of the religious life may radically contradict our duty from an ethical point of view. God's will may deny our strongest human feelings and deepest moral convictions. In *Fear and Trembling* (1843), Kierkegaard makes this point through an extended discussion of God's command to Abraham to kill his son, Isaac. Issued without apparent justification or reason, this command apparently violates both the natural emotional ties of parental love and the most basic principles of morality. God's absolute and unconditional command marks, for Kierkegaard, the strict separation of the religious from the ethical sphere, even though Abraham is not in the end required to sacrifice his son. The story of Abraham reveals faith as a 'monstrous paradox', 'a paradox capable of making a murder into a holy act well pleasing to God, a paradox which gives Isaac back to Abraham, which no thought can grasp because faith begins precisely where thinking leaves off'.[121]

In the end, there is little doubt that Kierkegaard recommends the resolute choice of religious faith. But his existential resolution of the dilemmas of aesthetic and ethical life arguably still owes much to Romanticism. He finds the absolute basis of existence in a love of God that is as passionate and as much beyond merely human rationality as Romantic love. Crucially for subsequent philosophical reflection on love and sexuality and unlike Hegel, Kierkegaard remains sensible of Romanticism's 'existential' insight that, for the modern individual, there is an essential relationship between love and the subjective meaningfulness of life. Love is the only means of mitigating the stark opposition between freedom and necessity which, as both Kant and Hegel recognized, plagues the 'spiritual' individual inhabiting a physical world. In love, '[t]he individual feels drawn to the other individual by an irresistible power, but precisely in this is sensible of his freedom.'[122] It is this reconciliation of freedom and necessity that accounts for love's existential import: 'Precisely in the necessity the individual feels himself free, is sensible in this of his whole individual energy, precisely in this he senses the possession of all that he is.'[123] It is only where the connection to this meaningful core is preserved that the individual's freedom can be genuine or, to use the language of the existentialist tradition Kierkegaard helped to inspire, authentic.

5 Phenomenology of Sexual Experience

Those not convinced by Kierkegaard's ultimate leap of Christian faith are left with his view of the essential but essentially problematic place of love and sexuality in human existence. The later existentialist tradition attributed to his influence explores this feature of existence most explicitly in the philosophy of Jean-Paul Sartre (1905–80), perhaps the pre-eminent exponent of modern existentialism. Sartre takes advantage of the 'phenomenological' method suggested by Hegel and, after Kierkegaard, most influentially developed by Edmund Husserl (1859–1938) and Martin Heidegger (1889–1976). Rather than attempt to make objective, theoretical pronouncements about the ultimate nature of reality or knowledge, phenomenology sets out to explore and describe human experience as it is experienced from the perspective of the subject. But in contrast to earlier phenomenologists after Kierkegaard, Sartre's analyses do not focus exclusively on epistemological and ontological questions. He provides striking descriptions of the complete range of human experience with particular emphasis on the experience of love and sexuality.

At the heart of Sartre's philosophy and the key to his understanding of sexuality is a radical concept of human freedom which owes much to Kierkegaard's account of subjective truth and the necessity of choice. In Sartre's terms, for humanity 'existence precedes essence'. In other words, unlike other animals, let alone inanimate things, human beings are free to define what they will become. We are not confined by a pre-given 'essence' but can choose, indeed we *must* choose what we are. This basic idea is developed in complex and sometimes abstruse detail in his most important and difficult work, *Being and Nothingness* (1943). Here Sartre describes how freedom results from the mysteriously undetermined 'nothingness' of consciousness or (in terms ultimately derived from Hegel) what he calls the 'for-itself' (*pour-soi*). The for-itself exists in radical opposition to the causally determined, objective 'being' of material reality, which is merely 'in-itself' (*en-soi*). Only the for-itself is able to escape the determinism of the world of things and hence break the 'circuit of being'. By itself, '[b]eing can generate only being.'[124] The negativity of consciousness is closely related to our conceptual grasp on reality, the fact that we inhabit a conceptualized world. Only the for-itself is able to conceive the world in different ways according to our ideas and imagination. Through consciousness we can imagine alternative futures, conceive of possibilities that we may or may not ultimately realize and project these possibilities on to the world. The negativity of consciousness in that sense is the foundation of our freedom.

But with absolute freedom comes absolute responsibility, and responsibility is a burden. Kierkegaard discusses the burden of freedom as a kind of 'dread', or what Heidegger terms 'anxiety' (*Angst*). So great is the burden of responsibility that we are constantly tempted to deny our freedom in what Sartre calls 'bad faith' (*mauvaise foi*). We fall into bad faith when, despite the fact of our radical freedom, we insist on seeing ourselves as having no choice but to live or to act in a certain way. We disclaim responsibility for our actions by attributing them to our biology, character or circumstances. In other words, we explain our choices as the result of a substantial and essential self and renounce our actual self-defining existence, which transcends such categories and limitations. For Sartre, Freudian psychoanalysis is, in these terms, just another excuse for bad faith, encouraging us to attribute our actions, attitudes and even jokes and slips of the tongue to unconscious sexual impulses and complexes acquired in early childhood. In fact, Freud's theory is particularly pernicious, because it alleges motivating factors not previously suspected and so creates previously unthought-of opportunities for bad faith.[125]

Given his suspicion of psychoanalysis and its prominence in the intellectual culture of his time, it is not surprising that sexuality presents Sartre with an archetypal instance of bad faith. He considers a certain homosexual who, though repeatedly acting on his inclinations, guiltily denies that he is a 'paederast'.[126] Surely, this is a case of an insincere individual who is acting in bad faith? It is not, however, the homosexual who is in bad faith but his 'critical' friend, who demands from him a forthright and sincere 'confession' of his 'sinful' nature. In fact by refusing to identify himself or, as we might now say, 'come out' as a certain kind of person, the homosexual shows, albeit in a confused way, that he is aware of his freedom. On the other hand, the critical friend who wants the homosexual to refer his actions to an essential and substantial 'homosexuality' is really inviting him to deny his freedom and engage in 'bad faith'. The sincere individual 'constitutes himself as a thing' by claiming to be essentially what, according to Sartre, he has freely chosen to be. In fact, a sincere confession further compounds bad faith by seeking to distance the perpetrator from his guilty self. The confessing self stakes a claim to moral superiority over his sinning counterpart:

> He derives a *merit* from his sincerity, and the deserving man is not the evil man as he is evil but as he is beyond his evilness. At the same time the evil is disarmed since it is nothing, save on the plane of determinism, and since in confessing it, I posit my freedom in respect of it; my future is virgin; everything is allowed to me.[127]

The descent into bad faith is, however, almost impossible to avoid. Even the homosexual who avoids the bad faith of sincere confession is still liable to fall into bad faith. He does so when he claims that he is essentially *not* a homosexual in the same substantial or essential sense – 'the sense in which this table *is not* an inkwell' – that his friend has asked him to admit that he *is*.[128] Sexuality remains a matter of free choice, so one neither is nor is not essentially homosexual or otherwise.

The doctrine of radical freedom is qualified by Sartre's awareness of what he calls 'facticity' (a term derived from Heidegger). The for-itself of consciousness is emphatically not disembodied and unconditioned. It is conditioned by its situation in the world. Facticity connotes the fact that 'the for-itself *is*' both 'in so far as it appears in a condition which it has not chosen' and 'in so far as it is thrown into a world and abandoned in a "situation"'. The for-itself '*is* in so far as there is in it something of which it is not the foundation – its *presence to the world*'.[129] But the for-itself must not be conceived, after the manner of philosophical dualism, as a spiritual substance or thing that is somehow just located within and connected to a material body: 'Being-for-itself must be wholly body and it must be wholly consciousness; it can not be *united* with a body.'[130] The body as 'being-for-itself' is 'a point of view and a point of departure': it is the perspective from which the world as an 'instrumental complex' unfolds and the centre from which consciousness projects its possibilities.[131] Sartre expresses the 'existential' as opposed to 'objective' relation of consciousness to the body-as-point-of-view by saying not that consciousness 'exists *in*' its body, but that 'consciousness *exists* its body'.[132] The essentially embodied state of consciousness also implies (and is implied by) a primary relation between my consciousness and the Other's. Because another for-itself is ontologically inseparable from *its* body, the existence of another for-itself cannot be in doubt and there is no need to demonstrate the existence of other minds.

Sartre's phenomenological account of an embodied and intersubjectively situated for-itself provides the basis for an illuminating, if not exactly reassuring, account of sexuality. All forms of relationship between one for-itself and another involve conflict and struggle. The first hint of conflict comes with the 'look'. According to Sartre, when we conceive of another for-itself, we conceive of another perspective or point of view on the world. The perception, the 'look', of the Other 'unfolds a spatiality which is not my spatiality'. In Sartre's dramatic terms, this creates an absence or 'hole' at the heart of my world, for when the Other looks at me and I recognize the Other as a subject, I risk being reduced to the status of mere object or in-itself. Subjected to the gaze of the Other, I become an object for his freedom.[133] I live 'my being as it is written in and by the Other's freedom' and apprehend myself as nature.[134] The experience of being looked at is therefore closely related to shame. The 'apprehension of myself as nature' makes me associate my body with sinfulness and is thus the phenomenological equivalent of the 'original fall'.[135]

Because the subjecthood of for-itself is always vulnerable in this way – always liable to collapse or to be collapsed into the mere thinghood of in-itself – relationships between people are inevitably unstable and fraught with conflict: 'Conflict is the original meaning of being-for-others.'[136] Subjects are condemned to an ultimately futile struggle for mutual recognition, recalling Hegel's dialectic of 'master and bondsman', in which victory is always a kind of defeat, and defeat is at the same time victory. Self and Other are condemned to an endless to-and-fro between two fundamental modalities of relationship with the Other, each ultimately impossible, each leading to its opposite – each 'the death of the other': 'To transcend the Other's transcendence, or, on the contrary, to incorporate that transcendence within me without removing from it its character as transcendence – such are the two primitive attitudes which I assume confronting the Other.'[137] And whereas Hegel's dialectic of master and bondsman is ultimately transcended, for Sartre there is only an endless cycle of victory and defeat.

According to the first mode of relationship, which Sartre epitomizes as 'love, language, masochism', the lover wishes to 'capture a "consciousness"', 'to possess a freedom as freedom'.[138] Sartre's account banishes any hint of Romantic, religious or philosophical loftiness from the experience of love in the western tradition. If anything, love is portrayed as an even more voracious and hubristic form of desire. Not content with possession of a mere body, the lover wishes to capture the other's for-itself as freedom or transcendence, even at the cost of his own subjectivity and freedom. This kind of love may be the occasion of an intense but fragile and transient experience of joy, when the burden of my responsibility is transferred to the Other along with my freedom. I no longer feel the need to justify myself or my actions: 'This is the basis for the joy of love when there is joy: we feel that our existence is justified.'[139]

But love in this mode ultimately proves to be an 'illusion'. The lover is invariably deceived by 'the game of mirrors which makes the concrete reality of love'.[140] A temporary respite from the uncertainties and instabilities of love is won only at the cost of a further denial of our subjectivity and freedom. In masochism I become fascinated 'by my self-as-object' and in this way can even enjoy rejection or abuse by the Other.[141] But masochism too is ultimately self-defeating, because even in its wilful abjection it nevertheless expresses a kind of freedom.[142] In fact, being all but invulnerable even to the cruelties and contempt of the Other, it represents freedom's most stubborn and least vulnerable manifestation. To the extent that masochism really represents the will of the *dominated* party – and, indeed, in sadomasochistic practices the ritual cruelties of the 'master' are typically scripted in advance by the 'slave' – masochism is adjacent to the second attitude towards the Other.[143]

The second mode of relationship is 'indifference, desire, hate, sadism' towards the Other. This attitude results from the opposite attempt to capture the Other's freedom, 'to look at the look', to escape being reduced to an object by reducing the other to that status.[144] For Sartre, this second modality is most clearly manifested in sexual desire. This claim is plausible once it is recognized that, despite his hostility to psychoanalysis as an invitation to bad faith, he accepts Freud's dramatic expansion of the concept of sexuality. For Sartre, sexuality is not essentially or originally a bodily or physiological relation. The fact that sexuality is relatively independent of physiology is demonstrated by the sexuality of the child – itself a 'discovery' of Freud – and that of the eunuch.[145] Nor, therefore, is sexuality intrinsically heterosexual or defined by its role in reproduction. Sex is not just desire for bodily pleasure from particular genital acts, but 'simply the desire of a transcendent object'.[146] The object of desire is 'a living body as an organic totality in situation and with consciousness at the horizon'.[147] The physical expressions of sexual desire are secondary to this more fundamental existential relation. At the same time, the tendency of desire is always to draw us towards the body. Desire lures us through the 'project of being swallowed up in the body'.[148] Indeed, the shaping of consciousness in the 'mould of desire' is necessary 'in order for my flesh to exist and for the Other's flesh to exist'.[149] Sexual experience thus makes an indispensable phenomenological contribution to our embodiment.

But the attempt to capture the freedom of another for-itself through desire is always vulnerable to the freedom of the Other and, as a result, desiring consciousness is always 'troubled with longing'.[150] The attempt to 'possess' the Other's body only in so far as it is possessed by consciousness and freedom is an ultimately futile project, because possession inevitably reduces the Other to an object:

> It is certain that I want to *possess* the Other's body, but I want to possess it in so far as it is itself a 'possessed' that is, in so far as the Other's consciousness is identified with his body. Such is the impossible ideal of desire: to possess the Other's transcendence as pure transcendence and at the same time as *body*, to reduce the Other to his simple *facticity* because he is then in the midst of my world but to bring it about that this facticity is a perpetual appresentation of his nihilating transcendence.[151]

The reduction of the Other to the status of pure object without transcendence or freedom leads to sadism. Sadism abandons any hope of capturing the Other as freedom and instead treats the Other simply and deliberately as an object.[152] This treatment of the Other's body as pure 'flesh' renders it literally obscene – as opposed to the 'graceful body' that expresses freedom.[153] But although the sadist inflicts pain on the literal object of his desires, his victim once again remains free. The attempt to capture freedom is doomed to failure, because for-itself can always transcend its situation.[154] In its frustration, sadism is always liable to be transformed into hatred, when the self relinquishes any project of union with the Other and pursues only its death.[155]

Sexuality thus represents a special but important case of what Sartre sees as the futility of the self, the 'useless passion' (*passion inutile*) that is always condemned to strive for an impossible goal. The for-itself invariably seeks to become in reality – in a substantial way or as 'in-itself' – whatever it posits as a goal for itself. This amounts to the ontologically impossible project of becoming a 'for-itself-in-itself'. The only entity that could realize this ontological condition is God. The for-itself can never achieve this state of perfection and fulfilment without ceasing to be what, as for-itself, it inevitably 'is', which is negativity or 'nothingness'. As Aronson explains:

> Consciousness can exist only as it sees the world as lacking, only as it rejects and surpasses it in order to give it meaning, only as it projects its possibilities as goals to be realized. Hence, consciousness is doomed to frustration. By nature consciousness is that which detaches itself from the world because the world is not enough; by its very nature the world is that which lacks.[156]

This futility is mirrored and confirmed, as we have seen, in the equally doomed pursuits of love and desire.

In effect, Sartre shares Schopenhauer's pessimistic view of human life as condemned to ceaseless striving and frustration. A self that is fundamentally 'will' or 'for-itself' can never exist in a stable state of fulfilment. Fulfilment can be experienced only as promise or nostalgia, never as a present reality. It is reliably attained only in the abandonment of all striving that is death or, for Freud, the 'nirvana' that is the object of an original 'death-wish'. This view of life, consciousness and desire finds its most overwhelming expression in the *Liebestod* of Wagner's *Tristan and Isolde*.[157] Both Schopenhauer and Sartre also echo themes from classical asceticism, conceiving human desire as intrinsically self-defeating. As Sartre puts it: 'But pleasure is the death and the failure of desire. It is the death of desire because it is not only its fulfillment but its limit and its end.'[158] Crucially, however, Sartre and Schopenhauer generalize the classic view of desire into an ontological truth. Futility is not confined to the classically devalued sphere of physical desire and satisfaction but is regarded as an inescapable feature of human existence in general. Conventional asceticism therefore makes little sense within their philosophies. The only alternative to a quasi-religious renunciation of life as such is a life lived as normal, albeit with an accompanying aura of pessimism and despair.

Sartre's melodramatic pessimism ultimately undermines his otherwise illuminating account of human relationships. The absolute demands of consciousness or the 'for-itself' certainly set a challenging problem. Sartre's exploration of the sadistic and masochistic modalities of love and desire points to important structural difficulties in human relationships. His account renders in systematic terms what has been explored less abstractly and more randomly in Romantic and post-Romantic literature. In effect, he recognizes that human relationships occur within a distinct and problematic conceptual space. In the process, the more extravagant hopes and fantasies of Romanticism are discredited. But Sartre tends to assume that the sadistic logic of desire and the masochistic logic of love determine the life-cycle of human relationships with grim inevitability, so that we are condemned to an endless relay between these equally unsatisfactory alternatives. More realistically, we can understand these alternative logics or modalities as dimensions of variation within which actual relationships may live, develop and die. Erotic relationships unavoidably co-exist with states of tension and possibility, but they are not ontologically condemned to frustration and failure.

6 Sex and Oppression

In *Being and Nothingness*, self and sexuality are analysed as if they were entirely unconditioned by society and power, unaffected by history and immune to politics. However, in his later writings Sartre came to recognize the need for a socially *situated* account of existence and, by implication, a more historical and political view of sexuality.[159] Much of the credit for this shift in Sartre's position belongs to his long-time partner and collaborator, Simone de Beauvoir (1908–86), and the phenomenologist and Marxist Merleau-Ponty (1908–61). Already in conversations during the early 1940s, when Sartre was writing *Being and Nothingness*, Beauvoir was arguing for a socially and politically situated conception of existence.[160] In fact, although she does not always make it clear, Beauvoir was at this time much closer to Merleau-Ponty, whose ambitious and promising programme, which he did not live to complete, effectively represented an ongoing dialogue with Sartre's philosophy, resolving, in the process, some of its tensions and inconsistencies.

The position effectively shared by Beauvoir and Merleau-Ponty follows, above all, from their insistence on the ontological inseparability of freedom and facticity, mind (or the 'for-itself') and body. The self and consciousness must be understood as thoroughly and irrevocably enmeshed in the physical world. If existence is essentially embodied, then we must recognize that mind is never purely mind, body can never be just body. Phenomenology's central insight into the *intentionality* of consciousness must be understood accordingly. Brentano and Husserl had pointed out that consciousness is distinguished by its intentionality – its essential relatedness to an *object* of consciousness. We have beliefs, fears or perceptions *of*, or *about*, things in the world. But if consciousness is essentially and not just contingently embodied, then its intentionality must be understood differently as well. In Merleau-Ponty's words, 'Consciousness is being-towards-the-thing *through the intermediary of the body*.'[161]

Nor is the self just a passive observer of the world. Beauvoir and Merleau-Ponty further insist on understanding intentionality in terms of the fundamental orientation of the embodied self to *action*. For Merleau-Ponty's version of Descartes's *cogito*, 'I can' rather than 'I think', should represent the fundamental starting-point of philosophical reflection.[162] Philosophy should be founded on the embodied and active self, not the 'thinking thing' which forms the basis of Descartes's philosophy and whose implications still permeate the existentialist ontology of Sartre. If the self is essentially and originally in active contact with this world, then we are not, as *Being and Nothingness* seems to suggest, forced to think of the self as an 'angelic' or godlike mind tragically confined in the painful grasp of materiality and contingency. Rather, the overcoming of resistance is intrinsic to human existence and freedom: 'It is the deep-seated momentum of transcendence which is my very being, the simultaneous contact with my own being and with the world's being.'[163] In *Pyrrhus et Cinéas* (1944) Beauvoir similarly finds the basic 'truth of humanity' in the unstoppable upsurge of our spontaneity, our irresistible urge to act and to achieve, to undertake projects in the face of an indifferent or recalcitrant reality.[164]

It follows that human freedom is never absolute or unconditioned. Freedom must always be understood in relation to a concrete situation: 'A man is simultaneously freedom and facticity; he is free, but not in the sense of that abstract freedom expounded by the Stoics; he is free in situation.'[165] Because the self's active transcendence always presupposes a degree of resistance, it is also possible for Beauvoir and Merleau-Ponty to countenance *degrees* of freedom and bondage. So it is implausible to suppose that the slave and the victim of torture remain absolutely free, as Sartre's conception of radical freedom implies. Sartrian for-itself always remains free, because it can always refuse to submit to violence, even at the cost of its own death. It seems uncontestable to Beauvoir, on the other hand, that the constraints of the 'external' situation of the slave or the victim of torture severely restrict and may even abolish his or her freedom altogether.

But significantly, human freedom is not only restricted by physical violence or coercion. As Hegel's dialectic of master and bondsman demonstrates, our ability to pursue our projects also depends on the attitudes of other people. Only the intersubjectivity of mutual recognition ultimately gives meaning to our projects and so enables us to act. By the same token, our freedom to act is always vulnerable to the absence of such recognition. To suffer the systematic denial of recognition is to live in a state of *oppression*. As Beauvoir puts it: 'Only man can be an enemy for man; only he can rob him of the meaning of his acts and his life because it also belongs only to him alone to confirm it in its existence, to recognize it in actual fact as a freedom. . . . It is this interdependence which explains why oppression is possible and why it is hateful.' Oppression denies the subject's transcendence, assigning to an active self the status of a mere thing. For a person reduced to the status of a thing, genuine existence is no longer possible: '. . . living is only not dying.'[166] Although oppression does not eliminate a person's freedom entirely, Beauvoir is at pains to emphasize that it is a real relationship with substantive implications for the freedom of its victims. In her early work of moral philosophy, the *Ethics of Ambiguity* (1947), Beauvoir attributes this condition to the proletariat, which can find freedom only by revolting against its capitalist oppressors.

However, Beauvoir's fullest and most influential exposition of oppression is developed in her account of woman as *The Second Sex* (1949), which is one of the founding texts of twentieth-century feminism. Beauvoir's central thesis is that the inferior position of women is the result not of biological differences but of systematic social oppression. Famously, '[o]ne is not born, but rather becomes, a woman.'[167] Contributing to woman's oppression are all those factors denying woman's transcendence, assigning her to a passive, merely decorative role, reducing her to the status of an inert thing. Beauvoir traces in great detail the effects of woman's status on every aspect of her life from childhood and education, marriage and domesticity to intellectual life, culture, work and politics. Early sections of the book consider the points of view of biology, psychoanalysis, Marxism and anthropology. Later sections consider literary representations and some of the characteristic fantasies and illusions of men and women. Through these many dimensions and virtually without historical exception, woman is treated not as the 'reciprocal Other' of man – an essentially equal party to symmetrical processes of mutual recognition – but as the permanent and 'inessential Other' to man, who is the sole representative of universal humanity.[168]

Beauvoir's detailed consideration of woman's oppression leads her to nuanced and subtle consideration of the nature of *sexual* relations between women and men. Beauvoir shares with Sartre (who declared that the for-itself is 'sexual in its very upsurge') the conviction that sexuality is much more than just an occasional and largely physical preoccupation. Our sexual life is rather, in Merleau-Ponty's words, 'one more form of original intentionality', which projects a 'manner of being towards the world, that is, towards time and other men'.[169] Beauvoir's post-Freudian recognition of the existential significance of sexual relationships is productively combined with an awareness of sexuality as a prime site of oppression. Whilst she does not deny that a woman's body presents certain challenges, she is at pains to emphasize that a woman's sexuality is not simply determined by biology or 'anatomical destiny'. It is their social and political situation that is responsible for the oppressive aspects of women's sexuality. So although Freud's notion of 'penis envy' relates to some aspects of the early sexual experience of girls, it is the social evaluation of boys and corresponding devaluation of girls that accounts for their feelings of inferiority.[170]

Narcissism, passivity and the cultivation of a self-disabling femininity are similarly induced in girls by their education and socialization. It is these processes, not their biology, which deny women the opportunities for activity and self-assertion reserved for boys.[171] Not surprisingly, a girl's first sexual experiences are also unsatisfactory. Puberty is found to be unpleasant, menstruation is encountered with horror. Passive fantasies of being the object of a man's love are replaced by equally self-defeating sexual longings:

> Allowing herself to be an object, she is transformed into an idol proudly recognizing herself as such; but she spurns the implacable logic which makes her still the inessential. She should like to be a fascinating treasure, not a thing to be taken. . . . She enjoys inflaming the male, but if she sees that she has aroused desire, she recoils in disgust.[172]

In a state of sexual oppression which defines women as prey, sex can only be experienced as a form of conquest and pollution. A woman's sexual organs are a cause of shame. Penetration and defloration are experienced as violations, which are attended with either the risks of conception or the inconveniences of contraception. Not surprisingly, sexual pleasure is a late and always uncertain attainment for women.[173]

Beauvoir also considers lesbian sexuality as, amongst other things, an alternative to the vicissitudes of heterosexual sex. Her central point is that homosexuality should not be regarded either as an unconditioned and unsituated choice or as the causally predetermined result of an underlying physiological condition. Homosexuality is just one possible choice, one instance of a human being's transcendence of her situation: '. . . anatomy and hormones only establish a situation and do not set the object towards which the situation is to be transcended.'[174] No doubt under Beauvoir's influence, Sartre puts forward a similar account of homosexuality in his biography of Jean Genet, published three years later. Here, in contrast to his earlier discussion of the radical freedom and bad faith of the homosexual, Sartre recognizes the importance of the individual's situation: 'I maintain that inversion is the effect of neither a prenatal choice nor an endocrinian malformation nor even the passive and determined result of complexes. It is an outlet that a child discovers when he is suffocating.'[175] The homosexuality of Sartre's heroic anti-hero is a chosen response to an impossible childhood and an unbearable society. It is Genet's stubborn assertion of freedom. Sartre also offers an unflattering but illuminating description of the alienated condition of the oppressed homosexual:

> . . . the homosexual never thinks of himself when someone is branded in his presence with the name *homosexual*. . . . His sexual tastes will doubtless lead him to enter into relationships with this suspect category, but he would like to make use of them without being likened to them. Here, too, the ban that is cast on certain men by society has destroyed all possibility of reciprocity among them. Shame isolates.[176]

Although Beauvoir's discussion of lesbianism is not free of disparaging remarks – a woman's return to heterosexual relations after a lesbian phase is described as making a 'favourable adjustment', an individual may be 'doomed to homosexuality' or 'inversion'[177] – she sees lesbianism as a choice that offers women certain advantages, including a calmer, more intimate, more sincere and more active sexual life. More fundamentally, homosexuality may be a way for women to regain their transcendence: 'Woman's homosexuality is one attempt among others to reconcile her autonomy with the passivity of her flesh.'[178] But there are many varieties of lesbian relationship, whose positive or negative value ultimately depends on the woman's particular situation and possibilities. In these terms, what is important is not the particular sexual orientation she chooses but the authenticity of her choice:

> The history of an individual is not a fatalistically determined progression: at each moment the past is reappraised, so to speak, through a new choice, and the 'normality' of the choice gives it no preferred value – it must be evaluated according to its authenticity. Homosexuality can be for woman a mode of flight from her situation or a way of accepting it. The great mistake of the psychoanalysts is, through moralistic conformity, to regard it as never other than an inauthentic attitude.[179]

Neither homosexuality nor heterosexuality has a determinate moral value simply as such. Their value depends on the particular circumstances and projects of the individuals involved.

As Debra Bergoffen has emphasized, Beauvoir's account also offers an alternative to Sartre's grim vision of the inescapable circuits of sexual domination and submission. In contrast to Sartre's view of love and sex as conflictual relationships tending inevitably to either sadism or masochism, Beauvoir envisages the possibility of genuinely reciprocal erotic relationships. If sex can be experienced apart from the futile 'battle of the sexes', then it may be possible for a woman to succeed 'in overcoming her passivity and in establishing a relationship of reciprocity with her partner'.[180] Indeed, under these conditions, erotic relationships might even offer a particularly favourable setting for reconciliation between our transcendence and immanence, between human subjectivity and the flesh. Beauvoir's rare philosophical appreciation of the potential of sex is worth quoting at some length:

> The dissimilarity that exists between the eroticism of the male and that of the female creates insoluble problems as long as there is a 'battle of the sexes'; they can easily be solved when woman finds in the male both desire and respect; if he lusts after her flesh while recognizing her freedom, she feels herself to be the essential, her integrity remains unimpaired the while she makes herself object; she remains free in the submission to which she consents. Under such conditions the lovers can enjoy a common pleasure, in the fashion suitable for each, the partners each feeling the pleasure as being his or her own but as having its source in the other. The verbs *to give* and *to receive* exchange meanings; joy is gratitude, pleasure is affection. Under a concrete and carnal form there is mutual recognition of the ego and of the other in the keenest awareness of the other and of the ego.[181]

On the basis of 'a mutual generosity of body and soul', '[t]he erotic experience is one that most poignantly discloses to human beings the ambiguity of their condition; in it they are aware of themselves as flesh and as spirit, as the other and as subject.'[182]

7 Eros and Civilization

Simone de Beauvoir explores the various ways in which an oppressive situation intrudes on the sexual lives of individual women (and even men) in damaging ways. But she does not clearly identify sexuality as a site of oppression independent of patriarchy. It was left to another thinker to develop a distinctively Marxist and Freudian approach to sexuality, which identifies sexual repression and repression of certain sexualities as a social and political condition and hence as the object of a distinctively sexual politics. The philosopher, political theorist, social critic and sometime guru of the sixties counterculture, Herbert Marcuse (1898–1979), was influenced by German Romanticism, Hegel and Marx, but also by Heidegger and phenomenology. Like Beauvoir and Merleau-Ponty, he was critical of the apolitical and ahistorical assumptions of the existentialism of *Being and Nothingness*.[183] His own synthesis of the ideas of Marx and Freud seeks to unlock the radical potential of Freud's ideas in the context of a materialist understanding of society and history.

The basic outline of Marcuse's synthesis of Marx and Freud emerges most clearly and systematically in *Eros and Civilization* (1955) – an explicit response to Freud's *Civilization and its Discontents* (1930).[184] In that work, Freud claims that the repression of the individual's erotic desires or 'eros' has been the inevitable price paid for civilization. Just to survive, human beings must delay and sometimes sacrifice sensual gratification in order to perform necessary social tasks. In Freudian terms, the unmitigated 'pleasure principle' or 'id' of the child, which seeks immediate gratification without any thought for the future or other people, must be tempered by the demands of the 'reality principle', which takes account of requirements for the future survival of self, family and society. Economic and cultural development depend on a certain 'investment' of energy – and corresponding sexual renunciation: 'The tendency on the part of civilization to restrict sexual life is no less clear than its other tendency to expand the cultural unit. . . . Here, as we already know, civilization is obeying the laws of economic necessity, since a large amount of the psychical energy which it uses for its own purposes has to be withdrawn from sexuality.'[185] As a result, the sexual life of the individual is significantly curtailed. The price of civilization explains the gap between Freud's radical assumptions about sexuality and his more conservative conclusions.[186] The consequence for the individual is the suppression of sexual impulses that are a normal feature of our originally 'bisexual disposition'. The 'polymorphously perverse' tendencies of the infant's untrammelled pleasure principle must be abandoned on the path to the socially approved, 'mature' reproductive sexuality of monogamous heterosexuality. What is more, as civilization has 'advanced', the renunciation of sexual gratification has considerably increased. The intensification of sexual repression has, according to Freud, reached a 'high-water mark' in the European civilization of his day.[187] Significantly, he is agnostic about the ultimate value of this civilization, for whose sake we sacrifice so much. And he refuses to prophesy whether its future development will require even greater instinctual renunciation.[188]

Marcuse accepts Freud's broad account of the instinctual costs of civilization. But he seeks to combine Freud's thesis with Marx's theory of economic exploitation and class struggle. Indeed, Marcuse might even be thought to take his cue from Freud's passing comment that in its restriction of sexual life 'civilization behaves towards sexuality as a people or a stratum of its population does which has subjected another one to its exploitation.'[189] The chief lesson of Marxism in this regard is the socially conditioned and, above all, contingent and changeable status of exploitation in all its forms. In the case of capitalism, Marx had argued that the appalling conditions of the industrial working classes of nineteenth-century England were the inevitable by-product of an exploitative social system, which had arisen over previous centuries and would eventually be transformed by working-class revolution. The class divisions of capitalism should be regarded not as permanent and unavoidable features of the human condition but as the object of revolutionary political transformation.

Of course, Marx understood exploitation in economic rather than sexual terms. But with the help of Freud's approach, Marcuse sees the possibility of extending Marx's basic mode of analysis to the topic of eros. According to Marcuse's revised model of the relationship between eros and civilization, the degree of sexual repression exacted by society varies according to the prevailing economic conditions. One important implication is to emphasize the unequal burden of sexual repression. The level of erotic repression depends on the prevailing economic system or 'mode of production' and its accompanying class relations. In class-divided societies like capitalism, exploited social groups are forced to work harder and with fewer rewards than members of the privileged or 'ruling' class. Other things being equal, the former will be erotically more repressed than the latter.[190] By the same token, a more equal society would reduce the sexual renunciation required from those currently disadvantaged. With Marx, Marcuse believes that the exploitative social relations of capitalism will eventually be transformed by socialist revolution, which will eliminate exploitation and the disproportionate sexual repression inflicted on the proletariat.

But the unnecessary sexual repression inflicted on the working class is only one example of what Marcuse, adapting a theoretical term from Marxian economics, calls 'surplus repression'.[191] From the perspective of Marxism, it seems clear that the degree of sexual repression necessary for civilization must ultimately depend on the productivity of labour. An unproductive society may require high levels of back-breaking work and correspondingly high levels of erotic renunciation. But the economic developments culminating in capitalism have gradually increased the productivity of society. Capitalism has only served to intensify and accelerate this process of 'accumulation', spurring rapid developments in industrial organization and the application of technology. But with this increased productivity, the reproduction of society requires, at least in theory, *less* necessary labour and *less* sexual renunciation. So although Freud might be right to claim that the *actual* sexual renunciation exacted by society has increased, this amounts to a dramatic increase in the amount of surplus as opposed to socially necessary repression.

Put another way, the economic productivity of contemporary society offers the enticing possibility of a radical liberation of eros.[192] Writing in the middle of the twentieth century, it seemed to Marcuse that the automation of the industrial process could liberate us entirely from the necessity of work, eliminating at the same time any real need for instinctual renunciation. But why then do the populations of 'civilized' societies fail to take advantage of this erotic potential? Drawing on the Frankfurt School's brand of critical Marxism, Marcuse points to a number of obstacles in the path of sexual liberation. In the first place, achieving a more equal socialist society is no easy matter. Even in the 1960s and 1970s, it seemed that the revolutionary will of the working class was waning. The 'successful' communist revolutions in Russia and China showed no tendency to unleash the erotic potential of the masses.[193] Socialist revolution, like psychoanalytic cure, has proved elusive.

Marcuse draws further on broader Frankfurt School's analyses to explain how capitalist society almost perversely intensifies sexual repression. Economic productivity has reached the point where everyone's basic needs can be satisfied with minimal labour. However, capitalism's drive constantly to expand its profitable production of commodities has led to the generation of what Marx called a 'wealth of needs'. Although this development potentially enriches civilization – as, from a different perspective, Freud describes – this potential has largely been squandered. The 'consumer society' promotes unnecessary consumption and 'false needs' for the sake of profit rather than genuine satisfaction. Capitalist societies 'generate needs, satisfactions, and values which reproduce the servitude of the human existence'.[194] Advertising and an acquisitive, materialistic and competitive culture inflate both the level of consumption and the amount of labour required to sustain it. We are persuaded to consume products that are, at best, unnecessary and, at worst, harmful or destructive. The burgeoning entertainment or 'culture industry' delivers products of dubious aesthetic and moral worth, which serve to inculcate conservative values and shore up support for an exploitative system. So-called 'free' time is really just 'the prolongation of work'.[195]

Surplus repression is further entrenched in capitalist society by what Marcuse calls the 'performance principle'. The performance principle is the psychological correlate of capitalism's relentless drive to expand. Like the more familiar 'work ethic' attributed to Protestantism, the performance principle values labour, productivity and efficiency as ends-in-themselves rather than as means to genuine human fulfilment.[196] The performance principle is clearly lethal for our erotic lives. It is not just that erotic pleasure can be sought only on the rare occasions when we are not working, thinking about work or recuperating. Even our 'free' time is organized by the culture and leisure industries, which incite us to additional activity more to encourage profitable consumption than for any intrinsic enjoyment or benefit. At the same time, our sexual lives are increasingly harnessed to the demands of capitalism. Sex is used to promote new and more expensive products, which are either, like cars, represented as magical substitutes for sexual prowess or, like cosmetic products, presented as necessary conditions of sexual attraction.[197] Within the narrow confines of normatively sanctioned heterosexuality, the performance principle promotes, particularly for men, a sexual culture of potency and proficiency rather than enjoyment.

Against the bleakly puritan demands of the performance principle, Marcuse proposes a liberating 'de-sublimation' of eros. We currently sacrifice considerable erotic enjoyment for no worthwhile good and, perhaps, with destructive consequences.[198] But unlike other sexual radicals such as Wilhelm Reich, Marcuse goes beyond the idea that it is enough simply to strive for fuller and more frequent orgasms.[199] Sexual liberation concerns not just the quantity but also the type of sexual activity. Unlike Reich, who sees homosexuality as a dysfunctional symptom of sexual repression, Marcuse values sexual 'perversions' like homosexuality as potentially liberating violations of the performance principle. Non-reproductive sexual activity is particularly valuable, because it unmistakeably puts human fulfilment above nature's or society's goal of reproduction. The non-genital focus of such sexuality eroticizes previously ignored or stigmatized erogenous zones. The liberation of eros potentially re-eroticizes a body previously captured by the repressive and de-eroticizing demands of civilization.

It would be a mistake, however, to see Marcuse as an uncritical or naïve advocate of the 'permissive society' of the 1960s. On the contrary, he warns of the dangers of a *repressive* de-sublimation of eros.[200] In a capitalist society, eros may escape from the unnecessary repressions of 'civilized' society only to be more thoroughly subjected to the profit motive and the general commodification of life. The proliferation of pornography and the sex industry reflects an exploitable sexual liberalization of this kind.[201] With the relaxing of sexual inhibitions, commodities can be more easily marketed with the help of sexual imagery and innuendo. Sex is still more about performance than pleasure. Nor does Marcuse welcome all varieties of sexual activity. He regards non-consensual sadism as an aggressive manifestation of the 'death instinct'. The 'dissolution of ordinary and orderly perception' through the use of narcotics represents a false and private solution.[202] Eros continues to be profitably harnessed to the performance principle, albeit in the guise of sexual permissiveness and uninhibited hedonism.

Marcuse's utopian vision of a 'libidinous civilization' assumes a quite different conception of eros and liberation.[203] Eros is surely playful, subversive and 'polymorphously perverse', but it is also potentially sociable, creative, loving, moral and even rational. Eros, in other words, is not equivalent to a naturally given and fixed array of instincts. Marcuse cannot legitimately be accused of a reductive biologism or naturalism of instincts. He advocates a 'biological' foundation for socialism, only because he believes that morality should be recognized as a biological 'disposition' of the organism which can provide 'an instinctual foundation for solidarity among human beings'.[204] Marcuse's 'aesthetic morality' is inspired by the Kant of the *Critique of Judgement* or Schiller's essay 'On the Aesthetic Education of Man'. It has little to do with the hedonism of Bentham or the naturalism of Darwin. Marcuse has an Aristotelian view of the human being as a 'rational animal'.[205] As a good student of Hegel, he finds the distinctiveness of the human species in its essentially *historical* being.

It follows that liberated eros may be civilized without being repressed. By the same token, the liberation of eros does not imply the end of civilization but only the end of conventional oppositions between work, art and play, between reason, sense and sensibility, between love, friendship and sex. Liberated eros is most clearly expressed in artistic creativity understood, in a Marxian way, as the epitome of genuinely human, productive activity. The division between the 'realm of freedom' and the 'realm of necessity' will be overcome in a society where work takes the form of creative and pleasurable production.[206] No longer a cipher for alienation and drudgery, labour will be an opportunity for the constructive expression of 'the erotic instincts as work instincts – work for the creation of a sensuous environment'.[207] Such a society would be dominated by an 'aesthetic ethos', but one 'pertaining to the senses' as much as to art. Against received views of the Frankfurt School's austere and elitist aesthetics, Marcuse's artistic utopia would be sexy and fun.

8 Politics and Anti-Politics of Sexuality

Marcuse's radical sexual politics was appropriated by the New Left and counter-culture of the 1960s and then by the gay and lesbian liberation movements of the following decades. But later waves of sexual activism would appeal to another thinker, the French post-structuralist Michel Foucault (1926–84). As David Halperin has remarked, just as radicals in the 1960s might have been carrying a copy of Marcuse's *Eros and Civilization* or *One-Dimensional Man*, sexual radicals and AIDS activists in the 1990s would be most likely to be carrying a copy of Foucault's *History of Sexuality*.[208] Foucault himself was a participant in the radical wing of the gay movement in France before his premature death from AIDS in 1984. But in fact, his relationship to the sexual politics of the last decades of the twentieth century is complex and ambivalent. Foucault's writings on sexuality have been taken as an outright rejection of the neo-Freudian theory of repression and liberationist politics associated with Marcuse. But Foucault's position is more accurately understood as being part amplification, part critical corrective to that and related approaches to sexual politics.

Foucault's philosophical 'anti-humanism' and 'critique of the subject' can be ascribed to the influence of the nineteenth-century German philosopher Friedrich Nietzsche (1844–1900). Foucault shares Nietzsche's scepticism at the post-Cartesian philosophy of the subject with its dogmatic confidence in both the certainty of human knowledge and the subject's privileged moral and epistemological status. He proposes to show how this philosophical subject, so often regarded as an unquestionable assumption and premise, has been produced by its history. According to one of his many programmatic statements, the objective of Foucault's work 'has been to create a history of the different modes by which, in our culture, human beings are made subjects'.[209] This statement exploits the ambiguity of the term 'subject'. According to Foucault, the philosophical subject is implicated, in a similarly ambivalent way, not only with political individualism and ideas of freedom but also with the individual's 'subjection' to authority and power. But Foucault proposes not so much to dispense with the subject as to provide an historical or, more precisely, 'genealogical' account of its emergence. The subject is no longer a premise, but still a prime object of investigation.[210]

Foucault's critical genealogy of the subject is pursued through a series of studies of the bio-medical and human sciences as well as related social institutions of the modern period, such as the clinic, the asylum and prisons.[211] But with the first volume of his *History of Sexuality*, he turns his attention to the ways in which the subject has been constituted in the West through a series of discourses of sexuality.[212] In the process, he directly challenges what he takes to be the fundamental assumption of a sexual politics that sets out to 'liberate' a 'repressed' subject from the confining power of an oppressive social order. His challenge to this 'repressive hypothesis' has two aspects. In the first place, he claims that liberationism unjustifiably posits an underlying 'natural' sexuality or essential sexual self, which can be liberated simply by removing the repressive 'veto' imposed by society. Foucault denies that there is any such 'natural' sexuality or essential self. Rather, our sexuality is in significant ways produced or, in the terms of subsequent debates, 'constructed' by the discursive practices or culture of society.

This relates to Foucault's second challenge to the repressive hypothesis, which concerns the central historical assumption of liberationist sexual politics, shared, as we have seen, by Freud and Marcuse, that the fate of sexuality in the West has, at least since the triumph of Christianity, been one of ever more rigorous and systematic repression. Foucault suggests instead that there has been a detailed and increasingly systematic incitement and production of sexuality. The evidence of Christian doctrine and practice as well as scientific sexology, medicine and the law of the modern period all demonstrate an obsessive and intensifying interest in sex. The history of sexuality in the West is not a story of the repression of a pre-given and fixed natural libido, which might be freed of this burden, but the painstaking elaboration of the modern construction of sexuality.[213]

Not surprisingly, Foucault's further studies of ancient Greek and Hellenistic sexual discourses question the familiar assumption that the pagan world was characterized simply by the laxity of its sexual norms, by its lower level of sexual repression.[214] Of course, ancient Greek sexual mores differ from contemporary ones in a number of ways. For example, the Greeks were less concerned with the sex of their partner (and homosexuality) than with the distinction between activity and passivity in sexual intercourse. The latter distinction was critical for the social status of male citizens and their supposed superiority to women and slaves. Even moral vices of immoderation (*akrasia*) and self-indulgence (*akolasia*), which result from lack of self-control, are condemned as *feminine* vices and as 'being passive with regard to the pleasures'.[215] It is from this perspective that '[t]he use of pleasures in the relationship with boys was a theme of anxiety for Greek thought – which is paradoxical in a society that is believed to have "tolerated" what we call "homosexuality".'[216] The Greeks' anxiety resulted from the fact that pederastic sexual relations involve a passive male partner. Their solution was carefully to regulate the appropriate status and age of the partners. In general, active homosexual acts were permitted as long as the passive participant was of lower status, being either a young man before the age of full citizenship or a slave. A male citizen, on the other hand, could lose any claims to the respect of his fellows and even certain legal rights were he to submit to such acts.[217]

But more important than these differences of sexual mores is the different place and meaning of sexual acts generally in the life and culture of ancient Greece. The Greeks not only had different sexual rules, they also understood the regulation of sexual activity in a very different way. In the first place, the Greeks do not seem to have regarded sex as a particularly dangerous pleasure or vice in comparison to other activities of moral concern. The pleasures and excesses of drinking, eating and sex were thought to present essentially similar problems.[218] Training for the control of sexual pleasures was not essentially different from the physical training of the gymnasium, to which the Greek term *askesis* originally referred.[219] Sexual activities were understood not so much in moral as in therapeutic or dietetic terms, as 'a matter of a regimen aimed at regulating an activity that was recognized as being important for health'.[220]

To the extent that the sexual discourses of Greek and Greco-Roman antiquity do manifest a moral concern, they emphasize *ethics* rather than *code*. In other words, they are concerned with a certain attitude of self-mastery rather than with the particular content of sexual norms or rules.[221] Where they advocate an attitude of sexual restraint or asceticism superficially similar to that of Christianity, they do so in a significantly different way. Above all, the 'concern with sexual austerity' is represented as a luxury and a matter of style rather than as a universal moral prescription.[222] As Foucault remarks of Greek sexual discourses of the fourth century BC, they were 'not directed toward a codification of acts . . . but toward a stylization of attitudes and an aesthetics of existence'.[223] These forms of self-control are recommended as specifically appropriate for social and political elites, whose 'aesthetics of existence' is a useful accessory to their rule over citizens and non-citizens of inferior status.[224]

Foucault's portrayal of ancient Greek and Hellenistic attitudes to sex provides the backdrop to his view of Christianity's distinctive contribution to the West's construction of sexuality. Christianity was not particularly innovative in the specific norms it sought to impose on sexual activity. Its championing of faithful monogamy and condemnation of all non-reproductive sex reflected values already ascendant in the Roman world.[225] The distinctive contribution of Christianity was twofold. Not only did it endeavour to transform these values from trappings of the elite into a universally prescriptive sexual morality, it also developed innovative techniques for the regulation of sexual behaviour.[226] The Church's 'pastoral' concern for its congregation was never simply prohibitive or negative but, like the shepherd caring for his flock, productive, self-consciously benevolent and at times even self-sacrificial. Furthermore, the Church deployed an individualized power which sought to discover and address the particularity of each person in its intricacy rather than simply to promulgate rules for the regulation of a population presumed homogeneous.

The archetype of the Church's pastoral power over its congregation is the Catholic confessional, which demonstrates an elaborate concern with the inner life of every individual and the most minute detail of his or her every whim and impulse. The confessional also represents, according to Foucault, an early instance of a cognitive and eventually scientific concern with the individual subject distinctive of western modernity. It is an important stage in the emergence of what Foucault calls the 'hermeneutics of the self'.[227] Christianity's preoccupation with the peculiarities of the individual self is one of a variety of such techniques that help to constitute the individual subject as a self-knowing and responsible subject. Whilst seeking exhaustive knowledge of the individual soul, the confessional helps to constitute the subject as responsible for itself, indeed as responsible for its every thought and desire. The confessional is a 'technique of the self'.[228] In that sense, too, the Church's pastoral concern with sexuality does not represent a primarily repressive or prohibitive power but a productive and constructive one, contributing over centuries to a distinctive configuration of the subject and sexuality.

A second line of descent for this configuration is the equally productive explosion of scientific discourses on sexuality, the emergence of a *scientia sexualis* from the nineteenth century onward. From the broader perspective of scientific rationalism in the West, some kind of empirical investigation of the facts of sexual life can be taken for granted as just another application of scientific method. The pioneers of scientific sexology catalogued with minute attention to detail all 'perverse' or 'deviant' variations from what was still generally assumed to be the 'natural' heterosexual norm. This science is also the source of categories like 'homosexuality' and, later and derivatively, 'heterosexuality'.[229] But these sciences display far less awareness of their own *moral* presuppositions. As Foucault points out, the West's *scientia sexualis* has quite different aims from the East's comparably sophisticated development of an 'erotic art' or *ars erotica*.[230] Almost completely lost to the western tradition (until quite recently) is any such exploration of alternative techniques for the increase of erotic pleasure through the selection of particular positions for intercourse, practices of meditation or even abstinence for the sake of an ultimately heightened pleasure.[231]

The role of scientific sexology in the genealogy of modern sexuality is related at the societal level to an emergent 'bio-politics of population'. Modern states have not only been concerned with the exploitation of labour, as Marxism encourages us to assume; at least from the late fifteenth century, states have also manifested an expanding and deepening pastoral concern for the health and fertility of their populations. The human resources for both material production and military force have been 'policed' by means of an increasingly sophisticated body of administrative policy and practice.[232] Like the Catholic Church's pastoral concern for its flock, the state's pastoral power is not involved in a straightforwardly repressive regulation of sexuality. No doubt repressive sexual prohibitions continue to suppress non-reproductive sexual acts such as sodomy and bestiality, but of equal if not greater significance, according to Foucault, are the *productive* interventions of the state, which are designed to enhance the health and fertility of the population.

The final stage of Foucault's schematic genealogy of sexuality is reached when Christianity's hermeneutic concern with the sexual recesses of the individual soul interacts with the bio-politics of the modern state. The result is that sex is promoted from what it was in the ancient world – a relatively unimportant fact about bodies and acts – to a crucial key to the individual's essential identity. The confessional practices of the Catholic Church and the categories of medical science come together in the depth-hermeneutic practices of

Freudian psychoanalysis. According to Foucault, the careful interrogation of the patient in therapeutic analysis really functions as an instance of power. In the process of supposedly uncovering deep and liberating truths about the self, psychoanalytic interpretations entice the subject into assuming responsibility for more and more regions of its life. At the same time, *sexual* instincts and motivations are identified as the underlying reality and key to the patient's personality and neuroses. What were once meaningless dreams, random slips or irrational symptoms are now traced to their deep, psycho-sexual roots. What were previously anomalous sexual acts without deeper significance are treated as clues to the individual's real sexuality and self.

The idea of sexuality as the key to individual identity is thus a product of late modernity. Today, as Halperin puts it,

> we understand 'sexuality' to refer to a positive, distinct, and constitutive feature of the human personality, to the characterological seat within the individual of sexual acts, desires, and pleasures – the determinate source from which all sexual expression proceeds. 'Sexuality' in this sense is not a purely descriptive term, a neutral representation of some objective state of affairs or a simple recognition of some familiar facts about us; rather, it is a distinctive way of constructing, organizing, and interpreting those 'facts'. . . .[233]

Foucault's history of sexuality implies that not only particular sexual categories and values but the category of sexuality itself is a modern product or 'construction'. Sexual constructionism also implies that particular sexualities are products of modernity as well. If the modern notion of sexuality is the product of a distinctively western genealogy, then there is a sense in which homosexuality did not really exist in ancient Greece either. The concept of homosexuality that first emerged in the nineteenth century was an expression of the modern construction of sexuality, because it conceived sexual orientation as a persistent and usually exclusive disposition towards sexual partners of the same sex, a disposition supposedly revealing some deep truth about the subject. In Halperin's provocative terms, there have only been (now somewhat more than) 'a hundred years of homosexuality'.[234] In ancient Greece individuals might perform a variety of sexual acts both socially approved and stigmatized, but those acts were not regarded as evidence of an underlying sexuality.

As a result, a certain version of gay and lesbian history which aims to chart the heroism and sufferings of a previously hidden but continuing community is invalidated. Any liberationist politics positing an eternal and essential sexual identity similarly risks 'playing into the hands of power': 'We must not think that by saying yes to sex, one says no to power; on the contrary, one tracks along the course laid out by the general deployment of sexuality.'[235] This kind of sexual politics risks reinforcing the role of sexuality as a useful relay for other social purposes and powers. Foucault's critique of essentialism implies that the path of sexual resistance should not be calibrated to some supposedly natural but previously repressed sexual essence. The point is rather to escape altogether from the 'subjected subject' integral to the West's distinctive deployment of sexuality. The goal is

> not to try to liberate the individual from the state, and from the state's institutions, but to liberate us both from the state and from the type of individualization which is linked to the state. We have to promote new forms of subjectivity through the refusal of this kind of individuality which has been imposed on us for several centuries.[236]

On Halperin's reading, what is required instead is a 'creative process' of resistance.[237] The de-naturalization of normative structures of sexuality should open up spaces for creativity. The political struggles of sexual minorities can be understood as seeking not the liberation of a repressed self, but *escape* from one kind of self for the sake of another.[238] To this end, Halperin explores the possibilities of radically non-normative forms of sex such as sado-masochism. Sado-masochistic practices are interpreted not as the unleashing of previously suppressed and stigmatized sexual desires but as 'practices of freedom', where freedom is to be understood as freedom *from* (rather than of) the self and sexuality. They are more about transcendence than expression of the self. Sado-masochism may, in Foucault's own words, be conceived as 'the purposeful art of a freedom perceived as a power game'.[239] In these terms, the very intensity of sado-masochistic pleasure and pain may contribute to the 'desubjectivation' of the self.

The *jouissance* of sado-masochistic orgasm can even be understood as a highly disciplined and self-transcending form of 'ascesis'.[240] Indeed, sado-masochistic practices are ascetic in the stronger sense of offering greater distance from sexuality and even sex. Sado-masochism is often other than primarily genital and does not always involve orgasm. Even when it *is* genital and orgasmic, it is unconventionally so.[241] It may thus be a way of enhancing and multiplying pleasures between sex and love – in a place somewhere between 'purely sexual encounters' and 'the merging of identities in love'.[242] Mark Vernon supports the view that Foucault's ultimate aim was a 'way out' of sexuality and even liberation from sex.[243] From this perspective, it appears that Foucault's intense preoccupation with Christian asceticism was never purely academic and certainly not hostile in intent. On the contrary, he regards Christian practices of renunciation and asceticism as potentially useful and beneficial.[244] According to Vernon, Foucault's ultimate value is a form of friendship conceived in spiritual rather than sexual terms – a conclusion that comes surprisingly close to Platonism.[245]

Despite Foucault's doubts about the politics of sexual liberationism, he nevertheless contributes to a distinctively political discourse and experience of sexuality. Throughout his life, he was actively, if idiosyncratically, involved in the gay movement. But more fundamentally, Foucault's critical genealogy of sexuality cannot be construed as a straightforward refutation of sexual politics. The West's distinctive configuration of self and sexuality is presented as a product of its history but not, for that reason, as just one morally and politically indifferent variation in the anthropological gallery of sexual constructions. Rather, it is presented as an object of critique and resistance. Foucault's history of sexuality theorizes an important dimension of the colonization of the self by power. Sexuality and self are seen as objects and, in certain ways, also products of power. Both are at stake in what is thus properly conceived as a sexual politics, even if that politics cannot uncritically rely on some supposedly pre-political conception of either the self or its sexual dispositions.

It is also misleading to exaggerate the contrast between Marcuse's 'repressive' and Foucault's 'productive' view of power and their corresponding views of the politics of sexuality. Properly understood, Marcuse's views are not vulnerable to Foucault's polemic against essentialism and naturalism. Although Marcuse does not always clearly rule out such an interpretation, he does not appeal to the idea of pre-repressive or essential sexuality. The 'liberation of eros' is seen not as the release of unmodified and primitive natural impulses but as an essentially constructive and even creative endeavour. Liberated eros is understood in aesthetic, social and even moral terms. Furthermore, Marcuse emphatically warns of the dangers of a potentially 'repressive de-sublimation' of eros. An uncritical dismantling of society's repressive sexual prohibitions will only further capitalism's tendency to exploit and commodify all aspects of life. Marcuse has no reason to deny that playing into the hands of this aspect of power would involve a considerable 'production' of sexual acts and experiences, a production that he has even less reason to understand as emancipatory.[246]

By the same token, although Foucault is best known for his characterization of power as productive in relation to sexuality, the evidence he presents is really persuasive only in support of the *discursive* productivity of power. In both religious and scientific contexts, the overriding preoccupation with sex has certainly led to a lot of talk about sex. And as Foucault points out, an indirect consequence of this discursive attention has been an intensification of the relationship between the subject and its sexual acts through the ongoing construction of 'sexuality'. But neither the state's bio-politics of population nor the Church's obsessive cataloguing of sin have been systematically productive of sexual *acts*, except perhaps in the strictly approved sense of reproductive sexual acts within monogamy. Surely, the discursive productivity of power has more often contributed to a restriction of sexual acts and opportunities. But whether power has been predominantly productive or repressive of sexual acts, for both Marcuse and Foucault sexuality is never innocent of power relations. Both Marcuse's politics of sexuality and Foucault's rhetorical anti-politics are, in these terms, no less sexual-political constructions. The politics of sexuality remains indispensable.

Afterthoughts

> In this activity the basic philosophical questions are how much guidance we are entitled to expect and where we can expect to find it. In seeking such guidance, we can never move from something that is merely contextual – the ideals and the institutions, the intuitions and the practices of our situation – to another thing that is beyond context. We can merely hope to broaden the range of our experience, and to deepen the distance of judgement, from which we evaluate the living possibilities of the present.
>
> R. M. Unger[1]

The main critical aim of the foregoing discussion has been to question, and, it is hoped, to resist, the narrowing of sexual experience in the name of some clear and definitive configuration of reason, sexuality and the self. We have seen how distinctive attitudes towards sexual experience are deduced from three basic constellations of reason, self and sexuality identified broadly as ascetic idealism, hedonist realism and Romanticism.[2] It hardly needs emphasizing at this stage that these basic orientations to the self and sexuality have exerted a profound influence on the lives of people in the West and, through them, many others. This influence has surely been disproportionate to what might be thought to be their legitimate philosophical content and insights. In fact, the clarity and often violence of their implications reflects a shared feature of these otherwise very different philosophical constructions. At the heart of each is the reifying and prioritizing, the absolutizing of one faculty or dimension of the self at the expense of the overall coherence and richness of human experience. Reason or rationality, sensuality, love or passion are conceived as essentially distinct faculties, capacities or forces and then assigned a privileged status as a systematic source of authoritative norms, values or even the meaning of life as a whole.

So with ascetic idealism, a reified faculty of reason is treated as a transcendent source of truth and morality and as the basis for the proper order of nature and society. Reason assumes ascendancy over other human faculties, inclinations and activities and, in particular, over a sexuality assigned to our merely physical, merely animal nature. In accordance with this construction, sex has been subjected to the prohibitions of an ascetic sexual morality that persists to this day, somewhat dissipated and diffused but still retaining surprising vigour and vehemence. Only essentially reproductive sexual activities are granted a conditional exemption. But this way of conceiving human life and sexuality does not so much perfect sexual morality as stunt and deform it. It is not only that it invalidates certain varieties of human sexuality and stigmatizes those people associated with them; the problem is also that reason is disqualified from any useful discrimination *within* the realm of sexual and sensual enjoyments, which is regarded as intrinsically questionable, intrinsically *beyond* reason.

In the realist tradition of rationality the situation is, in this respect, essentially the same. In its hedonist currents at least, rationality is conceived more modestly as a mere instrument at the service of a person's preferences and inclinations. Sexual activities and pleasures are, to that extent, rehabilitated. But although no longer treated as a moral and metaphysical absolute, rationality is still effectively reified as a separate faculty of reasoning, deliberation and calculation. It is detached and abstracted from the rest of a person's life, activities and experience. It is the individual's desires and inclinations, served ('organized' or 'maximized') by a now merely instrumental rationality, which are effectively given absolute status. Particular sensual inclinations are, though positively rather than negatively evaluated, as little subject to qualitative discrimination or 'rational' judgement as they are in the tradition of transcendent reason. Morality enters the scene only externally either by way of prudential calculations to maximize the individual's satisfaction over time or through moral consideration of the other people's satisfactions.

Romantic and post-Romantic constellations of reason, sexuality and the self react against both of these absolutizing constructions of reason and rationality, but they do so only by absolutizing some combination of love and sexual passion instead. A single dimension of human life is, once again, treated as the pre-eminent source of value and meaning. Once more, the overall coherence and balance of a person's life is put at risk. The absolute commitment to love or passion risks undermining our obligations to other people and devaluing other areas of our experience and activity. At the extreme, passionate love may even result in the sacrifice of a life. If only through the plethora of works of art and entertainment that it has inspired, Romanticism has undoubtedly exerted profound effects on the generations subject to its influence. This influence both reflects and reinforces the undoubted existential importance of love and friendship in *our* lives at least. But the Romantic insistence that passionate love and sexual relationship are the necessary and sufficient basis of a happy and meaningful life is surely exaggerated. Human relationships are as often destroyed as they are enhanced by the weight of these Romantic expectations.

More often, though, in the contemporary West we live in a *post*-Romantic world. The existential need for meaning and human relationship is no longer underwritten by any religious or metaphysical guarantee. As a result, Romantic themes are more pervasive in other contexts and modalities. Proust provides only the most definitively and subtly pessimistic of accounts of passionate love as an inescapable form of psychological bondage. Although not unchallenged, Freud's preoccupation with the all-pervasiveness of the various incarnations of the sex instinct has undoubtedly left its mark as well, not only on much psychotherapeutic practice but also on broader cultural conceptions and on the self-understanding of individuals. But Romantic themes have their most prolific after-life in the ever-present fantasies of the culture industries. Ideas and images born in the context of an aspiring Romantic idealism, which was highly critical of industrial and commercial society, are endlessly recycled for the sake of a materialistic, commercialized and often cynical hedonism. Although this claim inevitably goes beyond the scope of the present discussion, it might be said that the dominant cultural construction of contemporary sexuality is an uneasy and unstable hybrid of Romanticism and hedonism.

What scope does this leave for a philosophically illuminating conception of the place of reason and love, passion and sex within the whole of a human life? Certainly, any adequate conception of human love and sexuality cannot ignore the complex of attributes and relationships implied by notions of reason or rationality. A genuinely human sexuality will be, in some sense, a rational or reasonable sexuality. But reason does not have to be understood as an essentially separate faculty definable without any essential reference to other aspects of a person's activity and experience. It is idealist traditions, with their reliance on some kind of dualism of earthly and eternal reality or body and soul, which have insisted most strongly on regarding reason as a separate faculty exclusive to human beings.[3] For a holistic conception of reason, on the other hand, it is plain that reason can only be articulated in terms of the mutual relationship, the overall organization and interactions of the various dimensions of human experience and activity. For this conception, it also seems obvious that human rationality is a matter of degree.

From this perspective, the most fully realized human life is not, as Aristotle and subsequent idealist and religious traditions have supposed, a life devoted exclusively or, at least, as much as possible to rational contemplation; it is a life in which balance and coherence are maintained. In these terms, a human life completely lacking any sexual or sensual dimension is just as diminished, just as inadequate and incomplete, as a life confined to the unthinking pursuit of bestial pleasures. A fully realized human life depends instead on the complex mutual relationship and interaction of sense, thought and activity, feeling and relationship, experience, memory and foresight. Nor should it be seen as any objection to this view that no clear and definitive moral imperatives can easily be deduced from it. That should rather be seen as an advantage in the context of a tradition rarely characterized by moral reticence on the part of the advocates of ascetic, hedonist and Romantic views. After all, whatever a fully realized human life might look like, it must surely be a complex and multidimensional achievement. And even if not everything is permitted, there may be many ways to live a successful life.

Of course, there is nothing intrinsically wrong with exclusively intellectual, contemplative or spiritual pursuits. But neither is there any absolute reason why we should not occasionally enjoy merely animal pleasures or enjoy pleasures in a bestial way. The nature that we share with animals is not *ipso facto* suspect and contemptible. But it is also worth noting that the holism of human reason and experience implies that the 'merely' physical or biological level of human life is always potentially, and so always *in fact*, more than that. For a human being, even the bestial enjoyment of sex always occurs in the context of the possible awareness that this enjoyment is merely bestial. We may enjoy our temporary descent into animality, but as long as we enjoy it *as such* or with that awareness, then we have not really (completely or 'successfully') descended to the animal level after all.[4] On the other hand, a holistic view of reason does require, of course, that sexual activity occurs in ways that are at least compatible with our distinctively human characteristics.

This holistic approach to reason and sexuality is easily reconciled with the view of humans as essentially historical and cultural beings. The distinctive humanity and rationality of human beings is manifest, above all, in the culturally diverse and historically evolving ways in which human activities are conducted. Recognition of the irreducibly cultural nature of all human activities and capacities is implicit in Hegel's understanding of the whole of human experience in terms of an historical process of development or 'dialectic'. Human life is not only distinguished by such exclusively human achievements as religion, art, science and philosophy, which, as Hegel shows, are themselves best understood in social and historical terms; even physical activities such as eating and sex are realized in culturally and historically differentiated ways. If we abstract from Hegel's ultimately unsustainable teleology – his positing of an ascertainable meaning and goal of history – then his perspective encourages us to recognize the variety of ethical standards or forms of 'ethical life' governing human sexual practice.

At the same time, even Hegel's teleology seems somewhat less implausible when we understand it in the context of a holistic conception of reason. As Montaigne's explicitly *anti*-systematic and *anti*-teleological reflections make clear, the proliferation of 'experience', whether individual or societal, offers us the means, through memory, historical knowledge and, of course, the process of writing itself, for a more complex, multidimensional and even saner conduct of life.[5] By the same token, this adoption of the perspective of the experiencing subject complicates and ultimately undermines the historicist and relativist tendency to view human life and sexual morality from an external position of indifference. The perspective of the living or, more precisely, existing and evaluating subject is explored further by Kierkegaard and elaborated in the existentialism and phenomenology of Sartre, Beauvoir and Merleau-Ponty.[6]

Although the implications of this shift of perspective are surprisingly complex, it seems clear at least that it places greater demands on sexual ethics.[7] Sexuality is influenced by culture and history not only from the *outside* – in the sense that individuals born in different societies and times inherit significantly different ethical standards and conceptions – but also *internally*, through the subject's own appropriation of diverse ethical traditions, which overlay and in subtle or significant ways transform their inherited ethical position. It follows that the contribution of these different discourses and traditions must ultimately be resolved at the subjective level as well. A philosophical resolution of the conflict between value systems, however plausible in abstract terms, must be subjectively convincing for the concrete individuals concerned. Although there may, in the end, be something approaching 'objective' ethical principles governing sexual activity, they will always be in a significant sense principles *for someone* and so also principles *for a particular historical setting*.

A second complication comes from recognition of the political dimension of reason and sexual experience. Certainly, the West's ascetic-idealist preoccupation with sex has been long, intense and, in many ways, regrettable. For just as long, opponents of this peculiar obsession have resorted either to some version of the hedonist cause of innocent bodily pleasures, to Romantic enthusiasm or, perhaps, post-Romantic cynicism about passionate love. It is only in the twentieth century that an explicitly *political* concept of sexual oppression emerges from the related but divergent approaches of Freud, Sartre, Beauvoir, Merleau-Ponty, Marcuse and Foucault.[8] From this perspective, sex is not only one significant channel for the gendered or patriarchal oppression of women; sex is, in its own right, an important vehicle of relationships of power, exploitation and subordination between people. What is more, sex, sexual orientation and even the West's related constructions of sexuality and the subject can be seen as not only targets but also to a certain extent *products* of power. Sexuality and the subject are thus inevitably objects of political as well as ethical thought and action. But by the same token, as Foucault's critical discussion implies, the subject's sexuality provides, at best, a problematic and always questionable – if nonetheless unavoidable – basis for political engagement.

More encouragingly, these problems can be recognized, from a different perspective, as invitations to further experience. It would be wrong to conclude that philosophy has little to offer simply because it promises no clear and definite conclusions. It is philosophical approaches that deliver all-too-clear and definitive conclusions that have had the most unfortunate effects. For a holistic conception of philosophical reflection, on the other hand, the aim is rather to maintain and enhance the mutual communication and illumination of the different dimensions of our experience, thought and activity. Reflection in this sense is concerned with openness rather than determinateness of mind. It aims not towards some definite and confined conclusion but an unending expansion, articulation and rearticulation of human experience. To return to R. M. Unger's words above, 'We can merely hope to broaden the range of our experience, and to deepen the distance of judgement, from which we evaluate the living possibilities of the present.'[9]

Notes

Acknowledgements

1 The bibliography is available online via my homepage (*http://arts.anu.edu.au/sss/west/*).

Introduction

1 F. Nietzsche, *On the Genealogy of Morals*, III, 12, p. 119.
2 R. M. Schott, *Cognition and Eros*, p. viii and *passim*.
3 A fascinating discussion of reason and gender, which examines many of the philosophers considered here, is G. Lloyd, *The Man of Reason*. For an overview of contrasting understandings of reason or rationality in European philosophy, see my *An Introduction to Continental Philosophy*. Philosophical conceptions of the body and gender are traced illuminatingly in T. Laqueur, *Making Sex*.
4 Foucault's argument will be considered towards the end of this study: ch. 4, §8.
5 D. Halperin, *One Hundred Years of Homosexuality*, ch. 1.
6 See, for example, E. Grosz, *Sexual Subversions*, L. J. Nicholson, ed., *Feminism/Postmodernism* and M. Gatens, *Feminism and Philosophy*.
7 For an introduction to these fields, see A. Jagose, *Queer Theory*.
8 See ch. 3, §5 and ch. 4, §5–8.
9 See below, ch. 2, §4 for J. S. Mill's discussion of 'nature' and cf. ch. 1, §4. For an account of the impact of scientific sexology, see, for example, R. Porter and M. Teich, *Sexual Knowledge, Sexual Science*, L. Bland and L. Doan, eds, *Sexology in Culture*, J. Weeks, *Coming Out* and J. D. Steakley, *The Homosexual Emancipation Movement in Germany*.

10 I have only recently realized how much a reading of Nietzsche's *Beyond Good and Evil* has influenced my thinking.
11 See below, ch. 4, §8.
12 See ch. 4, §3. Holistic approaches are not, of course, confined to so-called 'continental' philosophy but are also to be found in 'English-speaking' and 'analytical' philosophy. See, for example, N. H. Smith, ed., *Reading McDowell*, esp. R. J. Bernstein, 'McDowell's Domesticated Hegelianism', pp. 9–24.
13 See H.-G. Gadamer, *Truth and Method* for a subtle hermeneutic analysis of human 'understanding'.
14 G. W. F. Hegel, *Philosophy of Right*, preface, p. 13.

Chapter 1 The Ascetic Idealism of Reason

1 Plato, *Complete Works*, 'Timaeus', pp. 1224–91, trans. D. J. Zeyl, §§90b–c, p. 1289. The extent to which Plato's *Timaeus* and *Theaetetus* present the aim of the virtuous and philosophical life as 'becoming like God' is discussed by J. Annas, *Platonic Ethics*, ch. III.
2 Plato, *Complete Works*, 'Epigrams', pp. 1742–5, trans. J. M. Edmonds, rev. J. M. Cooper, no. 3, p. 1743. Cf. G. Lloyd, *The Man of Reason*, chs 2–3, T. Gomperz, *Griechische Denker*, vol. II, p. 320, G. Vlastos, *Platonic Studies*, p. 26, n. 78. For Whitehead, above, see A. N. Whitehead, *Process and Reality*, p. 63.
3 Plato, *Complete Works*, 'Lysis', pp. 687–707, trans. S. Lombardo, esp. §§210ff., pp. 694ff. On Plato's homosexuality see Vlastos, *Platonic Studies*, p. 25, n. 74.
4 Plato, *Complete Works*, 'Symposium', pp. 457–505, trans. A. Nehamas and P. Woodruff, §193a, p. 476.
5 Ibid., §§191e–192b, p. 475.
6 Ibid., §192c, p. 475 and cf. M. Foucault, *The Use of Pleasure*, pp. 232ff. and D. Halperin, *One Hundred Years of Homosexuality*, ch. 6, pp. 131ff.
7 Plato, *Complete Works*, 'Symposium', §§211c–d, p. 493.
8 See Vlastos, *Platonic Studies*, pp. 38–42.
9 Plato, *Complete Works*, 'Symposium', §§215–22c, pp. 497–504. Cf. M. Nussbaum, *Sex and Social Justice*, ch. 12, p. 312.
10 See Vlastos, *Platonic Studies*, pp. 31–4.
11 Plato, *Phaedrus*, pp. 47ff.
12 Ibid., §§241c–d, p. 58.
13 Ibid., §§238a–c, pp. 54–5.
14 Ibid., pp. 62–4 and 72–3.
15 Ibid., pp. 67–9.
16 Ibid., p. 67.
17 The chronology of Plato's works adopted here is conventional but not uncontroversial. Cf. J. M. Cooper, Introduction to Plato, *Complete Works*, pp. xiiff.

18 Plato, *Complete Works*, 'Republic', pp. 971–1223, trans. G. M. A. Grube, rev. C. D. C. Reeve, bk VII, §§514–18, pp. 1132–6. Cf. 'Phaedo', pp. 49–100, trans. G. M. A. Grube, §§65ff., pp. 56ff.
19 The intended lesson of this analogy is, however, contentious. Julia Annas argues persuasively that the political analogy is designed to illuminate the moral situation, and not the reverse: see Annas, *Platonic Ethics*, ch. IV, esp. pp. 93–5.
20 Plato, *Complete Works*, 'Republic', bk IV, §441e, p. 1073.
21 Plato, *Complete Works*, 'Gorgias', pp. 791–869, trans. D. J. Zeyl, §507b, p. 851.
22 B. S. Thornton, *Eros*, pp. 130–1. Plato's views on hedonism are, in fact, varied. He attacks hedonism directly in *Gorgias* (cf. Thornton, pp. 127–9), but in *Protagoras* Socrates apparently defends a hedonist position: see Annas, *Platonic Ethics*, ch. VII.
23 See R. M. Schott, *Cognition and Eros*, pp. 32–41 and cf. Gomperz, *Griechische Denker*, vol. I, bk I, ch. 5, pp. 103–5 and W. K. C. Guthrie, *A History of Greek Philosophy*. On the long-standing controversy over the possible influence of Judaic thought on Pythagoras, see J. B. Schneewind, *The Invention of Autonomy*, ch. 24, esp. pp. 536–40 and 542–3.
24 Plato, *Complete Works*, 'Meno', pp. 870–97, trans. G. M. A. Grube, §§82ff., pp. 881ff.; 'Phaedo', esp. §§114c–e, p. 97.
25 Plato, *Complete Works*, 'Timaeus', §§69d–72d, pp. 1271–3.
26 Ibid., §§90b–c, p. 1289. As has been mentioned in note 1 of this chapter above, Annas (*Platonic Ethics*, ch. III) provides useful discussion here.
27 Plato, *Complete Works*, 'Timaeus', §§90d–91a, p. 1289.
28 Ibid., §§91b, p. 1290. This account is echoed by St Augustine (see below, §3). Cf. R. Ward, 'Why Unnatural? The Tradition behind Romans 1:26–7' on the 'natural use of the genitals' in Plato and Augustine.
29 Plato, *Complete Works*, 'Timaeus', §§86d–e, p. 1286.
30 Plato, *Complete Works*, 'Laws', pp. 1318–616, trans. T. J. Saunders, VIII, §§841d–e, pp. 1502–3.
31 J. Boswell, *Christianity, Social Tolerance, and Homosexuality*, pp. 13–14, n. 22 and p. 27.
32 Cf. Nussbaum's claim that, although suspicious of bodily appetites and orgasm, Plato never categorically condemns homosexuality, even in the *Laws*: *Sex and Social Justice*, ch. 12, esp. pp. 312–21, where she also discusses *Gorgias*, *Symposium*, *Republic* and *Phaedrus*.
33 P. Hadot, *Philosophy as a Way of Life*, pp. 21–2. Cf. M. C. Nussbaum, *The Therapy of Desire*, esp. chs 1 and 13.
34 Hadot, *Philosophy as a Way of Life*, p. 93.
35 See Schott, *Eros and Cognition*, ch. 2.
36 On the proper translation of *philia*, see Vlastos, *Platonic Studies*, pp. 3–5.
37 W. Jaeger, *Aristotle*.

38 On Plato's theory of Forms see above, pp. 13–14.
39 Aristotle, 'Metaphysics', *The Complete Works of Aristotle*, vol. II, pp. 1552–728, trans. W. D. Ross, bk I, 9, §§990b–993a, pp. 1565–9.
40 Ibid., esp. bks VII–IX, pp. 1623–61.
41 See R. Beiner, *Practical Judgment*, ch. 4, pp. 72–82 and H.-G. Gadamer, *Truth and Method*, pp. 312ff.
42 Aristotle, 'Nicomachean Ethics', *Complete Works*, vol. II, pp. 1729–867, trans. W. D. Ross, rev. J. O. Urmson, bk I, 2, §1095a, p. 1730.
43 Ibid., bk VII, 1, §1145b, p. 1809.
44 Gadamer, *Truth and Method*, p. 312.
45 Aristotle, 'Nicomachean Ethics', bk VII, 12, §1153a, p. 1822.
46 Ibid., bk III, 10, §1117b, l. 25, p. 1764.
47 Ibid., bk II, 3, §1104b, p. 1744.
48 Ibid., bk III, 4, §1113a, l. 33, p. 1758. Cf. Thornton, *Eros*, p. 135.
49 Aristotle, 'Nicomachean Ethics', bk III, 10, §1118a, l. 32, p. 1765.
50 Ibid., bk III, 10, §1118b, p. 1765 and bk VII, 12, §1153a, p. 1822.
51 Ibid., bk III, 12, §1119b, p. 1767.
52 Ibid., bk VII, 8, §1150b, p. 1818.
53 Ibid., bk VII, 5, §§1148b–1149a, pp. 1814–15.
54 Ibid., bk IV, 11, §1118b, p. 1766.
55 Nussbaum, *Sex and Social Justice*, pp. 321–2.
56 On the proper translation of *philia*, see n. 36 above.
57 Aristotle, 'Nicomachean Ethics', bk VIII, 2, §§1155b–1156a, pp. 1826–7.
58 Ibid., bk VIII, 3, §1156b, p. 1827.
59 Ibid., bk X, 12, §1171b, p. 1852.
60 Ibid., bk IX, 11, §1171a, p. 1851.
61 Cf. I. Singer, *The Nature of Love*, vol. I, p. 90.
62 Aristotle, 'Nicomachean Ethics', bk VIII, 1, §1155a, p. 1825. Cf. A. W. Price, *Love and Friendship in Plato and Aristotle*, esp. ch. 3.
63 Jaeger, *Aristotle*, p. 244.
64 See L. Faderman, *Surpassing the Love of Men*, esp. pp. 66–7. Cf. below, ch. 2, §2, esp. pp. 60–1.
65 Aristotle, 'Nicomachean Ethics', bk IX, 8, §§1168b–1169a, p. 1847.
66 Ibid., bk X, 7, §§1177a–1177b, pp. 1860–1.
67 Ibid., bk X, 8, §1178b, p. 1863.
68 Ibid. This interpretation, as well as Aristotle's emphasis on the value of living with one's friends, proved congenial to later monastic traditions of Christianity.
69 Jaeger, *Aristotle*, pp. 437 and 239–40.
70 Aristotle, 'Nicomachean Ethics', bk X, 8, §1179a, p. 1863.
71 Ibid., bk X, 9, §1179b, p. 1864.
72 Ibid., bk II, 1, §1103b, p. 1743.
73 Ibid., bk X, 9, §§1179a–1181b, pp. 1864–7.
74 Ibid., bk X, 9, §1181b, p. 1867 and see Aristotle, 'Politics', *Complete Works*, vol. II, pp. 1986–2129, trans. B. Jowett.

75 See pseudo-Aristotle, 'Problems', *Complete Works*, vol. II, pp. 1319–527, trans. E. S. Forster, IV, 26, §§879b–880a, pp. 1356–7 and cf. K. J. Dover, *Greek Homosexuality*, III, D, pp. 168ff. and Price, *Love and Friendship*, appendix 4, 'Aristotle on Erotic Love', esp. pp. 239ff.
76 Aristotle, 'Nicomachean Ethics', bk VIII, 4, §1157a, p. 1828.
77 Price, *Love and Friendship*, pp. 245–6.
78 Aristotle, 'Nicomachean Ethics', bk IX, 1, §1164a, p. 1839. Cf. Price, *Love and Friendship*, ch. 4, pp. 104ff. and appendix 4, pp. 239ff.
79 Aristotle, 'Nicomachean Ethics', bk VIII, 5, §1157b, p. 1829.
80 See, for example, the 'neo-Aristotelian' approach of Nussbaum, *Sex and Social Justice*, esp. ch. 12.
81 Aristotle, 'Politics', bk I, 2, §§1252b–1253a, p. 1987.
82 Aristotle, 'Parts of Animals', *Complete Works*, vol. I, pp. 994–1086, trans. W. Ogle.
83 See W. Schubart, *Religion und Eros*, esp. chs 1–6.
84 Leviticus 20.13 and cf. 8.22.
85 Boswell, *Christianity, Social Tolerance and Homosexuality*, ch. 4, pp. 93–9. Jeremy Bentham pointed out (*c.*1785) that the sin of the Sodomites was at least aggravated by violence and inhospitality (MSS, Box LXXII, 187–205, 'Penal Code, Paederasty', folio 188c).
86 On Mark 10.7–9 see Schubart, *Religion und Eros*, ch. 9, pp. 198–9.
87 Bentham suggests that Jesus, who is also compared with Socrates, may have indulged in 'eccentric pleasures of the bed' (MSS, Box CLXI(b), 215–523, 'Not Paul but Jesus, Asceticism', 1816–18, esp. folios 483–6 and 494). Cf. Schubart, *Religion und Eros*, ch. 9, pp. 196–7 and pp. 202ff.
88 On Matthew 19.12 see Schubart, *Religion und Eros*, ch. 9, p. 200. The work of Peter Brown and Wayne A. Meeks offers an excellent guide to the intricate variety and social origins of the divergent attitudes to sexual renunciation in the early Christian world. See P. Brown, *The Body and Society* and W. A. Meeks, *The Origins of Christian Morality*.
89 Boswell, *Christianity, Social Tolerance and Homosexuality*, p. 293.
90 See Plotinus, *The Enneads*.
91 St Augustine, *City of God*, bk VIII, ch. 5, p. 304.
92 Ibid., bk VIII, ch. 9, p. 311.
93 Ibid., bk XII, chs 25–6, pp. 504–6.
94 Ibid., bk XI, ch. 21, p. 451.
95 Brown, *The Body and Society*, p. 200.
96 S. M. Okin, *Women in Western Political Thought*, p. 150.
97 The term 'bugger' derives from the Old French *bougre*, meaning 'heretic', and reflects the supposedly Bulgarian sources of Catharism (*Concise Oxford Dictionary*).
98 St Augustine, *Confessions*, bk III, vii, §12, p. 43.

99 See, for example, ibid., bk 4, x, §15, pp. 61–2. This is the ultimate source of Christianity's moralized order of nature, which is most clearly developed in the writings of Aquinas (see next section).
100 Augustine, *City of God*, bk V, ch. 9, pp. 190–4.
101 Cf. Brown, *The Body and Society*, p. 408.
102 Augustine, *City of God*, bk XIV, ch. 16, p. 577. But Plato also worries that without the ingenious efficacy of the bowels, 'gluttony would make our whole race incapable of philosophy and the arts, and incapable of heeding the most divine part within us' (*Complete Works*, 'Timaeus', §91b, p. 1290).
103 Augustine, *City of God*, bk XIV, ch. 16, p. 577.
104 Ibid., bk XIV, ch. 19, p. 581.
105 Ibid., bk XIV, ch. 16, p. 577.
106 Augustine, *Confessions*, bk X, xxix, §41, p. 203.
107 Augustine, *City of God*, bk XIV, ch. 23, esp. p. 586.
108 Ibid., bk XIV, ch. 18, p. 579.
109 Ibid., bk XIV, ch. 20, p. 582.
110 Ibid., bk XIV, ch. 26, p. 591 and cf. chs 21–2, pp. 583–4.
111 Ibid., bk XIV, ch. 23, p. 585.
112 Ibid., bk XIV, ch. 26, p. 591 and bk XIV, ch. 16, p. 577.
113 Augustine, *Confessions*, bk VIII, vii, §17, p. 145.
114 Ibid., bk IV, iv, §7, p. 57.
115 Ibid., bk IV, iv, §9, p. 57 and vi, §11, p. 59.
116 Ibid., bk IV, vi, §11, p. 59.
117 Ibid., bk III, i, §1, p. 35.
118 Ibid., bk III, vii, §13, p. 44.
119 Ibid., bk III, viii, §15, pp. 45–6.
120 Augustine, *City of God*, bk VII, ch. 21, pp. 278–9.
121 Ibid., bk VII, ch. 26, p. 286. In their fondness for *castrati*, the Popes of the Italian Renaissance were to neglect this bit of patristic doctrine.
122 Ibid., bk VII, ch. 26, p. 287.
123 Brown, *The Body and Society*, p. 404.
124 St Thomas Aquinas, *Summa Theologiae*. See N. Kretzman and E. Stump, eds, *The Cambridge Companion to Aquinas*, J. A. Weisheipl, *Friar Thomas D'Aquino* and E. Gilson, *The Philosophy of St Thomas Aquinas*.
125 See J. A. Aertsen, 'Aquinas's Philosophy in its Historical Setting' in Kretzman and Stump, eds, *The Cambridge Companion to Aquinas*, ch. 1, esp. pp. 14–24.
126 On the comparison between Augustine and Aquinas, see Weisheipl, *Friar Thomas D'Aquino*, pp. 285–92.
127 St Thomas Aquinas, *Philosophical Texts*, pp. 261–2.
128 Ibid., pp. 312–13.
129 Ibid., p. 285.
130 Ibid., p. 162.
131 Ibid., p. 170. See above, pp. 27–9.

132 On Aquinas' relation to Aristotle, see J. Owens, 'Aristotle and Aquinas' in Kretzman and Stump, eds, *The Cambridge Companion to Aquinas*, ch. 2.
133 See above, §2, pp. 24–6 and cf. Schneewind, *Invention of Autonomy*, p. 19.
134 See below, ch. 2, §§2ff.
135 Cf. C. Taylor, *Hegel*, ch. 1, pp. 6–11.
136 Aquinas, *Philosophical Texts*, pp. 358–9.
137 Ibid., p. 358.
138 Ibid., p. 359.
139 Ibid.
140 Aquinas, *Summa Theologiae*, vol. 20, 1a2ae, §31, art. 7, p. 23.
141 Ibid., vol. 20, 1a2ae, §31, art. 7, p. 25.
142 Ibid. Though, as even some earlier medieval writers had observed, some animals do engage in homosexual activity.
143 Aquinas, *Philosophical Texts*, p. 325. On Christian mysticism, see below, ch. 3, §1.
144 Ibid., p. 323.
145 As a member of a celibate order, Aquinas is ready to admit that reproduction should be regarded as the duty of the human *species* as a whole rather than of every individual member within it: *Summa Theologiae*, vol. 28, 1a2ae, §94, art. 3, pp. 85–7.
146 Ibid., vol. 43, 2a2ae, §154, art. 11, p. 245.
147 Ibid., vol. 43, 2a2ae, §154, art. 12, p. 247.
148 Ibid., vol. 43, 2a2ae, §154, art. 12, p. 247 and p. 249.
149 Ibid., vol. 43, 2a2ae, §154, art. 12, p. 249.
150 Boswell, *Christianity, Social Tolerance and Homosexuality*, p. 293.
151 See I. Primoratz, *Ethics and Sex*, ch. 7, p. 71.
152 Aquinas, *Summa Theologiae*, vol. 43, 2a2ae, §142, art. 4, p. 47 and vol. 20, 1a2ae, §31, art. 7, p. 25.
153 This approach to rationality, pleasure and sexuality is considered in ch. 2, esp. §§3–5.
154 I. Kant, *Critique of Pure Reason*, I, Part I, 1, A28, p. 73 and cf. note, pp. 73–4. See Schott, *Cognition and Eros*, pp. 101–2.
155 See above, p. 20.
156 Schott, *Cognition and Eros*, pp. 103–5.
157 Ibid., pp. 152–3 and cf. I. Kant, *The Critique of Judgement*, Introduction, VII, pp. 29ff.
158 For a rebuttal of such criticism, see H. J. Paton, *The Categorical Imperative*, ch. III, §3, pp. 48–50.
159 I. Kant, *Groundwork of the Metaphysics of Morals*, 4:402, p. 57 (italicized in original) and cf. 4:421, p. 73.
160 See G. W. F. Hegel, *Phenomenology of Spirit*, part C.BB.B, III, §588, p. 358.
161 See below, ch. 2, §5.
162 Hegel, *Phenomenology of Spirit*, part C.BB.B, III, §589, p. 359.

163 I. Kant, *Lectures on Ethics*, 'Self-mastery', p. 138.
164 Ibid., p. 140. On Plato's analogy between state and individual, see above, p. 14 and n. 19.
165 I. Kant, *Anthropology from a Pragmatic Point of View*, bk III, §81, p. 174.
166 Kant, *Groundwork of the Metaphysics of Morals*, 4:429, p. 80.
167 Kant, *Lectures on Ethics*, 'Friendship', pp. 201–2.
168 Ibid., p. 203.
169 Ibid., p. 207.
170 Kant, *Lectures on Ethics*, 'Duties Towards the Body in Respect of Sexual Impulse', pp. 164–5.
171 Ibid., p. 163.
172 Ibid., pp. 166–7.
173 Kant, *Lectures on Ethics*, '*Crimina Carnis*', p. 170.
174 Ibid., p. 169.
175 Ibid., p. 170.
176 Cf. Schneewind, *Invention of Autonomy*, p. 6.

Chapter 2 Rationality in the Service of Desire

1 T. Hobbes, *Leviathan*, I, 6, p. 35.
2 Cf. I. Singer, *The Nature of Love*, vol. I, ch. 7, pp. 122ff.
3 Ovid, *Ovid in Love*, bk III, 'Vice and Veto', p. 93. Cf. *Erotic Poems*, 'Amores', bk 3, p. 143.
4 Ovid, *Erotic Poems*, 'Amores', bk 2, p. 122.
5 Ovid, *Erotic Poems*, 'The Art of Love', bk 3, p. 219: 'I was about to warn you against rank goatish armpits/And bristling hair on your legs.'
6 Epicurus, *Extant Remains*, §85, p. 57.
7 Lucretius, *De Rerum Natura*, bk 5, 1203, p. 473.
8 Ibid., bk 6, 41, p. 495.
9 Epicurus, *Extant Remains*, §82, p. 53.
10 Ibid., §§124–5, p. 85.
11 Lucretius, *De Rerum Natura*, bk 3, 59–64, p. 193.
12 Ibid., bk 3, 843–51, pp. 253–5 and cf. *On the Nature of the Universe*, l. 851, p. 121: '. . . even that contingency would still be no concern of ours once the chain of our identity had been snapped.'
13 'When behaving indecently in the market-place, he wished it were as easy to relieve hunger by rubbing an empty stomach': Diogenes Laertius, 'Diogenes' in *Lives of Eminent Philosophers*, vol. II, IV, 46, p. 47.
14 Lucretius, *De Rerum Natura*, bk 2, 20–36, p. 97.
15 Epicurus, *Extant Remains*, p. 139.
16 Ibid., p. 123.
17 Ibid., pp. 115 and 123.

18 Ibid., p. 109.
19 Lucretius, *De Rerum Natura*, bk 4, 1037–46, p. 357.
20 Ibid., bk 4, 1052–4, p. 359.
21 Lucretius, *On the Nature of the Universe*, bk 4, 1070–2, p. 163; cf. *De Rerum Natura*, p. 359.
22 Lucretius, *De Rerum Natura*, bk 4, 1073–120, pp. 361–3.
23 Ibid., bk 4, 1149–70, pp. 365–7.
24 On the tradition of courtly love see below ch. 3, §1, pp. 93–5.
25 C. S. Lewis, *The Allegory of Love*, p. 135.
26 G. de Lorris and J. de Meun, *The Romance of the Rose*, lines 19,671ff., p. 304.
27 Ibid., lines 19,599–657, pp. 302–3.
28 See E. McLeod, *The Order of the Rose*, pp. 65ff. and cf. M. Brabant, ed., *Politics, Gender, and Genre*, *passim*.
29 See C. de Pizan, *The Book of the City of Ladies* (*La cité des dames*). In fact, de Pizan effectively attacks *both* parts of the *Romance* when she points out the dangers for women lurking in the lofty ideals propagated by men: cf. C. de Pizan, *A Medieval Woman's Mirror of Honor: The Treasury of the City of Ladies*, bk I, ch. 27, p. 143. This work was first published only in 1497 as *Le trésor de la cité des dames* but originally written in 1405 as *Le livre des trois vertus*.
30 The surprising resilience of pagan sexual realism under the aegis of Church authority is emphasized by J. Boswell, *Christianity, Social Tolerance, and Homosexuality*, esp. pt III. On courtly love, see below ch. 3, §1, pp. 93–5.
31 See J. Huizinga, *The Waning of the Middle Ages* and J. Burckhardt, *The Civilization of the Renaissance in Italy*, pt III, 'The Revival of Antiquity'.
32 R. G. Collingwood, *Speculum Mentis*, ch. 1, p. 26.
33 Significantly, according to Collingwood, this eventual independence was only possible *because* of the long subservience to religion: ibid., ch. 1, pp. 29–30.
34 Ibid., ch. 1, p. 30.
35 See J. Saslow, *Ganymede in the Renaissance* and A. A. Kuzniar, ed., *Outing Goethe and his Age*. Cf. Collingwood, *The Principles of Art*, pp. 70 and 84–5. It is worth asking whether the West's intense appreciation of Greek culture at the expense of important Middle Eastern and Egyptian influences is a reflection of this homophile scholarly tradition (cf. M. Bernal, *Black Athena*, ch. 4, pp. 212–14).
36 B. P. Copenhaver and C. B. Schmitt, *Renaissance Philosophy*, p. 25 and cf. P. O. Kristeller, *Renaissance Thought*, ch. 1, pp. 8–11 and 22.
37 See, for example, A. Bray, *Homosexuality in Renaissance England*.
38 Valla's *On Pleasure* was reissued in 1431 under the less provocative title of *On the True and False Good*.
39 On Francis Bacon, see below pp. 60–1.
40 Copenhaver and Schmitt, *Renaissance Philosophy*, p. 148.
41 Cf. ch. 1, §1, pp. 11–12 above.

42 M. Ficino, *Commentary on Plato's Symposium on Love*, p. 72.
43 Ibid., p. 73.
44 Ibid., p. 168.
45 Ibid., p. 155.
46 Ibid., pp. 172–3.
47 Ibid., p. 135.
48 Ibid., p. 165 and cf. p. 161.
49 Ibid., p. 168.
50 Singer, *The Nature of Love*, vol. 2, p. 195.
51 See L. Faderman, *Surpassing the Love of Men*, pt I, B, esp. ch. 1, pp. 65–7.
52 G. Dall'Orto, 'Marsilio Ficino', p. 160.
53 See R. Norton, *Mother Clap's Molly House*.
54 F. Bacon, 'New Atlantis' in *Philosophical Works of Francis Bacon*, p. 725.
55 Ibid.
56 F. T. Stevens, 'Erasmus's "Tigress"', p. 137. On Renaissance attitudes to homosexuality, see Bray, *Homosexuality in Renaissance England*, esp. pp. 68f. The Renaissance ideal of friendship is notably represented in the writings of Michel de Montaigne: see below ch. 4, §1.
57 C. Taylor, *Hegel*, p. 4.
58 On the distinction here between 'reason' and 'rationality', see above pp. 2–3.
59 F. Bacon, *On the Advancement of Learning*, bk I, V, §12, p. 35.
60 See ibid. and R. Descartes, 'Discourse on the Method of Rightly Conducting the Reason' in *Philosophical Works of Descartes*, vol. 1.
61 Hobbes, *Leviathan*, pt 1, ch. 5, pp. 25–6. For discussion of Hobbes, see M. Oakeshott, Introduction to ibid. and Q. Skinner, *Reason and Rhetoric in the Philosophy of Hobbes*.
62 Hobbes, *Leviathan*, I, 6, p. 38.
63 Ibid., I, 6.
64 Ibid., I, 11, p. 63.
65 Ibid., I, 11, p. 64.
66 Ibid., I, 13, p. 83.
67 Ibid., I, 11, p. 67.
68 Ibid., I, 15, p. 104.
69 Ibid., I, 13, p. 82.
70 Ibid., II, 21, p. 142 and cf. ch. 18 on the extensive rights of the sovereign.
71 Ibid., II, 21, p. 143 and cf. I, 11, pp. 63ff.
72 See p. 48 and n. 1.
73 Hobbes, *Leviathan*, II, 27, p. 195.
74 Ibid., IV, 46, pp. 446–7.
75 See C. Pateman, *The Sexual Contract*, pp. 43–50.
76 See ibid. The patriarchal foundations of modern political thought are also explored in, for example, J. B. Elshtain, *Public Man, Private*

Woman, S. M. Okin, *Women in Western Political Thought* and H. Pitkin, *Fortune is a Woman*.

77 See I. O. Wade, *The Intellectual Development of Voltaire*.

78 'Si Dieu n'existait pas, il faudrait l'inventer': Voltaire, 'Épître à l'auteur du livre des *trois imposteurs*', p. 258.

79 He claims that seeing 'two or three young Jesuits take advantage of a few students' should not lead the observer to conclude that Ignatius Loyola had approved of such relations: Voltaire, 'The Love Called "Socratic" ', p. 13.

80 Ibid., p. 12.

81 Ibid.

82 Ibid.

83 Ibid., p. 13.

84 Ibid. Kant relies on essentially the same argument: see above, ch. 1, §5, p. 45.

85 On Plato's view of knowledge, see above, ch. 1, §1, pp. 13–14.

86 D. Hume, *A Treatise of Human Nature*, bk I. On the debate between empiricists and rationalists, see B. Aune, *Rationalism, Empiricism, and Pragmatism*.

87 Hume, *Treatise of Human Nature*, bk I, pt III, esp. Sns I–IV.

88 B. Russell, *The Problems of Philosophy*, ch. 6, p. 35.

89 Hume, *Treatise of Human Nature*, pp. xix–xxi.

90 D. Hume, 'Enquiry Concerning the Principles of Morals' in *Enquiries Concerning the Human Understanding and Concerning the Principles of Morals*, Sns I–III, §§133–63, pp. 169–204.

91 D. Hume, *Essays*, 'Of Suicide', pp. 577–89.

92 Hume, *Essays*, 'Of Polygamy and Divorces', p. 181.

93 Ibid., pp. 185ff.

94 Ibid., pp. 188–9.

95 Hume, *Essays*, 'Of Love and Marriage', p. 562.

96 Ibid., p. 560.

97 Hume, *Essays*, 'Of Moral Prejudices', pp. 538–9.

98 Hume, *Essays*, 'Of Suicide', p. 580.

99 Hume, *Treatise of Human Nature*, bk II, pt II, Sn. XI, pp. 394–6.

100 Hume, *Essays*, 'Of Love and Marriage', pp. 560–2. On Plato's *Symposium*, see above pp. 11–12. On Ficino's commentary, see above pp. 58–60.

101 D. Hume, *The History of England*, vol. II, ch. XIV, pp. 328–9.

102 Ibid., vol. II, ch. XIV, p. 344.

103 Ibid., vol. II, ch. XIV, p. 334.

104 Ibid., vol. II, ch. XIV, pp. 360–1.

105 See J. Bentham, 'An Introduction to the Principles of Morals and Legislation'.

106 See L. C. Boralevi, *Bentham and the Oppressed*, esp. ch. 3; J. E. Crimmins, *Secular Utilitarianism*, esp. ch. 9. See also L. Crompton, *Byron and Greek Love*, esp. chs 1 and 7.

107 J. Bentham, 'Essay on "Paederasty" ' and 'Offences against Taste'. For the unpublished manuscripts concerning sexual nonconformity, see D. G. Long, *The Manuscripts of Jeremy Bentham.*
108 As Crompton observes, these deprecatory remarks occur in the 1785 essay intended for publication but not in contemporaneous or subsequent notes. See L. Crompton, 'Jeremy Bentham's Essay on "Paederasty" ', p. 385.
109 J. Wolfenden, *Report of Great Britain Committee on Homosexual Offences and Prostitution* and H. L. A. Hart, *Law, Liberty and Morality.*
110 Bentham, 'Essay on "Paederasty", Part II', pp. 100–1.
111 Ibid., pp. 99–100.
112 ibid., pp. 97–8.
113 Bentham, Manuscripts, Box CLXI(a), folio 6.
114 Bentham, MSS, LXXIV(a), folio 218.
115 Bentham, 'Essay on "Paederasty", Part II', p. 92.
116 Bentham, MSS, LXXIV(a), folios 123–9.
117 Bentham, 'Essay on "Paederasty", Part I', pp. 391–2 citing Montesquieu, 'De l'esprit des lois': 'Il faudrait le proscrire quand il ne ferait que donner à un sexe les faiblesses de l'autre, et préparer à une vieillesse infâme par une jeunesse honteuse' (my translation).
118 Ibid., pp. 398–401.
119 Bentham quoted at Boralevi, *Bentham and the Oppressed*, p. 48. On Voltaire, see above pp. 65–7.
120 See J. I. Israel, *Radical Enlightenment.*
121 J. Bentham, 'Essay on "Paederasty", Part I', p. 402.
122 Bentham, 'Essay on "Paederasty", Part II', pp. 104–6.
123 Bentham, 'Essay on "Paederasty", Part I', p. 397.
124 Boralevi, *Bentham and the Oppressed*, p. 60. See also pp. 26–7 above.
125 Bentham, MSS, CLXI(b), folios 483–6. See also ch. 1, n. 87 above.
126 J. Bentham (Gamaliel Smith), *Not Paul, but Jesus.*
127 Bentham, 'Essay on "Paederasty", Part II', pp. 101–2. Cf. MSS, LXXIV(a), folios 141 and 195. If Bentham seems to display an unusual ignorance in this judgement, it is worth recalling that it would take more than a century for medical science to recognize the harmlessness of masturbation.
128 Bentham, 'Essay on "Paederasty", Part II', p. 101.
129 Cf. P. Singer, 'Heavy Petting', which is a response to M. Dekkers, *Dearest Pet.*
130 J. S. Mill, 'Bentham' in *Mill on Bentham and Coleridge*, pp. 42–68.
131 J. S. Mill, 'Utilitarianism', ch. II, p. 9.
132 J. Rawls, *A Theory of Justice*, ch. VII, §65, pp. 424–33 and cf. Mill, 'Utilitarianism', ch. II, pp. 8–10.
133 See F. H. Bradley, *Ethical Studies*, essay II, pp. 116ff. For a hint of Bradley's views on sex, see his 'On the Treatment of Sexual Detail in Literature'.

134 Mill, 'Utilitarianism', ch. II, pp. 8–10. However, Mill approaches the spirit of Bentham's views on sexuality in his essay on 'Nature': see below.
135 See A. P. Robson and J. M. Robson, eds, *Sexual Equality*.
136 Mill, 'Nature', pp. 64–5.
137 Ibid., p. 62.
138 Ibid., pp. 62–3.
139 Ibid., p. 64.
140 Mill, 'Utilitarianism', ch. IV, pp. 32–3.
141 On the economic interpretation of utilitarianism, see J. Plamenatz, *The English Utilitarians*, ch. VII and cf. R. E. Goodin, *Utilitarianism as a Public Philosophy*.
142 La Mettrie's radical materialism is developed in *L'Homme machine* or *Man the Machine* (1747): see J. O. de La Mettrie, *Machine Man and Other Writings*. Cf. Israel, *Radical Enlightenment*, pt V, ch. 37.
143 My translation: 'La mort est la fin de tout; après elle, je le répète, un abîme, un néant éternel; tout est dit, tout est fait . . . *La farce est jouée*.' La Mettrie, 'Système d'Épicure' in *De la volupté*, p. 182.
144 La Mettrie, 'Anti-Sénèque' in *De la volupté*, pp. 58–9.
145 Ibid., pp. 44–5.
146 My translation: 'Étouffer les dons de la nature, c'est être indigne de vivre.' La Mettrie, 'L'école de la volupté' in *De la volupté*, p. 135.
147 My translation: 'Je déplore le sort de l'humanité, d'être, pour ainsi dire, en d'aussi mauvaises mains que les siennes.' La Mettrie, 'Anti-Sénèque', p. 94. La Mettrie describes Montaique as the 'first Frenchman who has dared to think' (ibid., pp. 44–5).
148 My translation: '. . . car je ne vois pas qu'on ait rien de mieux à faire que de vivre.' Ibid., p. 68. On Epicureanism, see §1 above.
149 My translation: 'Tout âme, ils font abstraction de leur corps; tout corps, nous ferons abstraction de notre âme.' Ibid., p. 28.
150 Ibid., p. 29.
151 See Bentham, 'Introduction to the Principles of Morals and Legislation', ch. IV, pp. 151–4.
152 My translation: '. . . la volupté est à l'âme ce que le plaisir est au corps.' La Mettrie, 'L'école de la volupté', in *De la volupté*, p. 137.
153 My translation: 'Telle est la vraie volupté; l'esprit, et non l'instinct du plaisir, l'art d'en user sagement, de le ménager par raison, et de le goûter par sentiment.' Ibid., p. 142.
154 La Mettrie, *L'art de jouir* (1748) and *La volupté* (1750).
155 My translation and insertions: 'Aristote favorisait la ***** pour empêcher la multitude des citoyens, sans se soucier du précepte, *crecite* etc. On avait autrefois plus publiquement un G*** qu'on n'a aujourd'hui une maîtresse; cela est prouvé par la lecture de tous les Anciens qui célèbrent librement *l'oeuvre immonde, qui fait sans l'autre une moitié du monde*.' La Mettrie, 'Anti-Sénèque', pp. 54–5. This passage was omitted from the Berlin edition of 1774: see La Mettrie, *Oeuvres philosophiques*, p. 113.

156 My partial translation: 'Avec quelle délicatesse cet ancien auteur nous expose tous les genres de voluptés.' La Mettrie, 'L'école de la volupté', pp. 122–3 (120ff.).
157 My translation: 'Certes si les joies puisées dans la nature sont des crimes, le plaisir, le bonheur des hommes est d'être criminels. "*Heu! miseri, quorum gaudia crimen habent!*"' La Mettrie quoting Montaigne, 'Anti-Sénèque', p. 58.
158 Ibid., p. 91.
159 See above, §4, pp. 77–8.
160 See, for example, N. Schaeffer, *The Marquis de Sade* and Marquis de Sade, *The Complete Marquis de Sade*.
161 This view of nature foreshadows the harsh naturalism of social Darwinist and racist theories of the nineteenth and twentieth centuries.
162 My translation: '. . . ce n'est qu'en étendant la sphère de ses goûts et de ses fantaisies, que ce n'est qu'en sacrifiant tout à la volupté, que le malheureux individu connu sous le nom d'homme, et jeté malgré lui sur ce triste univers, peut réussir à semer quelques roses sur les épines de la vie.' Marquis de Sade, *Philosophie dans le boudoir*, 'Avant-propos: Aux libertins', p. 8.
163 My translation: '. . . la vertu n'est qu'une chimère, dont le culte ne consiste qu'en des immolations perpétuelles, qu'en des révoltes sans nombre contre les inspirations du tempérament. De tels mouvements peuvent-ils être naturels? La nature conseille-t-elle ce qui l'outrage?' Ibid., p. 46.
164 '. . . la propagation n'est nullement le but de la nature; elle n'en est qu'une tolérance.' Ibid., p. 115.
165 Ibid., p. 35.
166 Ibid., pp. 71–2.
167 My translation: '. . . l'homme est-il maître de ses goûts? Il faut plaindre ceux qui en ont de singuliers, mais ne les insulter jamais: leur tort est celui de la nature; ils n'étaient pas plus les maîtres d'arriver au monde avec des goûts différents que nous ne le sommes de naître ou bancal ou bien fait.' Ibid., p. 15.
168 Ibid., p. 175.
169 Ibid., p. 57.
170 Ibid., pp. 63–4.
171 Ibid., pp. 234–6.
172 Ibid., p. 97.
173 Ibid., pp. 40 and 82–3. In fact, Aristotle appears to refer to the same phenomenon, albeit as a kind of 'menstrual discharge' – 'Generation of Animals' in *Complete Works*, vol. I, §727b, pp. 10–11: '. . . yet often no conception takes place unless the liquid of the menstrual discharge is present in a right proportion'.
174 Cf. L. Bland and L. Doan, eds, *Sexology in Culture* and J. D. Steakley, *The Homosexual Emancipation Movement in Germany*. Sade's work can also be reinterpreted and rehabilitated as daringly crit-

ical philosophy of existence or as stark anticipation of the horrors of National Socialism and genocide.

175 S. de Beauvoir, 'Faut-il brûler Sade?' quoted in Singer, *The Nature of Love*, vol. II, p. 348.

176 Cf. P. Klossowski, *Sade My Neighbour*, esp. pp. 18 and 22.

177 Sade, *Philosophie dans le boudoir*, p. 222.

178 'L'imagination est l'aiguillon des plaisirs'. Ibid., pp. 88–90.

Chapter 3 Passion beyond Reason

1 My translation: 'Die begeisterte Diotima hat ihrem Sokrates nur die Hälfte der Liebe offenbart. Die Liebe ist nicht bloß das stille Verlangen nach dem Unendlichen; sie ist auch der heilige Genuß einer schönen Gegenwart. Sie ist nicht bloß eine Mischung, ein Übergang vom Sterblichen zum Unsterblichen, sondern sie ist eine völlige Einheit beider.' F. Schlegel, *Lucinde* in *Lucinde. Friedrich Schleiermacher, Vertraute Briefe über Friedrich Schlegels* '*Lucinde*', p. 67.

2 See §2.

3 See above, ch. 1, §§1–4.

4 The word 'pagan' comes from the Latin *paganus* ('villager', 'rustic'): *Concise Oxford Dictionary*.

5 An early guide to such practices is, ironically, St Augustine, *City of God*, II and VII: see above, pp. 32–3.

6 F. Nietzsche, *The Birth of Tragedy*.

7 See H. Chadwick, *The Early Church*, ch. 2, pp. 33ff.

8 I. Singer, *The Nature of Love*, vol. I, p. 170.

9 See above ch. 1, §3, pp. 27–9.

10 Cf. Singer, *Nature of Love*, vol. I, pp. 111–20.

11 A classic study of Christian mysticism is W. James, *The Varieties of Religious Experience*, esp. Lectures XVI–XVII.

12 St Teresa of Ávila, 'The Book of Her Life' in *The Collected Works of St Teresa of Ávila*, vol. I, ch. 20, p. 183.

13 St Teresa of Ávila, 'Meditations on the Song of Songs' (*c*.1566–75) in *Collected Works*, vol. II, ch. 2, p. 232 and cf. 'Book of Her Life', ch. 20, p. 184.

14 St John of the Cross, 'The Ascent of Mount Carmel' in *The Collected Works of St John of the Cross*, bk 3, ch. 25, §6, p. 312.

15 Ibid., bk 3, ch. 25, §6, p. 312.

16 Teresa of Ávila, 'The Interior Castle' in *Collected Works*, vol. II, VI, ch. 4, p. 381.

17 St Augustine, *Confessions*, *passim*.

18 Teresa of Ávila, 'The Book of Her Life', ch. 20, p. 182.

19 Teresa of Ávila, 'Meditations on the Song of Songs', ch. 6, p. 253.

20 Ibid., ch. 3, p. 237.

21 Ibid., ch. 6, p. 254.
22 Ibid., ch. 6, p. 253.
23 See K. Kavanaugh, 'The Book of Her Life – Introduction' in *The Collected Works of St Teresa of Ávila,* vol. I, esp. pp. 15–35.
24 Teresa of Ávila, 'The Book of Her Life', ch. 20, p. 179–80 and 'Interior Castle', VI, ch. 4, p. 384. This does not mean, however, that mysticism should simply be dismissed in Freudian terms as a 'sublimation' of repressed sexual urges.
25 Teresa of Ávila, 'Meditations on the Song of Songs' ch. 6, p. 252 and ch. 7, p. 258.
26 Teresa of Ávila, 'The Book of Her Life', ch. 20, pp. 172ff.
27 Teresa of Ávila, 'Meditations on the Song of Songs', ch. 1, p. 218.
28 Teresa of Ávila, 'Interior Castle', VI, ch. 2, p. 370. On the relation between religion and sexuality in women, see S. de Beauvoir, *The Second Sex*, p. 318.
29 Teresa of Ávila, 'The Book of Her Life', ch. 20, p. 178.
30 Ibid., ch. 29, pp. 251–2.
31 Teresa of Ávila, 'Interior Castle', VI, ch. 2, p. 369.
32 Teresa of Ávila, 'Meditations on the Song of Songs', ch. 1, pp. 220–1.
33 Ibid., ch. 4, p. 244.
34 Ibid., ch. 1, p. 221.
35 Singer, *Nature of Love*, vol. I, p. 43.
36 D. de Rougemont, *Passion and Society*, pp. 63ff. On Manicheanism, see above, ch. 1, §3, pp. 27–9.
37 Rougemont, *Passion and Society*, pp. 78ff. and 101. For criticism of Rougemont, see R. Scruton, *Sexual Desire*.
38 A. Capellanus, *The Art of Courtly Love*, bk I, p. 28.
39 Ibid., bk I, pp. 31 and 32.
40 Ibid., bk I, pp. 32–5.
41 Ibid., bk III, pp. 187–212.
42 Ibid., bk I, p. 30.
43 For a useful overview of Rousseau's thought as well as discussion of accusations of totalitarianism see T. O'Hagan, *Rousseau*, esp. ch. 5.
44 The traditions of idealist reason and hedonist rationality are considered in chs 1 and 2 above.
45 J.-J. Rousseau, *Émile, or Education*, bk I, p. 5.
46 Rousseau, 'Discourse on the Origin of Inequality' in *The Social Contract and Discourses*, pt I, p. 64. For his criticism of Hobbes's more pessimistic view of the state of nature, cf. p. 65.
47 Ibid., pt I, p. 66, n. 2.
48 Rousseau, *Émile*, bk IV, p. 174.
49 Rousseau, 'Discourse on the Origin of Inequality', pt I, p. 66, n. 2.
50 Rousseau, *Émile*, bk IV, p. 175.
51 The classic account of negative liberty is I. Berlin, 'Two Concepts of Liberty' in *Four Essays on Liberty* and cf. Introduction, pp. xxxviii–xxxix.
52 Rousseau, *Social Contract*, I, 8, pp. 177–8.

53 Sometimes Rousseau seems to assume that there were no continuing monogamous relationships, no marriage or family life in the state of nature, only occasional and transitory sexual couplings. At other times, he appears to treat the basic nuclear family as the original context for sexual relations. In both cases he assumes that nothing resembling love exists in the primitive state of social evolution. See S. M. Okin, *Women in Western Political Thought*, ch. 6, esp. pp. 109–15.
54 Rousseau, 'Discourse on the Origin of Inequality', pt II, p. 81.
55 Rousseau, 'Discourse on the Arts and Sciences' in *The Social Contract and Discourses*, pt I, p. 8.
56 Ibid., pt I, pp. 12–13.
57 Rousseau, *Émile*, IV, p. 175.
58 Ibid.
59 Ibid.
60 Cf. R. D. Masters, *The Political Philosophy of Rousseau*, pp. 38 and 51–2.
61 Cf. A. Bloom, *Love and Friendship*, pp. 50–6.
62 J.-J. Rousseau, *La Nouvelle Héloïse: Julie, or the New Eloise*, pt I, Letter L, p. 115.
63 Rousseau, *Émile*, V, p. 411.
64 Rousseau, *The New Eloise*, pt II, Letter II, pp. 162–3.
65 Ibid., pt I, Letter XLVI, p. 108.
66 M. Wollstonecraft, *A Vindication of the Rights of Woman*, ch. 5, p. 86.
67 Rousseau quoted at ibid., ch. 5, p. 88.
68 Ibid., ch. 3, p. 54, note.
69 Ibid., ch. 2, p. 35.
70 Ibid., ch. 4, p. 80.
71 Ibid., ch. 3. p. 52.
72 Ibid., ch. 2, p. 34 and cf. pp. 98–9.
73 Ibid., ch. 8, pp. 151–2.
74 Ibid., ch. 12, p. 182.
75 For a discussion of this allegation, see V. Sapiro, *A Vindication of Political Virtue*, pp. 138ff. and cf. C. Tomalin, *The Life and Death of Mary Wollstonecraft*.
76 Wollstonecraft, *Vindication*, ch. 5, p. 100.
77 Ibid., ch. 2, p. 35.
78 Ibid., ch. 5, pp. 118–22.
79 E. Burke, *A Philosophical Enquiry into the Origin of our Ideas of the Sublime and Beautiful*.
80 Cf. Singer, *Nature of Love*, vol. II, pp. 285–8.
81 See, for example, F. Schlegel, *On the Study of Greek Poetry*.
82 On Kant's philosophy, see above ch. 1, §5. Cf. my *Introduction to Continental Philosophy*, pp. 16–27.
83 See K. Ameriks, *The Cambridge Companion to German Idealism* and esp. P. Guyer, 'Absolute Idealism and the Rejection of Kantian Dualism'.

84 J. B. Robertson, 'Memoir of the Literary Life of Friedrich von Schlegel' in F. Schlegel, *The Philosophy of Life, and Philosophy of Language, in a Course of Lectures*, p. lvi.
85 On Kierkegaard, see below ch. 4, §4. F. Schlegel, 'Philosophy of Language' in *The Philosophy of Life, and Philosophy of Language, in a Course of Lectures*, p. 360.
86 Ibid., p. 507.
87 Ibid., p. 363.
88 Ibid., p. 358.
89 Ibid., pp. 361ff.
90 Ibid., p. 361.
91 Ibid., p. 371.
92 Schlegel, 'Philosophy of Life' in *The Philosophy of Life, and Philosophy of Language, in a Course of Lectures*, pp. 37–8.
93 Ibid., pp. 28–9.
94 Ibid., p. 38.
95 Ibid., pp. 39–43.
96 Schlegel, 'Philosophy of Language', p. 371.
97 Schlegel, 'Philosophy of Life', p. 31.
98 This argument appears in light phenomenological disguise in Scruton, *Sexual Desire*, p. 307: 'Without the fundamental experience of the otherness of the sexual partner, an important component of erotic love is therefore put in jeopardy.'
99 See p. 87 and n. 1.
100 Schlegel, *Lucinde*, p. 24.
101 M. B. Helfer, '"Confessions of an Improper Man"', p. 174.
102 My partial translation: 'Erinnere Dich, wie wenig uns immer . . . alles befriedigte, was über die Liebe als Reflexion gesagt und als Darstellung gedichtet ist, wie wir uns beklagten, daß man aus der Sinnlichkeit nichts zu machen weiß, als ein notwendiges Übel, das man nur aus Ergebung in den Willen Gottes und der Natur wegen erdulden muß, oder geistlose und unwürdige Libertinage, die sich rühmt, einen tierischen Trieb etwa bis zur Höhe der Kochkunst hinauf verfeinert und humanisiert zu haben.' F. Schleiermacher, *Vertraute Briefe über Schlegels Lucinde* in F. Schlegel, *Lucinde. Friedrich Schleiermacher, Vertraute Briefe über Friedrich Schlegels 'Lucinde'*, p. 97.
103 My translation: 'Ein Libertin mag verstehen mit einer Art von Geschmack den Gürtel zu lösen. Aber jenen höhern Kunstsinn der Wollust, durch den die männliche Kraft erst zur Schönheit gebildet wird, lehrt nur die Liebe allein den Jüngling.' Schlegel, *Lucinde*, p. 22.
104 Ibid.
105 Ibid., pp. 9ff. and *passim*.
106 Ibid., p. 15.
107 My partial translation from the following passage: '. . . daß die Frauen allein, die mitten im Schoß der menschlichen Gesellschaft Naturmenschen geblieben sind, den kindlichen Sinn haben, mit dem man die Gunst und Gabe der Götter annehmen muß.' Ibid., p. 61.

108 My translation: 'Du fühlst alles ganz und unendlich, Du weißt von keinen Absonderungen, Dein Wesen ist Eins und unteilbar.' Ibid., p. 10.
109 Ibid., p. 29.
110 Ibid., p. 12.
111 Ibid., p. 223 and cf. Helfer, ' "Confessions of an Improper Man" ', pp. 182ff.
112 My translation: 'Junge Männer aber, die ihm einigermaßen glichen, umfaßte er mit heißer Liebe und mit einer wahren Wut von Freundschaft.' Ibid., p. 39.
113 My translation: 'Es läßt sich denken, daß er, der sich eigentlich alles erlaubt hielt und sich selbst über das Lächerliche wegsetzen konnte, eine andre Schicklichkeit im Sinne und vor Augen hatte als die, welche allgemein galt.' Ibid., p. 50.
114 Ibid., 'On Fidelity and Jest', p. 65.
115 Ibid., p. 55.
116 My partial translation from the following passage: 'Es ist Ehe, ewige Einheit und Verbindung unsrer Geister, nicht bloß für das was wir diese oder jene Welt nennen, sondern für die eine wahre, unteilbare, namenlose, unendliche Welt, für unser ganzes ewiges Sein und Leben.' Schlegel, *Lucinde*, p. 11.
117 Ibid.
118 Ibid., pp. 28–9.
119 Schlegel, 'Philosophy of Language', p. 506.
120 Schleiermacher, *Vertraute Briefe*, pp. 109–10.
121 See M. Praz, *The Romantic Agony*.
122 From the perspective of Christian theology, the Romantic Christianity of Schlegel and Schleiermacher made an important contribution to the greater acceptance of inter-personal love in Lutheran Christianity. See Robertson, 'Memoir' in Schlegel, *Philosophy of Life*.
123 See above, §§2 and 3.
124 In his later writings, Goethe, like Schlegel, canvasses a more conservative solution. In *Wilhelm Meisters Wanderjahre*, as in Rousseau's *Julie*, Romantic love is transcended in abnegatory submission to the individual's social obligations.
125 Cf. R. Aronson, *Jean-Paul Sartre: Philosophy in the World*, chs 3–5.
126 See R. G. Collingwood, *The Principles of Art*, bk I, V, §3, p. 84; cf. Bradley, 'On the Treatment of Sexual Detail in Literature' and R. Grant, *The Politics of Sex*.
127 See Rougemont, *Passion and Society* and T. W. Adorno and M. Horkheimer, 'The Culture Industry: Enlightenment as Mass Deception' in *Dialectic of Enlightenment*, pp. 120–67.
128 On classical sexual realism, see above ch. 2, §1.
129 A. Schopenhauer, *The World as Will and Representation*, vol. II. Cf. P. Gardiner, *Schopenhauer*, pp. 41–66. On Kant's philosophy, see above ch. 1, §5.
130 Schopenhauer, *The World as Will and Representation*, vol. I, esp. bk II, §§17ff, pp. 95ff. On Spinoza, see below ch. 4, §2.

131 Schopenhauer at Gardiner, *Schopenhauer*, p. 177 and cf. pp. 176–80.
132 Schopenhauer, *The World as Will and Representation*, vol. II, ch. 44, p. 533.
133 Ibid., vol. II, ch. 44, pp. 533–4.
134 Ibid., vol. II, ch. 44, p. 538.
135 Ibid., vol. II, ch. 44, p. 542. Cf. R. Dawkins, *The Selfish Gene*.
136 Schopenhauer, *The World as Will and Representation*, vol. II, ch. 44, p. 535.
137 Ibid., vol. II, ch. 44, p. 535.
138 On Aquinas' development of this tradition, see above ch. 1, §4.
139 Schopenhauer, *The World as Will and Representation*, vol. II, ch. 48, pp. 603ff.
140 On Manicheanism, see above, ch. 1, §3, pp. 27–9. On the Marquis de Sade, see above, ch. 2, §5.
141 Schopenhauer, *The World as Will and Representation*, vol. II, ch. 44, appendix, p. 562.
142 Ibid., vol. II, ch. 44, appendix, p. 563. It is surely coincidence that Schopenhauer's remarks on pederasty were published shortly after his fifty-fourth birthday, when, according to Aristotle, men enter their second pederastic phase.
143 Ibid., vol. II, ch. 34, p. 406. Nietzsche diagnoses Schopenhauer's ascetic aestheticism in *Genealogy of Morals*, III, 6, pp. 103–6.
144 Cf. Gardiner, *Schopenhauer*, pp. 176–80.
145 See S. Freud, *Introductory Lectures on Psychoanalysis* and *Psychopathology of Everyday Life*.
146 On the Oedipus complex and the role of childhood sexuality in neurosis, see Freud, *Introductory Lectures on Psychoanalysis*, Lecture 21, pp. 373–82 and *passim*.
147 S. Freud, *On Sexuality*, Essay I, pp. 45–6.
148 Ibid., I, p. 57n.
149 Ibid., III, p. 127.
150 Ibid., I, p. 57n.
151 J. Neu, 'Freud and Perversion', p. 92.
152 See S. Freud, 'Civilization and its Discontents' and cf. below ch. 4, §7.
153 Freud quoted by Neu, 'Freud and Perversion', p. 89 and cf. S. Freud, *Leonardo*.
154 Freud, *Essays on Sexuality*, Preface to 4th edn, p. 43. On the relation between Freud and Plato, cf. G. Vlastos, *Platonic Studies*, pp. 27–8.
155 On Marcuse, see below ch. 4, §7.
156 Cf. K. Lewes, *Psychoanalysis and Male Homosexuality*.
157 See C. Waters, 'Havelock Ellis, Sigmund Freud and the State', pp. 168ff. and esp. p. 175.
158 A. S. Neill, *Summerhill*, p. 207. Cf. R. Hemmings, *Fifty Years of Freedom*, esp. ch. 10.

159 Neill, *Summerhill*, p. 207.
160 For idealist and hedonist approaches, see above chs 1 and 2.

Chapter 4 Perspectives on Reason and Sexuality

1 R. M. Schott, *Cognition and Eros*, p. 190.
2 M. de Montaigne, *The Complete Essays*, II, 12, 'An Apology for Raymond Sebond', p. 566.
3 Ibid., p. 599.
4 Ibid., p. 560. On Montaigne's distinctive approach to scepticism, see R. E. Flathman, *Freedom and its Conditions*, ch. 3.
5 Montaigne, *Essays*, II, 12, 'An Apology for Raymond Sebond', pp. 552–3.
6 Montaigne, *Essays*, I, 33, 'On Fleeing from Pleasures at the Cost of One's Life', pp. 244–5.
7 Montaigne, *Essays*, I, 31, 'On the Cannibals', p. 231.
8 Ibid.
9 Ibid., p. 236.
10 Montaigne, *Essays*, II, 12, 'An Apology for Raymond Sebond', p. 524.
11 Montaigne, *Essays*, I, 30, 'On Moderation', p. 223.
12 Montaigne, *Essays*, II, 12, 'An Apology for Raymond Sebond', p. 526.
13 Montaigne, *Essays*, I, 30, 'On Moderation', p. 226.
14 Montaigne, *Essays*, III, 5, 'On Some Lines of Virgil', p. 994.
15 Ibid., p. 1010.
16 Ibid., pp. 1009–10.
17 Montaigne, *Essays*, I, 30, 'On Moderation', p. 225.
18 Montaigne, *Essays*, II, 12, 'An Apology for Raymond Sebond', p. 526.
19 Ibid., p. 563.
20 Montaigne, *Essays*, III, 5, 'On Some Lines of Virgil', pp. 969–70, 998, 1003–4 and 1008–11.
21 Ibid., p. 956.
22 Ibid.
23 Ibid., p. 993.
24 Ibid., pp. 992–3.
25 Ibid., p. 992.
26 Ibid., p. 1003.
27 Ibid., p. 991 and Montaigne, *Essays*, 1, 28, 'On Affectionate Relationships', p. 211.
28 Montaigne, *Essays*, III, 5, 'On Some Lines of Virgil', pp. 961–4.
29 Ibid., pp. 975–82.
30 Ibid., p. 959.
31 Ibid., p. 1016.
32 Ibid., p. 966.
33 Ibid., p. 1012.
34 Ibid., p. 1001.

35 Ibid., pp. 964–5 and 973.
36 Montaigne, *Essays*, I, 28, 'On Affectionate Relationships', pp. 213–14.
37 Ibid., pp. 214–15.
38 Ibid., p. 217. Cf. Augustine's similar reaction to the loss of his young friend: see above, p. 31.
39 See J. Salazar, 'Michel Eyquem de Montaigne', pp. 316–17.
40 Montaigne, *Essays*, III, 5, 'On Some Lines of Virgil', pp. 1009 and 953.
41 Ibid., pp. 1013–14. This thought is taken up by Voltaire: see above, p. 66.
42 Montaigne, *Essays*, I, 28, 'On Affectionate Relationships', p. 210. 'A' refers here to the first edition of 1580, 'C' to additional material for a new edition planned at the time of Montaigne's death.
43 Ibid.
44 Ibid., pp. 211–12.
45 J. B. Schneewind, *The Invention of Autonomy*, p. 52.
46 For the implications of these distortions, see above chs 1 and 2.
47 B. de Spinoza, 'The Ethics' in *The Chief Works of Benedict de Spinoza*, vol. II, pts I–II.
48 J. I. Israel, *Radical Enlightenment*, pp. 707–9. On La Mettrie see ch. 2, §5.
49 On the seventeenth- and eighteenth-century debates between empiricists and rationalists, see above ch. 2, §3, p. 67 and n. 86.
50 On Hobbes, see above ch. 2, §3.
51 B. de Spinoza, 'A Political Treatise' in *A Theologico-Political Treatise and A Political Treatise*, II, 4, p. 292. On the influence of Hobbes, see M. Gullan-Whur, *Within Reason*, pp. 289–91 and *passim*.
52 Spinoza, 'Ethics', pt III, prop. VI, p. 136.
53 T. Hobbes, *Leviathan*, I, 11, p. 64.
54 Spinoza, 'Ethics', III, 6 and 7, p. 136.
55 Cf. S. Hampshire, 'Spinoza and the Idea of Freedom', pp. 55–6 and on Sartre, cf. below, §5.
56 Spinoza, 'Ethics', pt III, prop. LVIII, p. 171. On Spinoza's concept of freedom and its relationship to Hobbes, see my 'Spinoza on Positive Freedom'.
57 S. Hampshire, *Spinoza*, pp. 136–7.
58 Spinoza, 'Ethics', pt V, prop. III and corollary, p. 248.
59 Ibid., pt V, prop. IV, note, p. 249.
60 Cf. Schneewind, *The Invention of Autonomy*, p. 220.
61 M. Gatens, *Imaginary Bodies*, ch. 9, p. 132.
62 Spinoza, 'Ethics', pt III, prop. XI and note, p. 138.
63 Ibid., pt IV, prop. XLV, note, p. 219.
64 Ibid., pt IV, appendix, prop. XXXI, p. 242.
65 Gatens, *Imaginary Bodies*, ch. 9, p. 132.
66 Spinoza, 'Ethics', pt IV, appendix, prop. XXX, p. 242.
67 Ibid., pt IV, appendix, prop. XIX, p. 240.
68 Ibid., pt IV, appendix, prop. XX, p. 240.

69 My translation: 'Et le *conatus* ainsi défini, c'est le désir.' A. Mathéron, 'Spinoza et la sexualité', p. 438.
70 Ibid., p. 439.
71 For discussion of Hegel's attitude to women, see G. Lloyd, *The Man of Reason*, chs 4–6.
72 See ch. 2.
73 On Kant's philosophy, see above ch. 1, §5.
74 See G. W. F. Hegel, 'Life of Jesus' and 'Fragment on Love' in *Early Theological Writings*. On Schlegel's 'religion of love', see above ch. 3, §3.
75 On Platonic and Christian traditions of 'idealist reason', see above ch. 1.
76 See above, ch. 1, §5.
77 On the utilitarianism of Bentham and J. S. Mill, see above ch. 2, §4.
78 G. W. F. Hegel, *The Philosophy of History*, pt IV, sn III, ch. III, p. 456.
79 On Rousseau's idea of moral freedom see above, p. 98.
80 G. W. F. Hegel, *Phenomenology of Spirit*, §§167–77, pp. 104ff.
81 Ibid., §§175–6, pp. 109–110.
82 Ibid., §175, p. 110.
83 On Marx's appropriation of the dialectic of master and bondsman see, for example, E. Kedourie, *Hegel and Marx: Introductory lectures*, esp. pp. 110ff.
84 For Sartre's illuminating phenomenological account of sexual relations in these terms, see below §5.
85 Hegel, *Phenomenology of Spirit*, §361, p. 218. Cf. Kant, above p. 44.
86 J. N. Findlay in ibid., analysis of §363, p. 542.
87 Hegel, *Phenomenology of Spirit* §225, pp. 135–6.
88 G. W. F. Hegel, *Philosophy of Right*, §161, addition, p. 262.
89 Ibid., §§162–3, p. 112.
90 Ibid., §§169 and 173, pp. 116–17.
91 Ibid., §§167–8, pp. 115–16.
92 Ibid., §§164–5, pp. 113–14.
93 Ibid., §166, pp. 114–15.
94 Ibid., §§170–2, pp. 116–17.
95 Ibid., §§174–5, pp. 117–18. In fact, Hegel spent some years as principal of a secondary school in Nuremberg and apparently managed to combine a genuine concern for his charges with a responsible educational programme: see T. Pinkard, *Hegel: A biography*, ch. 7, esp. pp. 304–7.
96 See for example T. Nicolacopoulos and G. Vassilacopoulos, *Hegel and the Logical Structure of Love*, esp. ch. 10.
97 See Pinkard, *Hegel*, *passim*.
98 See M. Richter, *The Politics of Conscience*, ch. 7, pp. 195 and 217. For F. H. Bradley's criticisms of J. S. Mill, see above p. 76 and n. 133.
99 Kierkegaard quoted in translator's preface to S. Kierkegaard, *Either/Or*, vol. I, p. xi.

100 First clearly formulated by Plato and Aristotle, these objections have been recycled with little variation by philosophers and theologians ever since. See above, ch. 1, §§1–2.
101 Kierkegaard, *Either/Or*, vol. I, pp. 60–1.
102 Ibid., p. 59.
103 Ibid.
104 Ibid., pp. 59–60.
105 Ibid., pp. 69 and 105.
106 Ibid., p. 26.
107 Ibid., p. 28.
108 Ibid., p. 30.
109 Ibid., p. 40.
110 Ibid., p. 286.
111 Ibid., p. 282.
112 Ibid., p. 174.
113 The perverse dialectic of mutual attraction and repulsion is definitively portrayed in Marcel Proust's *À la recherche du temps perdu*, whose narrator recounts in tireless detail the cycles of hope and despair, attraction and indifference that constitute the only reliable content of his love affairs.
114 Kierkegaard, *Either/Or*, vol. I, p. 178.
115 S. Kierkegaard, *Either/Or*, vol. II, pp. 38–40.
116 Ibid., pp. 70ff.
117 Ibid., pp. 66–7.
118 Ibid.
119 Ibid., p. 37.
120 Ibid., p. 91.
121 S. Kierkegaard, *Fear and Trembling*, p. 82.
122 Kierkegaard, *Either/Or*, vol. II, pp. 46.
123 Ibid., p. 44.
124 J.-P. Sartre, *Being and Nothingness*, pp. 24–5.
125 Ibid., pp. 48ff. and cf. J.-P. Sartre *Existentialism and Humanism*, pp. 28–9. On Freud, see above ch. 3, §5.
126 Sartre, *Being and Nothingness*, pp. 63–7.
127 Ibid., p. 65. Sartre's attitude to the emotions as a deliberate orientation to the world is developed in his *Sketch for a Theory of the Emotions*.
128 Sartre, *Being and Nothingness*, pp. 63–4.
129 Ibid., p. 79.
130 Ibid., p. 305.
131 Ibid., p. 326. The notion of the world as an instrumental complex is borrowed from Heidegger.
132 Ibid., p. 329.
133 Sartre uses the masculine form throughout.
134 Sartre, *Being and Nothingness*, pp. 262–3.
135 Ibid., p. 263.
136 Ibid., p. 364.

137 Ibid., p. 363. On Hegel's dialectic, see above §3.
138 Ibid., pp. 366–7.
139 Ibid., p. 371.
140 Ibid., p. 376. A similar view is presented in Kierkegaard's 'Shadowgraphs': see above, pp. 149–50.
141 Ibid., pp. 377–8. Kierkegaard did not consider this particular escape from the lover's endless 'reflection'.
142 Ibid., pp. 378–9.
143 See G. Deleuze, 'Coldness and Cruelty'.
144 Sartre, *Being and Nothingness*, pp. 379–80.
145 Ibid., pp. 383–4.
146 Ibid., pp. 384–5.
147 Ibid., p. 386.
148 Ibid., p. 389.
149 Ibid., p. 393.
150 Ibid., pp. 386–7.
151 Ibid., p. 394.
152 Ibid., pp. 396–9.
153 Ibid., pp. 401–2.
154 Ibid., pp. 405–6.
155 Ibid., pp. 410–12.
156 R. Aronson, *Jean-Paul Sartre*, p. 81.
157 On Freud's notion of the 'death-wish' as an essential counterpart of the pleasure principle see H. Marcuse, *Eros and Civilization*, ch. 2. On Schopenhauer and Wagner, see above ch. 3, §4.
158 Sartre, *Being and Nothingness*, p. 397.
159 E.g. J.-P. Sartre, *Jean Genet*.
160 See S. Kruks, 'Teaching Sartre about Freedom' and E. Fullbrook and K. Fullbrook, *Simone de Beauvoir*, esp. ch. 6, pp. 106ff.
161 M. Merleau-Ponty, *Phenomenology of Perception*, pp. 138–9, emphasis added.
162 Ibid., pp. 136–7.
163 Ibid., p. 377.
164 S. de Beauvoir, *Pyrrhus et Cinéas*, pp. 9–12.
165 Quoted at Fullbrook and Fullbrook, *Simone de Beauvoir*, p. 106.
166 S. de Beauvoir, *The Ethics of Ambiguity*, pp. 82–3.
167 S. de Beauvoir, *The Second Sex*, p. 295.
168 Ibid., pp. 16–18.
169 Merleau-Ponty, *Phenomenology of Perception*, pp. 157–8.
170 Beauvoir, *The Second Sex*, pp. 299ff.
171 Ibid., pp. 306ff.
172 Ibid., pp. 373–4.
173 Ibid., pp. 392ff.
174 Ibid., p. 425.
175 Sartre, *Jean Genet*, p. 78.
176 Ibid., p. 41, note.
177 Beauvoir, *The Second Sex*, pp. 425 and 437.

178 Ibid., pp. 426–7.
179 Ibid., p. 426.
180 Ibid., p. 421. Beauvoir's suggestions about the possibilities of erotic experience are developed at length in D. B. Bergoffen's *The Philosophy of Simone de Beauvoir*.
181 Beauvoir, *The Second Sex*, pp. 421–2.
182 Ibid., pp. 422–3 and cf. pp. 413 and 702.
183 H. Marcuse, 'Sartre's Existentialism', p. 175 and *passim*.
184 See also D. Kellner, *Herbert Marcuse and the Crisis of Marxism*, ch. 6 and V. Geoghegan, *Reason and Eros*, esp. ch. 3.
185 S. Freud, 'Civilization and its Discontents', IV, pp. 293–4.
186 See above, ch. 3, §5.
187 Ibid., IV, p. 294.
188 Ibid., VIII, pp. 339–40.
189 Ibid., IV, pp. 293–4.
190 In practice, though, disadvantaged social groups have sometimes enjoyed greater freedom from restrictive sexual norms: cf. J. D'Emilio and E. B. Freedman, *Intimate Matters*, pp. 122ff. and *passim*.
191 Marcuse, *Eros and Civilization*, pp. 43–4.
192 Ibid., chs 10–11, pp. 161ff. and cf. H. Marcuse, *An Essay on Liberation*.
193 Cf. H. Marcuse, *Soviet Marxism*.
194 Marcuse, *An Essay on Liberation*, introduction, p. 6.
195 T. W. Adorno and M. Horkheimer, *Dialectic of Enlightenment*, p. 137.
196 Marcuse, *Eros and Civilization*, pp. 50ff. and *passim*. Cf. Oakeshott 'On the Character of a Modern European State', which traces the origins of the productivist ethic to Francis Bacon.
197 On the direction of libido to technological objects see H. Marcuse, 'Some Social Implications of Modern Technology', p. 144.
198 Deeply influenced by the Vietnam War and the arms race, Marcuse perhaps unwisely sees the performance principle as evidence of the 'death-wish' postulated by Freud. H. Marcuse, *Five Lectures*, ch. 1, pp. 17–18.
199 See, for example, W. Reich, *The Invasion of Compulsory Sex-Morality*, pp. 51ff.: 'If the greater part of a society lives sex-economically, there can be no neuroses, simply because these disorders arise from inhibited genital life' (p. 51).
200 Marcuse, *Five Lectures*, ch. 3, pp. 56ff.
201 Marcuse, *An Essay on Liberation*, I, p. 9.
202 Ibid., II, p. 37.
203 Marcuse, *Five Lectures*, ch. 1, p. 22.
204 Marcuse, *An Essay on Liberation*, I, p. 10.
205 Ibid., I, pp. 16–17.
206 Ibid., I, pp. 20–2.
207 Ibid., IV, p. 91.
208 D. Halperin, *Saint Foucault*, pp. 15–16.
209 M. Foucault, 'Afterword: The Subject and Power', p. 208.

210 Foucault's account of 'genealogy' is presented in his essay 'Nietzsche, Genealogy, History'.
211 See for example M. Foucault, *Madness and Civilization* and *Discipline and Punish*.
212 M. Foucault, *The History of Sexuality*, vol. I.
213 See ibid., pts I–II.
214 M. Foucault, *The Use of Pleasure* and *The Care of the Self*.
215 Foucault, *The Use of Pleasure*, p. 86.
216 Ibid., p. 187.
217 Cf. D. Halperin, *One Hundred Years of Homosexuality*, ch. 5. According to Foucault, this is also the starting-point for the Socratic and Platonic reflections on love, which address the problem of 'how to make the object of pleasure into a subject who was in control of his pleasures' (*The Use of Pleasure*, p. 225).
218 Foucault, *The Use of Pleasure*, p. 50.
219 Ibid., p. 75.
220 Ibid., p. 98.
221 Ibid., p. 31.
222 Ibid., p. 23.
223 Ibid., p. 92.
224 Ibid., pp. 80–1.
225 Ibid., pp. 120–1. Cf. P. Brown, *Body and Society* and P. Veyne, *Roman Erotic Elegy*.
226 M. Foucault, *Religion and Culture*, p. 121.
227 Ibid., chs 12–13.
228 Ibid., pp. 162–3 and *passim*.
229 See Halperin, *One Hundred Years of Homosexuality*, ch. 1.
230 Foucault, *The History of Sexuality*, vol. I, pp. 67ff.
231 Foucault, *Religion and Culture*, pp. 118–19.
232 Foucault, *The History of Sexuality*, vol. I, pp. 140–5 and cf. G. Burchell et al., eds, *The Foucault Effect*. The contemporary sense of 'police' (from the early nineteenth century) as an organization officially devoted solely to the enforcement of law has lost the broader connotations of administrative policy.
233 D. Halperin, 'Is there a History of Sexuality?', p. 417. A similar position is developed by Martha Nussbaum, *Sex and Social Justice*, ch. 10.
234 Halperin, *One Hundred Years of Homosexuality*, ch. 1, esp. pp. 15ff. It would follow, as Halperin also argues, that heterosexuality has existed for an even shorter time, since that concept was formulated only *after* and in response to the 'invention' of homosexuality (p. 17).
235 Foucault, *The History of Sexuality*, vol. I, p. 157.
236 Foucault, 'Afterword: The Subject and Power', p. 216.
237 Halperin, *Saint Foucault*, p. 60.
238 Ibid., pp. 77–9.
239 Ibid., p. 111.
240 Ibid., p. 97.
241 Ibid., pp. 85ff.

242 Ibid., p. 81.
243 M. Vernon, 'I Am Not What I Am', p. 201.
244 Ibid., p. 208.
245 Ibid., pp. 206–9.
246 On Marcuse, see the previous section.

Afterthoughts

1 R. M. Unger, *Democracy Realized*, p. 18.
2 See above chs 1–3.
3 More recent zoology suggests that the exclusiveness of these attributes should be seen as a matter of degree: see, for example, M. Bright, *Animal Language*. For a recent philosophical argument for a stricter demarcation, see J. Bennett, *Rationality*.
4 It seems reasonable to suppose that animals are not aware, or at least are less aware, of their animality. Such suppositions are, in any case, philosophically suspect for most of us.
5 On Montaigne and Hegel, see above ch. 4, §§1 and 3. For a related view of the holism of human experience, see M. Oakeshott, *Experience and its Modes*.
6 On Kierkegaard, Sartre, Beauvoir and Merleau-Ponty, see above ch. 4, §§4–6.
7 Some of these implications are explored by J. Grimshaw, 'Ethics, Fantasy and Self-transformation'. For a variety of approaches to sexual morality, see, for example, I. Primoratz, *Ethics and Sex*, R. Scruton, *Sexual Desire*, L. Gruen and G. E. Panichas, eds, *Sex, Morality, and the Law*, A. Soble, ed., *The Philosophy of Sex*, R. Baker and F. Elliston, eds, *Philosophy and Sex* and M. Blasius and S. Phelan, eds, *We Are Everywhere*.
8 See above, ch. 3, §5 and ch. 4, §§5–8. And of course, many others have contributed to understanding the politics of sexuality.
9 See p. 179 and n. 1.

Bibliography

Adorno, T. W. and Horkheimer, M.: *Dialectic of Enlightenment*, trans. J. Cumming (Verso, London and New York, 1979).

Ameriks, K.: *The Cambridge Companion to German Idealism* (Cambridge University Press, Cambridge and New York, 2000).

Annas, J.: *Platonic Ethics: Old and new* (Cornell University Press, Ithaca, NY and London, 1999).

Aquinas, St Thomas: *Philosophical Texts*, trans. T. Gilby (Oxford University Press, Oxford and New York, 1951).

Aquinas, St Thomas: *Summa Theologiae*, trans. T. Gilby et al. (Blackfriars/Eyre & Spottiswoode, London, and McGraw-Hill, New York, 1964–8), 60 vols.

Aronson, R.: *Jean-Paul Sartre: Philosophy in the world* (Verso, London, 1980).

Aristotle, *The Complete Works of Aristotle*, ed. J. Barnes (Princeton University Press, Princeton, NJ, 1984), 2 vols.

Augustine, St: *City of God*, trans. H. Bettenson (Penguin, London and New York, 1984).

Augustine, St: *Confessions*, trans. H. Chadwick (Oxford University Press, Oxford and New York, 1991).

Aune, B.: *Rationalism, Empiricism, and Pragmatism: An introduction* (Random House, New York, 1970).

Bacon, F.: *Philosophical Works of Francis Bacon*, ed. J. M. Robertson (George Routledge, London, 1905).

Bacon, F.: *On the Advancement of Learning*, ed. G. W. Kitchin (Dent, London, 1973).

Baker, R. and Elliston, F., eds: *Philosophy and Sex* (Prometheus Books, Buffalo, NY, 1975).

Beauvoir, S. de: *Pyrrhus et Cinéas* (Gallimard, Paris, 1944).

Beauvoir, S. de: *The Ethics of Ambiguity*, trans. B. Frechtman (Citadel Press, Secaucus, NJ, 1948).

Beauvoir, S. de: *The Second Sex*, trans. H. M. Parshley (Penguin, Harmondsworth, 1972).

Beiner, R.: *Political Judgment* (Methuen, London, 1983).

Bennett, J.: *Rationality: An essay towards an analysis* (Routledge and Kegan Paul, London, 1964).

Bentham, J. (Gamaliel Smith): *Not Paul, but Jesus* (John Hunt, London, 1823).

Bentham, J.: 'Offences against Taste', Appendix to J. Bentham, *The Theory of Legislation*, ed. C. K. Ogden (Paul, Trench, Trubner, London, 1931).

Bentham, J.: 'An Introduction to the Principles of Morals and Legislation' in *A Fragment on Government, and An Introduction to the Principles of Morals and Legislation*, ed. W. Harrison (Basil Blackwell, Oxford, 1960).

Bentham, J.: 'Essay on "Paederasty" ', ed. L. Crompton in *Journal of Homosexuality*, 3, 4, 1978, pp. 383–405 (part I) and 4, 1, 1978, pp. 91–107 (part II).

Bergoffen, D. B.: *The Philosophy of Simone de Beauvoir: Gendered phenomenologies, erotic generosities* (State University of New York Press, Albany, NY, 1997).

Berlin, I.: *Four Essays on Liberty* (Oxford University Press, Oxford and New York, 1969).

Bernal, M.: *Black Athena: The Afroasiatic roots of classical civilization* (Vintage, London, 1991).

Bland, L. and Doan, L., eds: *Sexology in Culture: Labelling bodies and desires* (Polity Press, Cambridge, 1998).

Blasius, M. and Phelan, S., eds: *We Are Everywhere: A historical sourcebook of gay and lesbian politics* (Routledge, New York and London, 1997).

Bloom, A.: *Love and Friendship* (Simon & Schuster, New York and London, 1993).

Boralevi, L. C.: *Bentham and the Oppressed* (de Gruyter, Berlin and New York, 1984).

Boswell, J.: *Christianity, Social Tolerance, and Homosexuality: Gay people in Western Europe from the beginning of the Christian era to the fourteenth century* (University of Chicago Press, Chicago and London, 1980).

Brabant, M., ed.: *Politics, Gender, and Genre: The political thought of Christine de Pizan* (Westview Press, Boulder, CO and Oxford, 1992).

Bradley, F. H.: *Ethical Studies*, 2nd edn (Clarendon Press, Oxford, 1927).

Bradley, F. H.: 'On the Treatment of Sexual Detail in Literature' in *Collected Essays*, 2 vols (Oxford University Press, Oxford, 1935), vol. 2, pp. 616–27.

Bray, A.: *Homosexuality in Renaissance England* (Gay Men's Press, London and Alyson Publications, Boston, 1982).

Bright, M.: *Animal Language* (Cornell University Press, Ithaca, NY, 1984).

Brown, P.: *The Body and Society: Men, women, and sexual renunciation in early Christianity* (Columbia University Press, New York, 1988).

Burchell, G., Gordon, C. and Miller, P., eds: *The Foucault Effect: Studies in governmentality* (University of Chicago Press, Chicago, 1991).

Burckhardt, J.: *The Civilization of the Renaissance in Italy: An essay*, trans. S. G. C. Middlemore (Phaidon Press, London, 1960).
Burke, E.: *A Philosophical Enquiry into Our Ideas of the Sublime and the Beautiful*, ed. A. Phillips (Oxford University Press, Oxford and New York, 1990).
Capellanus, Andreas: *The Art of Courtly Love*, trans. J. J. Parry (New York, F. Ungar, 1959).
Chadwick, H.: *The Early Church* (Penguin, Harmondsworth, 1967).
Collingwood, R. G.: *Speculum Mentis, or the Map of Knowledge* (Oxford University Press, Oxford, 1924).
Collingwood, R. G.: *The Principles of Art* (Clarendon Press, Oxford, 1938).
Copenhaver, B. P. and Schmitt, C. B.: *Renaissance Philosophy* (Oxford University Press, Oxford and New York, 1992).
Crimmins, J. E.: *Secular Utilitarianism: Social science and the critique of religion in the thought of Jeremy Bentham* (Oxford University Press, Oxford and New York, 1990).
Crompton, L.: 'Jeremy Bentham's Essay on "Paederasty": An Introduction', *Journal of Homosexuality*, 3, 4, 1978, pp. 383–6.
Crompton, L.: *Byron and Greek Love: Homophobia in 19th-century England* (Gay Men's Press, Swaffham, 1998).
Dall'Orto, G.: 'Marsilio Ficino' in R. Aldrich and G. Wotherspoon, eds, *Who's Who in Gay and Lesbian History* (Routledge, London and New York, 2001), pp. 159–61.
Dawkins, R.: *The Selfish Gene* (Oxford University Press, Oxford and New York, 1989).
Dekkers, M.: *Dearest Pet: On bestiality*, trans. P. Vincent (Verso, London and New York, 2000).
Deleuze, G.: 'Coldness and Cruelty' in L. von Sacher-Masoch, *Masochism*, trans. J. McNeil (Zone Books, New York, 1989).
D'Emilio, J. and Freedman, E. B.: *Intimate Matters: A history of sexuality in America* (Harper and Row, New York and London, 1988).
Descartes, R.: *Philosophical Works of Descartes*, ed. E. S. Haldane and G. R. T. Ross (Dover, London, 1955), 2 vols.
Dover, K. J.: *Greek Homosexuality* (Duckworth, London, 1978).
Elshtain, J. B.: *Public Man, Private Woman: Women in social and political thought* (Princeton University Press, Princeton, NJ, 1981).
Epicurus: *The Extant Remains*, trans. C. Bailey (Clarendon Press, Oxford, 1926).
Faderman, L.: *Surpassing the Love of Men: Romantic friendship and love between women from the Renaissance to the present* (William Morrow, New York, 1981).
Ficino, M.: *Commentary on Plato's Symposium on Love*, trans. S. Jayne, 2nd rev. edn (Spring Publications, Dallas, 1985).
Flathman, R. E.: *Freedom and its Conditions: Discipline, autonomy, resistance* (Routledge, New York and London, 2003).
Foucault, M.: *Madness and Civilization: A history of insanity in the Age of Reason*, trans. R. Howard (Tavistock, London, 1971).

Foucault, M.: 'Nietzsche, Genealogy, History' in *Language, Counter-memory, Practice: Selected essays and interviews*, trans. D. F. Bouchard and S. Simon (Basil Blackwell, Oxford and Cornell University Press, Ithaca, NY, 1977).

Foucault, M.: *The History of Sexuality, Volume I: An introduction*, trans. R. Hurley (Penguin Books, Harmondsworth, 1978).

Foucault, M.: *Discipline and Punish: The birth of the prison*, trans. A. Sheridan (Penguin Books, Harmondsworth and New York, 1979).

Foucault, M: 'Afterword: The Subject and Power' in H. L. Dreyfus and P. Rabinow, *Michel Foucault: Beyond structuralism and hermeneutics* (Harvester, Brighton, 1982).

Foucault, M.: *The Use of Pleasure: The history of sexuality*, vol. 2, trans. R. Hurley (Penguin Books, London and New York, 1987).

Foucault, M.: *The Care of the Self: The history of sexuality*, vol. 3, trans. R. Hurley (Penguin Books, London and New York, 1990).

Foucault, M.: *Religion and Culture*, ed. J. R. Carrette (Routledge, London and New York, 1999).

Freud, S.: *Psychopathology of Everyday Life*, ed. A. A. Brill (Penguin Books, Harmondsworth, 1938).

Freud, S.: *Leonardo, and a Memory of His Childhood*, trans. A. Tyson (Penguin Books, Harmondsworth, 1963).

Freud, S.: *Introductory Lectures on Psychoanalysis*, trans. J. Strachey (Penguin Books, Harmondsworth, 1973).

Freud, S.: *On Sexuality: Three Essays on the Theory of Sexuality and other works*, trans. J. Strachey (Penguin Books, Harmondsworth, 1977).

Freud, S.: 'Civilization and its Discontents' in *Civilization, Society and Religion: Group Psychology, Civilization and its Discontents and other works*, trans. J. Strachey (Penguin Books, London and New York, 1991).

Fullbrook, E. and Fullbrook, K.: *Simone de Beauvoir: A critical introduction* (Polity Press, Cambridge, 1998).

Gadamer, H.-G.: *Truth and Method*, trans. J. Weinsheimer and D. G. Marshall, 2nd rev. edn (Continuum, New York, 1994).

Gardiner, P.: *Schopenhauer* (Penguin Books, Harmondsworth, 1963).

Gatens, M.: *Feminism and Philosophy: Perspectives on difference and equality* (Polity Press, Cambridge, 1991).

Gatens, M.: *Imaginary Bodies: Ethics, power and corporeality* (Routledge, London and New York, 1996).

Geoghegan, V.: *Reason and Eros: The social theory of Herbert Marcuse* (Pluto Press, London, 1981).

Gilson, E.: *The Philosophy of St Thomas Aquinas*, trans. E. Bullough (Books for Libraries Press, Freeport, NY, 1971).

Gomperz, T.: *Griechische Denker: Eine Geschichte der antiken Philosophie*, 3rd edn (Veit & Comp, Leipzig, 1911–12), 3 vols.

Goodin, R. E.: *Utilitarianism as a Public Philosophy* (Cambridge University Press, Cambridge and New York, 1995).

Grant, R.: *The Politics of Sex and Other Essays: On conservatism, culture and imagination* (St Martin's Press, New York, 2000).

Grimshaw, J.: 'Ethics, Fantasy and Self-transformation' in A. Soble, ed., *The Philosophy of Sex: Contemporary readings* (Rowman and Littlefield, Lanham, MD and Oxford, 1997), pp. 175–87.
Grosz, E.: *Sexual Subversions: Three French feminists* (Allen and Unwin, Sydney, 1989).
Gruen, L. and Panichas, G. E., eds: *Sex, Morality, and the Law* (Routledge, London and New York, 1997).
Gullan-Whur, M.: *Within Reason: A life of Spinoza* (Random House, London, 2000).
Guthrie, W. K. C.: *A History of Greek Philosophy* (Cambridge University Press, Cambridge, 1962–82), 6 vols.
Hadot, P.: *Philosophy as a Way of Life: Spiritual exercises from Socrates to Foucault* (Blackwell, Oxford and New York, 1995).
Halperin, D. M.: *One Hundred Years of Homosexuality, and other essays on Greek love* (Routledge, New York and London, 1990).
Halperin, D. M.: 'Is there a History of Sexuality?' in *The Lesbian and Gay Cultural Studies Reader*, eds H. Abelove, M. A. Barale and D. Halperin (Routledge, New York and London, 1993).
Halperin, D.: *Saint Foucault: Towards a gay hagiography* (Oxford University Press, Oxford and New York, 1995).
Hampshire, S.: *Spinoza* (Penguin Books, Harmondsworth, 1951).
Hampshire, S.: 'Spinoza and the Idea of Freedom' in P. F. Strawson, ed., *Studies in the Philosophy of Thought and Action* (Oxford University Press, Oxford, 1968).
Hart, H. L. A.: *Law, Liberty and Morality* (Oxford University Press, Oxford, 1963).
Hegel, G. W. F.: *Early Theological Writings*, trans. T. M. Knox and R. Kroner (University of Chicago Press, Chicago, 1948).
Hegel, G. W. F.: *Philosophy of Right*, trans. T. M. Knox (Oxford University Press, Oxford and New York, 1952).
Hegel, G. W. F.: *Phenomenology of Spirit*, trans. A. V. Miller (Oxford University Press, Oxford and New York, 1977).
Hegel, G. W. F.: *The Philosophy of History*, trans. J. Sibree (Prometheus Books, Buffalo, NY, 1991).
Helfer, M. B.: '"Confessions of an Improper Man": Friedrich Schlegel's *Lucinde*' in A. A. Kuzniar, ed., *Outing Goethe and His Age* (Stanford University Press, Stanford, CA, 1996).
Hemmings, R.: *Fifty Years of Freedom: A study in the development of the ideas of A. S. Neill* (Allen and Unwin, London, 1972).
Hobbes, T.: *Leviathan, or the Matter, Forme and Power of a Commonwealth Ecclesiasticall and Civil*, ed. M. Oakeshott (Basil Blackwell, Oxford, 1955).
Huizinga, J.: *The Waning of the Middle Ages: A study of the forms of life, thought and art in France and the Netherlands in the dawn of the Renaissance*, trans. F. Hopman (Doubleday, New York, 1954).
Hume, D.: *The History of England*, vol. II (Cadell and Davies, London, 1807).

Hume, D.: *A Treatise of Human Nature*, ed. L. A. Selby-Bigge (Clarendon Press, Oxford, 1888).

Hume, D.: *Enquiries Concerning the Human Understanding and Concerning the Principles of Morals*, ed. L. A. Selby-Bigge, 2nd edn (Clarendon Press, Oxford, 1902).

Hume, D.: *Essays Moral, Political, and Literary*, ed. E. F. Miller (Liberty Fund, Indianapolis, 1987).

Israel, J. I.: *Radical Enlightenment: Philosophy and the making of modernity 1650–1750* (Oxford University Press, Oxford and New York, 2001).

Jaeger, W.: *Aristotle: Fundamentals of the history of his development*, trans. R. Robinson, 2nd edn (Oxford University Press, Oxford and New York, 1934).

Jagose, A.: *Queer Theory* (New York University Press, New York and Melbourne University Press, Melbourne, 1996).

James, W.: *The Varieties of Religious Experience: A study of human nature*, rev. edn (Longmans, Green, New York and London, 1902).

John of the Cross, St: *The Collected Works of St John of the Cross*, trans. K. Kavanaugh and O. Rodriguez (Institute of Carmelite Studies, Washington, DC, 1991).

Kant, I.: *Lectures on Ethics*, trans. L. Infield (Methuen, London, 1930).

Kant, I.: *Critique of Pure Reason*, trans. N. Kemp Smith (Macmillan, London, 1933).

Kant, I.: *The Critique of Judgement*, trans. J. C. Meredith (Clarendon Press, Oxford, 1952).

Kant, I.: *Anthropology from a Pragmatic Point of View*, trans. V. L. Dowdell (Southern Illinois University Press, Carbondale and Edwardsville, IL, 1978).

Kant, I.: *Groundwork of the Metaphysics of Morals* in *Practical Philosophy*, trans. M. J. Gregor (Cambridge University Press, London and New York, 1996).

Kedourie, E.: *Hegel and Marx: Introductory lectures*, ed. S. Kedourie and H. Kedourie (Blackwell, Oxford and Cambridge, MA, 1995).

Kellner, D.: *Herbert Marcuse and the Crisis of Marxism* (Macmillan, Basingstoke, 1984).

Kierkegaard, S.: *Either/Or*, vol. I, trans. D. F. Swenson and L. M. Swenson (Princeton University Press, Princeton, NJ, 1971).

Kierkegaard, S.: *Either/Or*, vol. II, trans. W. Lowrie (Princeton University Press, Princeton, NJ, 1971).

Kierkegaard, S.: *Fear and Trembling*, trans. A. Hannay (Penguin, Harmondsworth and New York, 1985).

Klossowski, P.: *Sade My Neighbour*, trans. A. Lingis (Quartet, London, 1992).

Kretzman, N. and Stump, E., eds: *The Cambridge Companion to Aquinas* (Cambridge University Press, Cambridge and New York, 1993).

Kristeller, P. O.: *Renaissance Thought: The classic, scholastic and humanist strains* (Harper, New York, 1961).

Kruks, S.: 'Teaching Sartre about Freedom' in M. A. Simons, ed., *Feminist Interpretations of Simone de Beauvoir* (Pennsylvania State University Press, University Park, PA, 1995), pp. 79–95.

Kuzniar, A. A., ed.: *Outing Goethe and His Age* (Stanford University Press, Stanford, CA, 1996).

La Mettrie, J. O. de: *Oeuvres philosophiques* (Georg Olms Verlag, Hildesheim and New York, 1970), reprint of Berlin edition of 1774.

La Mettrie, J. O. de: *Machine Man and Other Writings*, ed. A. Thomson (Cambridge University Press, Cambridge and New York, 1996).

La Mettrie, J. O. de: *De la volupté: Anti-Sénèque ou le souverain bien, L'école de la volupté, Système d'Épicure*, ed. A. Thomson (Desjonquères, Paris, 1996).

Laertius, Diogenes: *Lives of Eminent Philosophers*, trans. R. D. Hicks (Loeb Classical Library, Harvard University Press, Cambridge, MA, 1958), 2 vols.

Laqueur, T.: *Making Sex: Body and gender from the Greeks to Freud* (Harvard University Press, Cambridge, MA and London, 1990).

Lewes, K.: *Psychoanalysis and Male Homosexuality* (Aronson, Northvale, NJ and London, 1995).

Lewis, C. S.: *The Allegory of Love: A study in medieval tradition* (Oxford University Press, Oxford, 1936).

Lloyd, G.: *The Man of Reason: 'Male' and 'Female' in Western Philosophy* (Methuen, London, 1984).

Long, D. G.: *The Manuscripts of Jeremy Bentham: A chronological index* (Bentham Committee, London, 1981).

Lorris, G. de and Meun, J. de: *The Romance of the Rose*, trans. F. Horgan (Oxford University Press, Oxford and New York, 1994).

Lucretius: *On the Nature of The Universe*, trans. R. E. Latham (Penguin, Harmondsworth, 1951).

Lucretius: *De Rerum Natura* (*On the Nature of Things*), trans. W. H. D. Rouse, rev. M. F. Smith (Harvard University Press, Cambridge, MA, and Heinemann, London, 1975).

McLeod, E.: *The Order of the Rose: The life and ideas of Christine de Pizan* (Chatto and Windus, London, 1976).

Marcuse, H.: *Soviet Marxism* (Columbia University Press, New York and Routledge and Kegan Paul, London, 1958).

Marcuse, H.: *Eros and Civilization: A philosophical inquiry into Freud* (Allen Lane, London, 1969).

Marcuse, H.: *An Essay on Liberation* (Allen Lane, London and Beacon Press, Boston, 1969).

Marcuse, H.: *Five Lectures: Psychoanalysis, politics, and Utopia*, trans. J. J. Shapiro and S. M. Weber (Beacon Press, Boston and Allen Lane, London, 1970).

Marcuse, H.: 'Sartre's Existentialism' in *Studies in Critical Philosophy*, trans. J. de Bres (Beacon Press, Boston, 1973), pp. 157–90.

Marcuse, H.: 'Some Social Implications of Modern Technology' in A. Arato and E. Gebhardt, eds, *The Essential Frankfurt School Reader* (Continuum, New York, 1982), pp. 138–62.

Masters, R. D.: *The Political Philosophy of Rousseau* (Princeton University Press, Princeton, NJ, 1968).

Mathéron, A. 'Spinoza et la sexualité' in *Giornale Critico della Filosofia Italiana*, 8, 4, 1977, pp. 436–57.

Meeks, W. A.: *The Origins of Christian Morality: The first two centuries* (Yale University Press, New Haven, CT and London, 1993).

Merleau-Ponty, M.: *Phenomenology of Perception*, trans. C. Smith (Routledge and Kegan Paul, London, 1962).

Mill, J. S.: 'Nature' in *Three Essays on Religion: Nature, The Utility of Religion and Theism*, 2nd edn (Longman, London, 1874).

Mill, J. S.: 'Utilitarianism' in *Utilitarianism, On Liberty, and Considerations on Representative Government*, ed. H. B. Acton (Dent, London, 1972).

Mill, J. S.: *Mill on Bentham and Coleridge*, ed. F. R. Leavis (Cambridge University Press, Cambridge and New York, 1980).

Montaigne, M. de: *The Complete Essays*, trans. M. A. Screech (Penguin Books, London and New York, 1991).

Neill, A. S.: *Summerhill* (Penguin Books, Harmondsworth, 1962).

Neu, J.: 'Freud and Perversion' in R. M. Stewart, ed., *Philosophical Perspectives on Sex and Love* (Oxford University Press, New York, 1995), pp. 87–104.

Nicholson, L. J., ed.: *Feminism/ Postmodernism* (Routledge, London and New York, 1990).

Nicolacopoulos, T. and Vassilacopoulos, G.: *Hegel and the Logical Structure of Love: An essay on sexualities, family, and the law* (Ashgate, Aldershot and Brookfield, VT, 1999).

Nietzsche, F.: *On the Genealogy of Morals, and Ecce Homo*, trans. W. Kaufmann (Random House, New York, 1967).

Nietzsche, F.: *The Birth of Tragedy*, trans. S. Whiteside (Penguin Books, London and New York, 1993).

Norton, R.: *Mother Clap's Molly House: The gay subculture in England 1700–1830* (Gay Men's Press, London, 1992).

Nussbaum, M. C.: *The Therapy of Desire: Theory and practice in Hellenistic ethics* (Princeton University Press, Princeton, NJ, 1994).

Nussbaum, M. C.: *Sex and Social Justice* (Oxford University Press, New York and Oxford, 1999).

Oakeshott, M.: *Experience and its Modes* (Cambridge University Press, Cambridge and New York, 1933).

Oakeshott, M.: 'Introduction' to T. Hobbes, *Leviathan*, ed. M. Oakeshott (Basil Blackwell, Oxford, 1955), pp. vii–lxvi.

Oakeshott, M.: 'On the Character of a Modern European State' in *On Human Conduct* (Clarendon Press, Oxford, 1975), pp. 185–326.

O'Hagan, T.: *Rousseau* (Routledge, London and New York, 1999).

Okin, S. M.: *Women in Western Political Thought* (Princeton University Press, Princeton, NJ, 1979).

Ovid: *The Erotic Poems: The Amores, The Art of Love, Cures for Love, On Facial Treatment for Ladies*, trans. P. Green (Penguin Books, Harmondsworth and New York, 1982).
Ovid: *Ovid in Love: Ovid's Amores*, trans. G. Lee (John Murray, London, 2000).
Pateman, C.: *The Sexual Contract* (Polity Press, Cambridge, 1988).
Paton, H. J.: *The Categorical Imperative: A study in Kant's moral philosophy* (Hutchinson, London, 1947).
Pinkard, T.: *Hegel: A biography* (Cambridge University Press, Cambridge and New York, 2000).
Pitkin, H.: *Fortune is a Woman: Gender and politics in the thought of Niccolò Machiavelli* (University of California Press, Berkeley and London, 1984).
Pizan, C. de: *The Book of the City of Ladies*, trans. E. J. Richards (Pan Books, London, 1983).
Pizan, C. de: *A Medieval Woman's Mirror of Honor: The Treasury of the City of Ladies*, trans. C. C. Willard (Persea Books, New York, 1989).
Plamenatz, J.: *The English Utilitarians* (Basil Blackwell, Oxford, 1949).
Plato: *Phaedrus* in *On Homosexuality: Lysis, Phaedrus, and Symposium*, trans. B. Jowett and E. O'Connor (Prometheus Books, Buffalo, NY, 1991).
Plato: *Complete Works*, ed. J. M. Cooper (Hackett Publishing, Indianapolis and Cambridge, 1997).
Plotinus: *The Enneads*, trans. S. MacKenna (Penguin Books, London and New York, 1991).
Porter, R. and Teich, M., eds: *Sexual Knowledge, Sexual Science: The history of attitudes to sexuality* (Cambridge University Press, Cambridge and New York, 1994).
Praz, M.: *The Romantic Agony* (Oxford University Press, London and New York, 1970).
Price, A. W.: *Love and Friendship in Plato and Aristotle* (Clarendon Press, Oxford, 1989).
Primoratz, I.: *Ethics and Sex* (Routledge, London and New York, 1999).
Rawls, J.: *A Theory of Justice* (Harvard University Press, Cambridge, MA, 1971).
Reich, W.: *The Invasion of Compulsory Sex-Morality* (Penguin Books, Harmondsworth, 1975).
Richter, M.: *The Politics of Conscience: T. H. Green and his age* (Weidenfeld and Nicolson, London, 1964).
Robson, A. P. and Robson, J. M., eds: *Sexual Equality: Writings of John Stuart Mill, Harriet Taylor Mill, and Helen Taylor* (University of Toronto Press, Toronto and London, 1994).
Rougemont, D. de: *Passion and Society*, trans. M. Belgion, rev. edn (Faber and Faber, London, 1956).
Rousseau, J.-J.: *Émile, or Education*, trans. B. Foxley (Dent and Dutton, London and New York, 1918).

Rousseau, J.-J.: *La Nouvelle Héloïse: Julie, or the New Eloise*, trans. J. H. McDowell (Pennsylvania State University Press, University Park, PA and London, 1968).

Rousseau, J.-J.: *The Social Contract and Discourses*, trans. G. D. H. Cole, rev. J. H. Brumfitt and J. C. Hall (Dent, London, 1973).

Russell, B.: *The Problems of Philosophy* (Oxford University Press, Oxford and New York, 1959).

Sade, D. A. F., Marquis de: *The Complete Marquis de Sade*, trans. P. Gillett (Holloway, Los Angeles, CA, 1966).

Sade, D. A. F., Marquis de: *Philosophie dans le boudoir* (Jean-Jacques Pauvert, Paris, 1970), *Oeuvres complètes*, vol. XXV.

Salazar, J.: 'Michel Eyquem de Montaigne' in R. Aldrich and G. Wotherspoon, eds, *Who's Who in Gay and Lesbian History* (Routledge, London and New York, 2001), pp. 316–17.

Sapiro, V.: *A Vindication of Political Virtue: The political theory of Mary Wollstonecraft* (University of Chicago Press, Chicago and London, 1992).

Sartre, J.-P.: *Sketch for a Theory of the Emotions*, trans. P. Mairet (Methuen, London, 1962).

Sartre, J.-P.: *Jean Genet: Actor and martyr*, trans. B. Frechtman (George Braziller, New York, 1963).

Sartre, J.-P.: *Existentialism and Humanism* (Haskell, New York, 1987).

Sartre, J.-P.: *Being and Nothingness*, trans. H. E. Barnes (Routledge, London and New York, 1989).

Saslow, J. M.: *Ganymede in the Renaissance: Homosexuality in art and society* (Yale University Press, New Haven, CT, 1986).

Schaeffer, N.: *The Marquis de Sade: A life* (Knopf, New York, 1999).

Schlegel, F.: *Lucinde. Friedrich Schleiermacher, Vertraute Briefe über Friedrich Schlegels 'Lucinde'* (Insel Verlag, Frankfurt am Main, 1964).

Schlegel, F.: *The Philosophy of Life, and Philosophy of Language, in a course of lectures*, trans. A. J. W. Morrison (AMS Press, New York, 1973).

Schlegel, F.: *On the Study of Greek Poetry*, ed. S. Barnett (SUNY Press, Albany, 2001).

Schneewind, J. B.: *The Invention of Autonomy: A history of modern moral philosophy* (Cambridge University Press, Cambridge and New York, 1998).

Schopenhauer, A.: *The World as Will and Representation*, trans. E. F. Payne (Dover, New York, 1966 and 1969), 2 vols.

Schott, R. M.: *Cognition and Eros: A critique of the Kantian paradigm* (Beacon Press, Boston, 1988).

Schubart, W.: *Religion und Eros*, 3rd edn (C. H. Beck'sche Verlag, Munich, 1952).

Scruton, R.: *Sexual Desire: A philosophical investigation* (Weidenfeld and Nicolson, London, 1986).

Singer, I.: *The Nature of Love*, 2nd edn (University of Chicago Press, Chicago and London, 1984), 3 vols.

Singer, P.: 'Heavy Petting', *Nerve*, 2001 (*nerve.com/opinions/Singer/heavyPetting/main.asp*).

Skinner, Q.: *Reason and Rhetoric in the Philosophy of Hobbes* (Cambridge University Press, Cambridge and New York, 1996).

Smith, N. H., ed.: *Reading McDowell: On mind and world* (Routledge, London and New York, 2002).

Soble, A., ed.: *The Philosophy of Sex: Contemporary readings* (Rowman and Littlefield, Lanham, MD and Oxford, 1997).

Spinoza, B. de: *A Theologico-Political Treatise and A Political Treatise*, trans. R. H. M. Elwes (Dover Publications, New York, 1951), vol. I.

Spinoza, B. de: *The Chief Works of Benedict de Spinoza: 'On the Improvement of the Understanding', 'The Ethics', Correspondence*, trans. R. H. M. Elwes (Dover Publications, New York, 1955), vol. II.

Steakley, J. D.: *The Homosexual Emancipation Movement in Germany* (Ayer, Salem, NH, 1993).

Stevens, F. T.: 'Erasmus's "Tigress": The Language of Friendship, Pleasure, and the Renaissance Letter' in J. Goldberg, ed. *Queering the Renaissance* (Duke University Press, Durham, NC and London, 1994), pp. 124–40.

Taylor, C.: *Hegel* (Cambridge University Press, Cambridge and New York, 1975).

Teresa of Ávila, St: *The Collected Works of St Teresa of Avila*, trans. K. Kavanaugh and O. Rodriguez (Institute of Carmelite Studies, Washington, DC, 1976/80), 2 vols.

Thornton, B. S.: *Eros: The myth of ancient Greek sexuality* (Westview Press, Boulder, CO and Oxford, 1999).

Tomalin, C.: *The Life and Death of Mary Wollstonecraft* (Penguin, Harmondsworth, 1977).

Unger, R. M.: *Democracy Realized: The progressive alternative* (Verso, London and New York, 1998).

Vernon, M.: ' "I Am Not What I Am" – Foucault, Christian Asceticism and a "Way Out" of Sexuality', postscript to M. Foucault, *Religion and Culture*, ed. J. R. Carrette (Routledge, London and New York, 1999).

Veyne, P.: *Roman Erotic Elegy: Love, poetry, and the West* (University of Chicago Press, Chicago, 1988).

Vlastos, G.: *Platonic Studies* (Princeton University Press, Princeton, NJ, 1973).

Voltaire, 'Epître à l'auteur du livre des *Trois imposteurs*' in *Oeuvres complètes de Voltaire* (Baudouin Frères, Paris, 1827), vol. 17, pp. 257–60.

Voltaire, 'The Love called "Socratic" ' in M. Blasius and S. Phelan, eds, *We Are Everywhere: A historical sourcebook of gay and lesbian politics* (Routledge, London and New York, 1997), pp. 12–13.

Wade, I. O.: *The Intellectual Development of Voltaire* (Princeton University Press, Princeton, NJ, 1969).

Ward, R.: 'Why Unnatural? The Tradition Behind Romans 1:26–27', *Harvard Theological Review*, 90, 1997, pp. 263–84.

Waters, C.: 'Havelock Ellis, Sigmund Freud and the State: Discourses of Homosexual Identity in Interwar Britain' in L. Bland and L. Doan, eds, *Sexology in Culture: Labelling bodies and desires* (Polity Press, Cambridge, 1998), pp. 165–79.

Weeks, J.: *Coming Out: Homosexual politics in Britain, from the nineteenth century to the present* (Quartet Books, London and New York, 1977).
Weisheipl, J. A.: *Friar Thomas D'Aquino: His life, thought, and works* (Basil Blackwell, Oxford, 1975).
West, D.: 'Spinoza on Positive Freedom' in *Political Studies*, XLI, 1993, pp. 284–96.
West, D.: *An Introduction to Continental Philosophy* (Polity Press, Cambridge, 1996).
Whitehead, A. N.: *Process and Reality: An essay in cosmology* (Cambridge University Press, Cambridge, 1929).
Wolfenden, J.: *Report of Great Britain Committee on Homosexual Offences and Prostitution* (HMSO, London, 1957).
Wollstonecraft, M.: *A Vindication of the Rights of Woman with Strictures on Moral and Political Subjects* in M. Wollstonecraft, *The Rights of Woman* and J. S. Mill, *On the Subjection of Women*, ed. P. Frankau (Dent and Dutton, London and New York, 1954).

Index

References to major entries are set in **bold** *type.*